THE

MEXICAN AMERICAN

HERITAGE

SECOND EDITION — REVISED

The offering of copal
to the four directions
Redwood Regional Park, East Oakland, California
La Danza Azteca de Berkeley,
California

THE

MEXICAN AMERICAN

HERITAGE

 **SECOND EDITION — REVISED**

WITH WRITING EXERCISES

INDEX WITH ILLUSTRATIONS

by

Carlos M. Jiménez

 **PUBLICATIONS**

A Division of Tonatiuh-Quinto Sol International, Inc.

Post Office Box 9275   Berkeley   CA   94709

Second Edition: April 1994

Third Printing: April 1995

Library of Congress Cataloging-in-Publication Data

Jiménez, Carlos M., 1951-
    The Mexican American heritage : with writing exercises / by Carlos
M. Jiménez. -- 2nd ed., rev.
        p.   cm.
    Includes Index.
    ISBN 0-89229-028-5
    1. Mexican Americans--History.   2. Mexico--History.   3. Mexican
Americans--History--Examinations, questions, etc.   4. Mexico-
-History--Examinations, questions, etc.   I. Title.
E184.M5J55   1994
973' .046872--dc20   94-590
                                                                            CIP

COPYRIGHT © 1994

by Carlos M. Jiménez

ISBN: 0-89229-028-5

Printed in Korea

TABLE OF CONTENTS

The Maya Indians were masters of mathematics, astronomy, the measurement of time, architecture and surgery, including brain surgery. (See page 33)

Chapter Two: LA CONQUISTA — 53

Chapter Two: WRITING EXERCISES —78

The siege of Tenochtitlan lasted eighty days. The Aztec warriors had numbered several hundred thousand. Of these, only about 40,000 survived. No one will ever know how many died of smallpox, thirst and hunger. As the Aztecs left their burning and destroyed city, Spanish soldiers were stationed along the roads and searched everyone for gold. **(See page 70)**

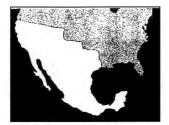

The earliest Mexican Americans...were promised that they could keep their land and other property in accordance with the laws of Mexico and the U.S. Unfortunately, as in the case of the treaties signed with the American Indians, the terms of this treaty were not lived up to by the U.S. Mexicans were not able to keep their lands, often because of violence or the threat of violence.
(See page 103)

Chapter Four:

THE MEXICAN REVOLUTION—PART I:

The Era of Porfirio Díaz — 117

Chapter Four: WRITING EXERCISES — 133

. . . Mexico would finally gain effective leadership in the person of Benito Juárez. The story of "Don Benito" is one of the most stirring in modern Mexican history. Born a pure-blooded Zapotec Indian in the Mexican state of Oaxaca, Benito was orphaned at the age of three and could not even speak Spanish as a boy. Eager for an education, Benito walked over forty miles from his village to the state capital, the city of Oaxaca. There he lived with an older sister who found the boy a job with a Franciscan order. His pay would be his school tuition. He not only learned Spanish quickly but was soon a top student. The only question was whether Benito should enter the priesthood or study law. He chose the legal profession . . . . In 1861 he was elected president of Mexico. **(See page 118)**

Chapter Five:

THE MEXICAN REVOLUTION—PART II:

Revolutionary Decade (1910-1920) and Beyond— 139

Chapter Five: WRITING EXERCISES — 182

Emiliano Zapata was perhaps Mexico's greatest hero of the revolution. From the central Mexican state of Morelos, Zapata fought for the lands and the liberty of his people. Having no interest in politics, he never sought the presidency for himself. **(See page 161)**

Lázaro Cárdenas was a Tarascan Indian . . . . He had been a revolutionary fighter as a boy and had risen to the rank of general. After his election in 1934, Mexico soon saw that Cárdenas would be unlike most Mexican presidents. Cárdenas then traveled extensively throughout the nation. He visited the rural poor, listened to their problems, studied solutions . . . .
(See page 175)

Luis Valdez

However, the day came when Mexican American youth sought to test the "freedom" and "equality" they were reading about in school. They tried to be "real Americans." The clothes that the young men wore, which came to be known as the "zoot suit," may have had their origins in the popular 1939 movie, *Gone With the Wind*. The zoot suits, or drapes, were probably the young men's way of trying to look "American."
(See page 199)

Chapter Six:

THE ZOOT SUIT YEARS — 191

Chapter Seven:

CESAR CHAVEZ
AND MEXICAN LABOR
IN THE SOUTHWEST — 223

Chapter Seven: WRITING EXERCISES — 241

During the 1930s, organizing among Mexican and Mexican American workers had become stronger and stronger. World War II, however, scattered the people both into the armed services and into other lines of work. The agricultural organizing was interrupted by the war and, therefore, it did not succeed in establishing a permanent and organized labor force. However, the effort was to surge again in the form of the first Mexican American labor union to actually succeed in altering not only working conditions, but also state and national labor legislation. This was accomplished by the United Farm Workers Union, which was led by César Chávez.
(See page 225)

Chapter Eight:

LOS CHICANOS — 249

Chapter Eight: WRITING EXERCISES — 274

It was also in the 1960s that the voices of Mexican Americans for change began to enter the national consciousness. The young farmworkers who supported César Chávez's union saw to it that America learned who they were. The call by César Chávez for a national grape boycott brought the plight of the campesinos and also of the Mexicans as a whole to the attention of the U.S. But these young protesters had adopted a different name for themselves. Just as the African Americans marching and protesting in places like Birmingham and Selma, Alabama, preferred to call themselves "Black," the followers of Chávez proudly proclaimed themselves "Chicanos." What was born in the midst of this decade of upheaval was a mass movement by Americans of Mexican descent: "The Chicano Movement of Aztlan." **(See page 249)**

Acknowledgements

This book began out of frustration. While teaching Mexican American Studies at Belmont High School in Los Angeles in 1978, I could not find an acceptable textbook. The school textbook room had copies of Rudolfo Acuña's *Mexican American Chronicle.* While interesting and thought provoking, the book's treatment of certain subjects ("The Mexican Revolution," "The Pachuco Era," for example) was so brief that it was almost impossible to teach a unit on these subjects, even though they were of great interest to my students. I consulted the California State List of Approved Textbooks and found three in the Mexican American Studies section. Two of these were out of print, and the other was Julian Nava's book which was written for elementary age students. Carey McWilliams's *North From Mexico* and Acuña's *Occupied America*, although both excellent, did not seem suited for students of high school age. What was needed was a basic Mexican and Mexican American history text that would help my students to understand themselves better at their current level of educational progress. This led me to begin an experiment during the spring semester of 1979 in which I selected topics of importance and high interest to my students and then wrote "research papers" (as if I were still in college). These reports became my "textbook" for the school year.

Instead of "staying one chapter ahead of the class" (something every teacher is forced to do at one time or another), I was staying a few pages ahead of my students in the actual writing of the class text! Each night, after teaching, as well as coaching a track team, I researched, wrote and typed as many pages as possible and made ditto copies the following morning. In this way, I had a "book" to use in my classes.

What kept me on this suicidal schedule was the fact that my students seemed to love it. They enjoyed the "Indian Mexico" and "La Conquista" sections, and by the time we got to "The Zoot Suit Years" they were eagerly awaiting the arrival of new pages, hot off my typewriter. Proudly they declared themselves my guinea pigs and encouraged me to write more.

At the same time, I began to include the teaching of writing in my history classes. In the past, virtually all of my college history exams had been of the essay or "blue book" type. Now I wanted to prepare my students for writing in history classes. But I knew I had to figure out a way to teach writing without trying to teach formal grammar. After all, what history teacher wants to teach nouns and verbs? This was how the writing exercises in the book began to evolve.

Then, in 1980, I participated in the UCLA Writing Project's Summer Institute for teachers. Under the direction of Rae Jeane Williams of UCLA, and Richard Dodge of Santa Monica College, I shared these writing exercises with the other teacher participants so that they could critique them or adapt them to their own uses.

At this time, Dr. Juan Francisco Lara was the Executive Director of the UCLA Center for Academic Interinstitutional Programs (CAIP) which administered the Writing Project. In 1983, I showed him my unpublished book. When I told him I had been using it while at Belmont High School and now at my present school, James A. Garfield High School in East Los Angeles, he expressed great interest and offered his assistance in seeking improvements.

After I had expanded and revised the manuscript, Dr. Lara sent copies to Dr. Adolfo Bermeo of Compton College and Shirlene Soto of California State University, Northridge, for factual and historical editing. Dr. Faye Peitzman and Dr. Ruth Mitchell, both of CAIP, also assisted greatly with their editing expertise.

Finally, at UCLA during the summer of 1987 I transferred the manuscript into a word processor. It was then that budget cuts dealt a blow to my project. Dr. Lara's office could not assist in the production of the book. I would not be stopped. Using photographs taken during various trips to Mexico, and illustrations made by one of my students, Eddie Lainez, at Garfield High School, I arranged to have some copies printed at a nearby high school's print shop.

In 1991, after further modifications of the manuscript, I forwarded the work to TQS Publications in Berkeley, California. They are the publishers of Rudolfo Anaya's internationally famous novel, *Bless Me, Ultima,* which I had used in my Chicano Literature classes for years. Would the number-one publishers of Chicano literature take an interest in my efforts? I was delighted when TQS accepted my manuscript for publication.

My wife, Virginia Peñaloza Jiménez, had prodded me to continue my work and to overcome my fears of rejection. To her I owe uncountable thanks.

Many thanks arc also due to my mother, Josephine C. Jiménez, for her help in editing and for providing me with the benefit of her forty-plus years in public education.

Similarly, I would like to thank all the students in my Mexican American Studies classes. For the past fourteen years, their enthusiasm and positive responses constituted the highest award any teacher can receive. Their new-found pride upon discovering their Mexican heritage has sustained my conviction that I was doing something meaningful and important. After all, as educators, what more essential objective do we have than to help teach our students who they are?

Carlos M. Jiménez
Los Angeles, California, 1991

To my father,

Oscar M. Jiménez,

I dedicate this book.

A native of Sonora, Mexico, he came with his family to the United States to escape the impending chaos of the Mexican Revolution. As millions of Mexicans have before and after him, he struggled to learn a new language and to adapt to a foreign culture. He served in the U.S. Navy and soon, after World War I, he won a track and field scholarship to the University of Southern California. There, he majored in Spanish and soon was teaching high school Spanish classes in Los Angeles. His enduring love of the teaching profession is what inspired me to become a teacher. I guess I inherited his love for Mexico as well. My only regret is that he never lived to see me also become a teacher, or to see this book published.

Foreword

The story of the Mexican Americans in the United States begins in the distant nights and days of prehistory, during an unrecorded "Age of Great Migrations" which became an incredible "Age of Discovery" for these ancestral peoples as they systematically explored and discovered a "New World" that spread out endlessly before their eyes and their every footstep.

In this new world of theirs, they explored and settled along the tundra, the mountains, plains, deserts, forests, and along rivers and lakes, as well as the coastlines of two vast continents. These people of pre-history went on to develop highly complex agricultural and hunting systems, a wide range of architectural styles, a considerable variety of philosophical concepts and structures, and medical systems which ranged from a calming tea to complicated surgery. Ultimately, through inventiveness, intelligence and highly developed rational thought, there evolved the mathematical genius and advanced knowledge of astronomy exhibited by the Mayan Indians, as well as the horticultural, architectural and calendric expertise of the Aztecs, only then to be thrust by European nations into the catastrophic throes of international wars, intrigue and the foreigners' unbridled drive toward conquest, power and riches, whatever the cost.

These are the foundations of Mexican American history, a history that in Mexico was among the first to eliminate slavery, one which, from the inception of contact with the United States, exerted great influence in architecture, agriculture, gold mining, the cattle industry, music, art and international trade. Mexican American history also became a major influence in the rise of the labor movement in the West, and it has been a major contributor to the development of what today is called jazz music.

The history of Mexican Americans is one of the printing press, for it has sustained a steady current of printed and graphic expression from the days of the Californio ranchos of the 1800s all the way to the present literary expression of the Chicano authors, journalists and artists, whose works we see every day.

Always active, always seeking a better life, and often still migrating in this search, the Mexican American population can best be compared to a river which at times runs full while at other times it encounters a drought but, regardless, continues to flow.

What I am saying, of course, is that the Mexican American population is not one that is "emerging" or "awakening." These concepts are a repetition of the old stereotype of the Mexican sleeping under the cactus, always said to be leaving everything for mañana, too lazy and disoriented to do anything.

Now, in *The Mexican American Heritage,* by Carlos M. Jiménez, this stereotype can be set aside forever, for in his work Jiménez has given us a panorama of Mexican American life as no other author has done before. It is a history which clearly shows that today's Mexican Americans are the descendants of people who have struggled for generations for a better life. Now, judging from this history book, it is clear that Mexican Americans continue this struggle in the present, and certainly this process will be continued into the future.

Octavio I. Romano-V., Ph.D.
Berkeley, California, 1992

INTRODUCTION

In the year 2017 it will be exactly 500 years since the first Spaniard, Francisco Hernández de Córdova, landed on what is today Mexico. Currently there is much debate over what would be the proper way to note the 500th year since the Europeans and Native Americans first came in contact with one another. Should we celebrate or condemn? Commemorate or educate? Should we note or bemoan?

Whatever the case may be, for Mexicans and Mexican Americans this anniversary is impossible to ignore. In many ways, it represents our beginning as the people we are today. In this light, Mexicans who speak Spanish, who practice the Catholic religion, who have Spanish surnames, and who have a unique *Mestizo* culture have existed only for these past 500 years.

Racially, culturally and linguistically we are still working on all of the ramifications of this *Mestizaje*. But one thing is certain: It is important for people of Mexican descent to know how they came to be what they are. In what is today Mexico, Mexican school children are afforded this opportunity. However, Mexican and Mexican American students living in what used to be Mexico, that is, the U.S. Southwest, are not so fortunate. For decades we have been tossed into an educational "melting pot" and have been taught history, literature, language and even science and mathematics from a Eurocentric point of view. As a result, millions of Mexican Americans living in the U.S. do not know who they are. At home, for example, many are likely to speak Spanish and be raised in accordance with the traditions of Mexico. But in their schools they are taught that they must be "American." This suggests that people of Mexican descent are not Americans and therefore need not learn the history of their ancestors. Thus, as is often true, many young people today have only the vaguest of clues as to why they have the names they do, why they are likely to have brown skin, why they are likely to be Catholic, to speak Spanish or to eat the foods they do. Tragically, their teachers probably do not know these things either. Equally tragic is the fact that U.S. born Mexican American students frequently use derogatory terms such as "wetback" when referring to recently arrived Mexican classmates. Similarly, Chicano students often are embarrassed because their parents do not speak English. Some students may even be embarrassed over their own names. Once, for example, while announcing students' names at a high school graduation ceremony in East Los Angeles, a teacher was told by a graduating senior with an obviously Spanish name to, "Say my name in *English,* please!"

In 1968, Chicano high school students in East Los Angeles walked out of their classes. They demanded a better education which would include more college preparatory classes as well as Mexican American history courses. Despite the subsequent adoption of many ethnic studies courses by high school districts, Mexican American studies and literature classes were not deemed sufficiently worthy of the University of California. Essentially, Mexican American students were told that if they wanted to attend the top colleges they could study Shakespeare or Greek mythology, but they could not choose to learn about their own people or their literature. Therefore, an entire generation of Mexican Americans grew up thinking that the only road to success was to forget about their own culture and to emulate European Americans.

Finally, after 24 years of refusals, in 1992 the University of California has agreed to accept Mexican American Studies as an "academic elective" for potential undergraduates. While some colleges and private universities have adapted to contemporary needs in higher education and accepted Mexican American history and culture courses for admission, it is now hoped that this belated action on the part of the University of California will inspire other institutions of higher education to follow suit.

While facing the future, will the unique linguistic and cultural heritage of Mexican American youth be incorporated and nurtured by our educational system? If so, then future generations of Mexican Americans may be better able to contribute in the workplace, the arts and the professions. Similarly, if such would come to pass, then certainly Mexican Americans in particular and Latinos in general will be better able to help shape our ever evolving democracy.

The history and lessons contained in this book are especially timely today as we approach the 500th anniversary of the beginning of the Mestizo people of Mexico. It is our hope that in the year 2017 we will commemorate the event with pride as we look back at the progress made over the years, not the least of which will be in having established the principle that all students deserve to be taught the history of who they are.

TO THE TEACHER

This text is designed as an introduction to some of the most interesting events in the heritage of Mexican Americans. It is not meant to be a comprehensive treatment of the subject matter. The idea, instead, is to whet the appetite of students and get them to want to know more and to come away with a changed attitude. Certain periods of Mexican history are therefore skipped over or referred to only briefly. The book is meant to correspond roughly to a one-semester course and obviously, within this time frame, some important items must be omitted.

What sets this book apart from other history texts is the inclusion of writing instruction exercises which follow each chapter. Instead of merely providing a list of questions for students to answer, the student is instructed step by step in how to answer history questions in well-written sentences, paragraphs and essays. The history or social studies teacher must believe in the importance of writing instruction for it to have value. These exercises can be used easily by students, and the teacher need not have formal training in the teaching of English. The exercises enhance the learning of content by allowing the student to write and think about the material.

For the benefit of teachers who might wish to use only one or two chapters of the book, each chapter is essentially self-contained and includes a full sequence of writing exercises.

Let me now explain how the writing exercises are structured.

Sentence or Fragment?

This assignment is the first in each chapter's exercises. It uses a content-oriented approach to the concept of the complete sentence. **This exercise need not be used if students are already writing complete sentences on their own.** I have found it useful through the years to do this exercise at least once, even with the best of classes, at the beginning of the semester. I offer a list of incomplete sentences (fragments) as well as complete sentences, using the material previously read by students. After reading one of the items out loud with the class, I ask: "Sentence or fragment?" One very simple rule is given: "A complete sentence makes sense when read alone." When students decide that one of the items is a fragment, they are asked to rewrite it so that it makes sense. They must also maintain historical accuracy when doing this revision. I generally do three or four items aloud with the class and then let them complete the exercise in class on their own, under my supervision, as I circulate around the room helping those who need it. When they are done writing out their revised fragments, we go over them orally. Again, I stress that their rewritten work must be factually correct, but I also stress that there is more than one correct way to revise a fragment. After completing such an exercise, students are more aware of what a sentence is and is not. **Some classes or individuals may never again need to do this exercise. Others may need to repeat it while studying a later chapter.** One such exercise is included for each chapter.

Short Answer Questions

These questions are designed to be answered in one or two sentences only. The students are to write out their own sentence answers following the previous exercise's rule: "A complete sentence makes sense when read alone." Again, I usually model two or three questions with the class and have them give me examples of factually correct answers which are also written in complete sentence form. My students do this as written work and I usually set a due date for the day of a test on that particular material.

Thus, by doing these written exercises, they are essentially studying. I can easily grade their papers while they are taking the examination. I generally grade such written work by giving a double grade; the top grade for historical accuracy and the bottom grade for writing correctness. I then average the two grades together for a final grade on the written work. I also weigh these written assignments roughly equal to the test.

A list of short answer questions often makes an excellent review sheet and we often spend class time going over these questions as the students take notes which they write into complete sentences to be handed in. **As with the *Sentence or Fragment?* exercise, more advanced classes may need to do this type of assignment only once or not at all.** But for the sake of making each chapter self-contained, one *Short Answer* assignment is provided for each chapter.

Single Paragraphs

Students learn best when a clear, visual model is provided. For this purpose, **a sample paragraph, written in response to a given question, is provided at the end of the *Indian Mexico* chapter.** The basic topic sentence, supporting details, and strong closure is stressed. Students then write their own paragraphs in response to the questions asked. They are instructed to be certain that their paragraphs are factually correct, that they follow acceptable paragraph form, and that each individual sentence represents a complete thought. Again, a list of paragraph questions is often used as a review sheet as I go over the questions and answers with the class, perhaps a day or two before an exam. The students learn note taking as I discuss various aspects of the answers to these questions. I then usually assign four or five paragraphs to be handed in on the day of the test. Sometimes I allow the students to select the questions they answer, suggesting that they try to anticipate topics on which they might be tested. The skill of writing single paragraphs not only allows the student to write about the material in some detail, but it is also an essential building block for the construction of essays.

Clustering and Identification Items/Paragraphs

Clustering is a useful method for generating ideas about specific topics. Once these ideas emerge in a cluster, paragraphs can be written using the cluster as a guide. I have used the idea of clustering in conjunction with the concept of the identification item. Many history classes in colleges and universities utilize identification items — basically important people, places and things from the historical content being studied. Teachers and professors pick out these items and students then write short paragraphs which attempt to answer two basic questions about them: Who or what is it and why is it important historically? By clustering first on certain identification items provided by the text (or by the teacher), students can then write ID paragraphs. Teachers should encourage students to continually ask themselves the two basic questions as they fill out their cluster. Clustering can be done by the class as a whole with the teacher writing an item on the board with a circle around it. In response to the two basic questions, the teacher adds whatever students suggest and writes their ideas arrayed around the central topic, like "satellite bubbles" as my students call them. (See page 49.) Students can also make clusters on their own by writing the ID item in the middle of a page with a circle around it. They then write whatever pops into their minds connected with the item. **For the *Indian Mexico* chapter, a sample cluster and ID para-**

graph are provided with detailed instructions for students. For all subsequent chapters a list of suggested ID items is provided. Clustering can also be used effectively when students are preparing to write their essays.

Essay Questions

Generally I provide two types of essay questions in the form of essay tests. Early in the semester when I have covered only the sentence fragment and complete sentence skills, I may give an essay test — for the Indian Mexico chapter for example. I instruct students to answer the essay question fairly freely. I tell them not to worry about paragraphs, thesis statements, or any other expository essay writing skills yet. In other words, what I want is fluency first, before form. But once the single paragraph and ID paragraph skills have been mastered by students, I introduce the expository essay. Such essays can take the place of other written work due on the day of the test, and the test itself may consist of only one essay question to be answered. **Clear instructions about the function of each component of an expository essay, along with a sample essay with explanations, are provided at the conclusion of** *The Mexican Revolution, Part II,* **chapter.** If the earlier building blocks of sentences, paragraphs, and ID paragraphs are learned well, my students have little trouble.

Expository essay form is essential for high school students' required term or research papers in other classes as well as history. Obviously, those heading for college will need to be able to write essays and research papers in this format. Clustering works well when students are preparing to write their essays. Clustering and/or some type of basic outlining is strongly suggested for students of junior or senior high age.

SPECIFIC USES OF WRITING EXERCISES

For Mexican American Studies teachers

What I have always done is to introduce the writing skills one step at a time at the end of each chapter. For example, at the end of *Indian Mexico,* my students do the Sentence or Fragment and the first half of the Short Answer exercises. At the end of the *La Conquista* section, I introduce the Single Paragraph skill and the Clustering/ID Paragraph ideas. After the *Loss of Aztlan* or *Mexican Revolution* chapter, we then begin to write expository essays. In this way the students progress through the sequence of writing skills as they progress through the content. By the end of the semester, therefore, they have completed both the content and the writing aspects of the course. As mentioned previously, I ask for essay exams exclusively but do not hold students responsible for expository essay form until it has been thoroughly explained and then practiced by the students.

Here is my rule of thumb for grading written work: *Do not hold students responsible for a given writing skill until you have specifically taught it to the class. But once you have taught it, hold them to account for it. The higher your expectations of the students, the better they will do.*

For teachers who plan to use only part of this book

As I have mentioned, a full sequence of writing exercises is provided for each chapter in the interest of making each self-contained. This is not to suggest that every class should do all the exercises. **I would suggest that teachers gauge the ability of their students and start them at the point in the sequence for which the class is ready.** For example, some basic classes might never get beyond the Sentence or Fragment and Short Answer assignments. Other classes might begin with and do only the essay writing. Tailor the exercises to fit your individual classes.

To all teachers

Students gain deeper understanding of history if they write about it, rather than merely responding to objective exams. By using a sequence of writing exercises such as I have presented, your students will gain a better grasp of the content. Additionally, similar writing exercises could easily be devised for other history classes with similar results.

A NOTE TO THE STUDENT
ABOUT THE WRITING EXERCISES

Why study writing? What is the purpose of writing exercises in a Mexican American history textbook? Your success and achievement, both in junior and senior high school as well as in college, depend upon your ability to express yourself clearly in writing. Historical material is excellent subject matter to write about. In this book there is a series of writing exercises at the close of each chapter. They are very different from the questions that come at the end of the chapter in most history books. These exercises are meant to help you to write better. What follows here is an explanation of the writing exercises you will find in this book as well as some important definitions of the basic components or parts of the writing process.

Sentence or Fragment? / Short Answer Questions

A sentence is any group of words that begins with a capital letter and ends with a period. As a junior or senior high school student you should attempt to write sentences that express complete thoughts or that make sense when read alone. Although many books or articles written by professional writers contain incomplete sentences or fragments, these writers certainly know the difference between a sentence and a fragment. They use fragments from time to time for purposes of style or to make their writing sound better. Why then should you not also write in fragments?

Master painters may use abstract or unusual figures in their paintings, but when they were learning to paint they learned first how to paint the hands, face and body clearly. In other words, they had to acquire the basic skills first. The same is true in writing. You must master the complete sentence and be able to tell a sentence from a fragment. This is the purpose of this exercise.

The Short Answer exercises are designed for you to practice writing your own complete sentences. And obviously, these exercises are meant to help you learn the history. If you can write about it, you have learned it!

ID and Single Paragraphs

Paragraphs are the essential building blocks of high school and college writing. Many college teachers use the ID paragraph for tests and exams. Paragraphs answer historical questions that are a bit more complicated than the short answer question. What is a paragraph?

A paragraph is a group of sentences that all deal with one main idea. Paragraphs are usually less than one page long. A paragraph must have a topic sentence, which usually comes at the beginning of the paragraph. The topic sentence states what the rest of the paragraph will cover. It tells the reader what the rest of the paragraph will be about. Try to stay on the topic and use the rest of the paragraph to provide as many facts, details, and other specific information you need, like names and dates to help you explain what the topic sentence stated. Once you have learned to write individual paragraphs, either as answers to questions or as ID paragraphs, you will have an excellent skill which can help you to be a better student. Paragraphs will also help you to move ahead to the next step in the writing process, the essay or composition.

Essays and Essay Tests

Many teachers, both in high school and college, assign essays and give essay tests. They will ask you a broad, detailed question with many aspects to it and expect you to answer it by writing an essay of several paragraphs. Essays need to be well planned and organized. The same basic procedures for planning an essay will apply to a take-home composition, a term or research paper, as well as an in-class essay exam.

At the conclusion of each chapter or section of the reading you will find the writing exercises themselves, along with detailed instructions and samples. By learning the skills of writing you will become a much better student.

Good Luck!

¡Buena Suerte!

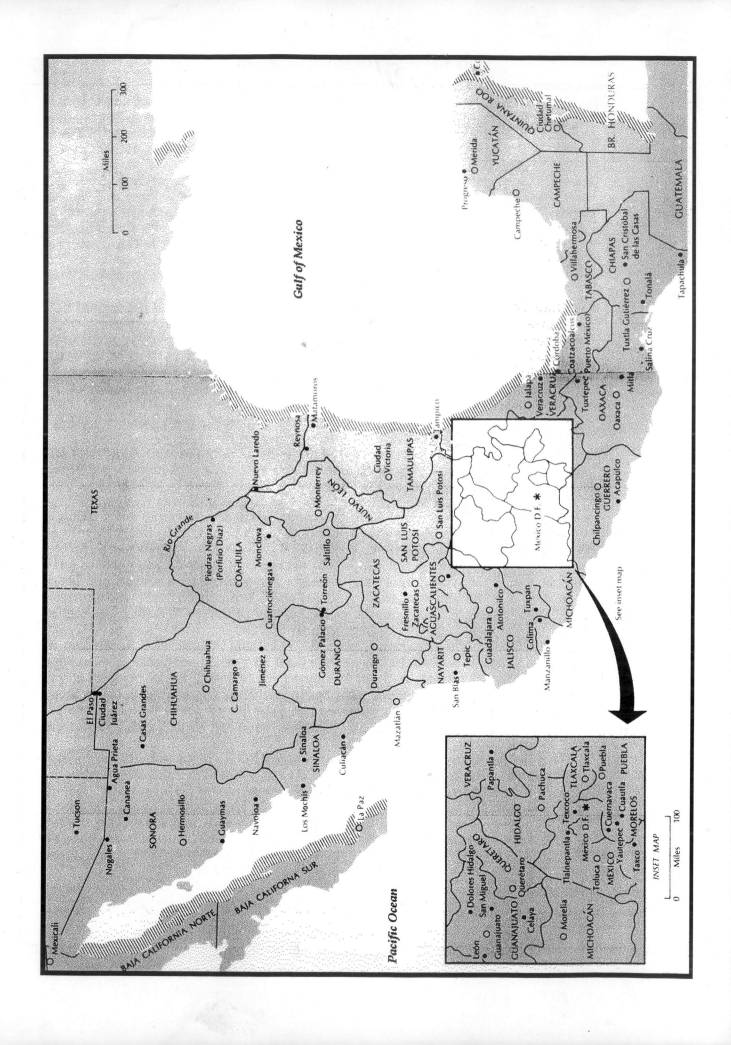

Chapter One

INDIAN MEXICO

1. Who are the Indians?

Between twenty and forty thousand years ago, the land we now call Mexico was peopled by Native Americans. These native (or indigenous) people are mistakenly referred to as "Indians." At one time, the entire American continent from Alaska in the north to the tip of what is now Argentina in the south was peopled entirely by these indigenous inhabitants.

When most of us who have been raised in the Hollywood and video culture of North America think of "Indians," we probably imagine war-whooping peoples who generally get shot by someone like John Wayne or Clint Eastwood at the end of the story. Despite a belated attempt by Hollywood in the 1990s to reform the image of Native Americans, most Mexican American teenagers probably have a somewhat negative and stereotypical view of these indigenous Americans.

But the truth tells a far different and richer story. Whether it be the Eskimos of Alaska, the Navajos and Cherokees of North America, the Toltecs and Aztecs of Mexico, the Mayans of Central America or the Incas of Peru, the rich, varied and complex societies established by these peoples directly contradict the stereotype of the American Indian as a "savage" who needed to be taught how to be "civilized" by the Europeans.

The story of the native peoples of the Americas who lived in what is now Mexico is the first step on a long voyage of cultural discovery for Mexican people. Who then are these "Indians"? A good place to begin would be to ask: "To what race do Indians belong?"

The concept of "race" is a difficult yet important subject to discuss. Understanding one's racial background is essential for a clear grasp of a person's true identity. For the purposes of this book, race will be taken to mean one's physical, biological or genetic heritage — in other words, what we see when we look in the mirror. In this volume, the terms Chicano, Asian, Black and White are capitalized in order to add emphasis to their historical importance.

Many anthropologists believe that very early in the mists of prehistoric human life there may have been only three "races" of people: the Black or Negroid race, the Asian or Oriental, and the White or Caucasian. To what race then would the Native American belong? If Indians are an integral part of the Mexican American's racial heritage, from which of the three races are we descended?

Our first clue is that the American continent was the last of the great land masses to have been inhabited by human beings. While prehistoric human bones dating back millions of years have been found in Africa and Asia, the Native Americans arrived here only twenty to forty thousand years ago. Where did they come from? To what race do they belong?

Geography gives us our next clue. Take a look at a map of the world. Find Alaska. Notice how close the tip of Asia comes to the western coast of Alaska. The narrow section of ocean that separates Asia from Alaska is known as the Bering Strait. Although there are several different theories, most scientists such as anthropologists and geologists tell us that during an ice age, perhaps 25,000 years ago, across the frozen Bering Strait from Asia it was possible to walk into the continent of America. Prehistoric tribes of Asian people, probably following wild game and seeking a warmer climate, migrated across the land bridge into the presumably uninhabited lands of what is today Alaska, Canada, the United States, Mexico, Central America and eventually all the way south into the area presently called South America. Is it possible that Native Americans are of the Asian race?

There are clear physical similarities between Native Americans and Asian people. They share a relatively short stature, limited body and facial hair, straight black hair on the head, a tendency to have high cheek bones, and an extra flap of skin on the eyelids (incorrectly called "slanted eyes"). All of these traits are shared by Asians and Native Americans. For further evidence, study the ancient Mayan and Aztec carvings and look closely at the faces you see. Or look at the Indian faces of a Diego Rivera mural. For that matter, you can also travel to Mexico or visit East Los Angeles and observe the "Indian" faces. The resemblance to Asian people is unmistakable. But how many Mexicans and Mexican Americans today realize that we are directly related to Asian people? The story of the Mexican American heritage is full of surprises!

Now that we know to what race Mexican Indians belong, let us travel thousands of years back in time and try to reconstruct how the great Mexican Indian civilizations were born.

2. Civilization — the Beginnings

The first prehistoric Asians, said to have crossed the Bering Strait into the American continent, were what we call "nomads." These Native American Indians obtained food by hunting wild game; fishing in the oceans, rivers and lakes; and by gathering wild fruits, nuts, roots and the berries yielded by nature. Their homes were quite often made of portable materials, or they resided temporarily in caves.

Their culture, that is, their way of life, revolved around those things most important to them: the hunt and the animals they depended on for food, as well as the forces of nature such as rain, lightning, thunder, the sun and the moon. They passed on their culture from generation to generation verbally as their sense of an oral language became gradually more and more complex. But they built no lasting dwellings or structures, left no great cities behind them, for their lives were a continual search for food. They had to follow game wherever it could be found.

A long time ago, however, one great discovery began the transformation of the nomadic wanderer into a highly civilized city dweller with a written language and history, many forms of artistic expression, complex architecture, and even knowledge of sciences such as astronomy and hydraulic engineering. That one great discovery was agriculture!

Curious prehistoric nomadic Indians must have wondered how a permanent supply of their most important wild plant foods, such as corn, could be obtained. Perhaps by accident, at some point the Native Americans of Mexico learned that if seeds were placed in moist earth they would sprout and produce mature fruits or vegetables. And once human beings had planted a seed in the ground for their use as a food supply, they were tied to the land. Now they must give up the nomadic life of continual wandering. They must water the seed, care for the land, wait for the seed to grow, and finally gain the harvest.

In what is now Mexico, archaeologists have found traces of agriculture dating back to 7000 B.C., or 9000 years ago. Such crops as corn, squash, chiles, avocados, and even cotton were cultivated throughout Mexico by ancient Indians. By 3400 B.C. agricultural advances, such as the combining of different varieties of corn, revolutionized Indian society. A steady and even surplus food supply allowed Mexican Indians to experiment with and even specialize their talents into great social achievements. They built their first permanent dwellings, erected temples to honor their gods, began to understand the cycles of the sun, moon and stars, developed the first calendars, the first writing systems, created methods for counting and accounting, and, in short, they became the first artists, musicians and scientists.

Thus it came to be that, in time, a flowering of the arts and sciences took place and produced the Classic Era of Indian Mexico. One of the great centers of this era was located at Teotihuacan, the "home of the gods."

3. Teotihuacan

The central Mexican Valley, or Anahuac Valley, traditionally has been a center of Mexican population, culture and society. Mexico City is located in the heart of the Anahuac Valley. This valley sits high in the clouds, over 8000 feet above sea level, yet it is surrounded by a ring of mountains and volcanoes which tower even higher over the valley's base. The excellent climate, abundant forest and grasslands, and extensive lakes promised good homes to successive migrations of nomadic Indians from the north. The first great city or metropolis of Mexico's Anahuac Valley was Teotihuacan. Teotihuacan came to be one of the most important and influential population centers in all of Classic Indian Mexico.

Plans for the great city of Teotihuacan may have been drawn up as early as 200 B.C. In total area the population center covered over twelve square miles. At its height there may have been as many as 100,000 inhabitants. The city had pyramids of immense size and great beauty, exquisitely carved stone temples dedicated to various gods, broad and straight avenues, lavish residences for the priestly class, and modest thatched roof dwellings for the average citizens.

Tourists who make the one-hour journey from Mexico City to Teotihuacan are immediately impressed by the two immense pyramids there: the Pyramid of the Sun and of the Moon. The Pyramid of the Sun is a massive edifice of over 200 feet in height and over 700 feet at its base. It is estimated that 10,000 workers toiled for twenty years or more to complete this monument to the sun. See Plate 19.

The temple of Quetzalcoatl is another important part of Teotihuacan. "Quetzalcoatl" means feathered or plumed serpent and refers to one of ancient Mexico's most important gods. Quetzalcoatl was the ruling god of Teotihuacan and his temple is adorned with huge, carefully carved snake heads ringed with feathers. This god was said to be responsible for teaching the Teotihuacanos art, farming and other cultural innovations. See Plates 20-21.

Pilgrims from other cities came to Teotihuacan to pray and worship at this home of the gods. The pyramids and temples were covered with a smooth stucco plaster and their walls were then painted to enhance their majesty. Elaborate religious festivals and rituals occurred at regular intervals in Teotihuacan. Processions of priests and other notables would come down the Avenue of the Dead and would then ascend the huge pyramids for specific religious worship. Resplendent in their elaborate robes, feather headdresses and exquisite jewelry, these Teotihuacan leaders must have presented a stirring spectacle. At its height, what a place Teotihuacan must have been!

Pottery which had long been made by the earlier nomadic groups now took the form of elaborate polychrome or multicolored ceramics. Woven goods such as clothing and blankets now were not merely functional but embroidered and fash-

Nopal

PLATE **1**

The Aztec Stone of the Fifth Sun (mistakenly called a calendar) is one of the Aztecs' greatest artistic accomplishments. Standing over twelve feet tall, it weighs twenty-five tons. Of great significance for the Aztecs, the sun god Tonatiuh can be seen in the center, sticking out his blade tongue, asking for the sacrifice of human hearts (clutched in his hands). The Aztecs believed there had been four previous creations and destructions of the universe and thus we see the four previous eras, or suns, represented in the four squares around the head of Tonatiuh. Around these four symbols we see the twenty-day signs which represent the eighteen Aztec months totaling exactly 360 days. Notice also the two gods who face off at the bottom of the stone. They represent the eternal struggle between good and evil.

PLATE 2

Detail of a mural by the noted Mexican artist Diego Rivera depicting life in Indian Mexico prior to the arrival of the Spanish. In this case we see the Aztecs engaged in ceramic arts beginning with the taking of suitable clay from the river bank, creating the ceramic pots and other vessels and finally the process of firing or hardening the finished product. We also see other Indian artists creating fine feather work as well as illustrating manuscripts.

PLATE **3**

This Diego Rivera mural shows one sector of the great Aztec capital of Tenochtitlan. Note the bright colors used to paint and decorate the massive pyramids; the fine clothing of the residents; and the feathered decorations and fans which the people used. Finally, we see the famous Indian practice of *Los Voladores,* or men who tie themselves to tall poles and then jump from the top, spinning or flying gracefully around the pole as the ropes slowly unwind until they reach the ground.

PLATE **4**

One of Diego Rivera's most famous murals, *El Mercado* (The Market) depicts the vast collection of goods available to the Aztec residents of Tenochtitlan. How many different foods and other articles for sale can you identify? The important looking gentleman seated at the left is a judge who would render rulings on the spot if anyone felt he or she had been cheated in the purchase or selling of merchandise. Finally, in the background, note the vast expanse of Tenochtitlan, Lake Texcoco's canals, and the broad and straight causeways which led to and from the city.

PLATE **5**

Detail from a Diego Rivera mural which shows the clash between the Aztec and Spanish armies during the conquest of Mexico in 1521. Note the different weapons used by the Aztecs (slings, bows and arrows, wooden clubs with obsidian tips) compared with those of the Spaniards (metal armor, shields and guns).

PLATE **6**

Another mural by Diego Rivera shows early developments in Mexico immediately after the defeat of the Indians by the Spanish. Indians are enslaved and even branded like animals by their Spanish masters as the process of establishing haciendas and reorganizing life in Mexico begins. Note the Spanish gentleman in the front with his Indian mistress. On her back is a Mestizo baby, born of a Spanish father and Indian mother. This baby represents the beginning of Mexico's Mestizo population.

PLATE 7

Far from being a long-dead and forgotten people, in many states of Mexico the Indians make up a large percentage of the population. They often speak their Indian languages, as well as Spanish. Here we see a Zapotec Indian woman with her baby as she strolls through a market in the State of Oaxaca.

PLATE **8**

ioned so as to please the eye as well as keep the wearer warm. Mural wall paintings which depicted historical or mythical scenes were likewise multi-colored. Wall sculptures, called bas-reliefs, joined three-dimensional sculptures of gods and goddesses to give the worshipers a clearer vision of their religion. Calendars quickly followed on the heels of mathematics and astronomical discoveries. Jewelry and delicate feathers adorned the residents of Teotihuacan. But as great as the Teotihuacanos were, they were not necessarily the most brilliant of Mexico's classic Indians. That distinction belongs to the Maya.

4. The Maya

The Mayan civilization was located mainly in the Yucatan Peninsula of what is today Mexico, Guatemala, El Salvador and Honduras. Their achievements were many: a writing system, advanced mathematics, accurate astronomy, great architecture, medical techniques and, of course, farming. By the year 300 A.D. they had developed several different varieties of corn. Their society was so well organized that a Mayan farmer had only to work about 48 days out of a year in order to grow enough food to feed his family. This left him enough free time for other work such as building roads, temples, pyramids and other public buildings for the state. The Mayan building period lasted roughly until 1300 A.D. or until the so-called Post-Classic era. The traveler to the land of the Maya today will be astounded to see Mayan pyramids, temples and even astronomical observatories still standing. See Plates 13 to 18. Unfortunately, we know less about the Maya than we would like, for of the 300 Mayan books found by the Spaniards, all but three were burned as "works of the devil."

Much of what we do know about the Maya is derived from their intricate system of picture writing, known as "glyphs," which the Mayans meticulously carved on their temples, walls and monuments. Recently, scientists have deciphered the glyph writings, which has led to exciting new information regarding their achievements and their history. New discoveries in the jungles of Central America seem to occur almost on a monthly basis. They add to our knowledge of these advanced people.

The Maya are probably best known for their mathematics. As early as 300 B.C. they had developed a practical use for the zero, an idea essential to any higher form of mathematics. This was a very advanced discovery; the zero was not widely used in Europe, for example, for another thousand years. The Maya also devised an excellent calendar, *more accurate than the one we use today,* by charting the heavens and the solar system. They could correctly predict astronomical eclipses of the moon, sun and Venus years in advance. They were true scientists in the sense of observing accurately, *for they could calculate time in millions of years.* Much of their science was closely tied to their religion. They were artists as well, excelling in ceramic pottery, mural painting, stone sculpture and weaving. Their building techniques are probably their most lasting achievements. As one looks at Mayan buildings, one is amazed by the precision of their craftsmanship and by the beauty of the carvings and sculptures. How were they able to cut and fit together so perfectly such huge pieces of rock without the use of metal tools or large draft animals such as oxen or elephants?

Recent archaeological discoveries show that the Mayans were also adept at surgery. Skulls have been found which had undergone operations in which the skull was opened, operations were performed on the brain, the incisions were closed, and the patient lived on for many more years. The Mayans were also able to provide fresh water to their inhabitants through aqueducts; homes were supplied with fresh running water by means of a system of troughs and valves which brought water from a main aqueduct. Even steam baths were popular.

They were curiously lacking in some techniques, however. They never made use of metal for anything other than jewelry, and while they put wheels on children's toys, they never thought to use the wheel as we use it today. This lack of technological development only makes their architectural achievements more amazing.

The religion of the Maya says much about them as a people. They believed that man and the earth were one and the same. Anything that existed was sacred and therefore to be respected. Their many gods took the forms of natural things such as corn, the rivers, mountains, lightning and thunder.

Far from being a long dead and forgotten people, fully 50% of the population of Guatemala today is Mayan. Large segments of the population of Mexico's Yucatan peninsula as well as parts of El Salvador and Honduras are heavily populated by Mayan Indians. These descendants of the first Mayans are in a sense caught between the past and the present. Many of them speak only their native Mayan language and not Spanish. Many continue to worship their Indian gods along with the newer Catholic one. One can see them today, especially in the mountains of Guatemala, living in much the same way as they did in the times of the great Mayan civilization. Their traditions in language, food, colorful clothing and religion continue. They are a dignified people who resist the influence of foreign cultures. See Plates 8 to 12.

The Mayans of today seem awed and a bit puzzled when they look at the great classic Mayan cities and buildings. They seem to be amazed at the accomplishments of their ancient ancestors. The Classic Mayans constructed many great cities. Among them are Tikal (in Guatemala), Palenque (Chiapas, Mexico), and Copan (Honduras). Tikal is possibly the most impressive of Mayan classic cities.

Settled before 320 A.D. it was a large metropolis similar to Teotihuacan in terms of population. In all, there are six pyramids in Tikal, the tallest standing over 230 feet high. There are also ball courts for the ceremonial ball game (which was like a combination of soccer and basketball), temples to the gods, palaces of the priests and nobles, ten reservoirs to provide drinking water, and several man-made lakes which were apparently for aesthetic or decorative purposes. Tikal, Palenque, Copan and the other great classic cities of the Maya are analogous or comparable to the great cities of classic or ancient Greece such as Athens and Corinth. For just as the people of Europe built upon the splendid achievements of the ancient Greeks, the people of Indian Mexico learned from and built upon the advances of the Classic Maya.

Unfortunately, Mexican Indian history did not proceed smoothly. Between 600 and 700 A.D. most of the classic cities of Mexico fell into decay and were abandoned by their inhabitants. Why and how did this occur? The question has plagued historians, anthropologists, and archaeologists for decades. Did crop failure, overpopulation, plague, locusts, or invasion by other tribes cause the downfall of Classic Indian Mexico? The most likely explanation is that it was not one of these possibilities but rather a combination. We do know that between 600 and 700 A.D., Teotihuacan was invaded and burned by peoples from the north. Thus Teotihuacan became the first classic city to decay. By 900 A.D. most of the great classic centers of Mexico were also abandoned.

But a new age would soon dawn over Indian Mexico. Newer cultures and peoples continued the development and history of Indian Mexico. This period is known as the Post-Classic time. The first great people of the Post-Classic era made their home near Teotihuacan, also in Mexico's central Anahuac Valley. They were the Toltecs.

5. The Toltecs

The Toltecs, or Tolteca, were the most influential Mexican Indians of the early Post-Classic era. Their influence was widely felt as they established a military empire which extended into northern Yucatan to include the Mayans of that time. Indeed, Post-Classic Mayan cities such as Chichen-Itza and Uxmal show much evidence of Toltec contact and even domination.

The Toltecs built their capital, Tula, only forty miles from Teotihuacan. From approximately 900 A.D. until 1100 A.D. the Toltecs were the dominant Mexican Indians. Their culture and way of life were so impressive that the word "Toltec" to later Mexican Indians meant smart or intelligent. Tula was the most important city in central Mexico between the time of Teotihuacan and the later rise of the Aztec capital city of Tenochtitlan. Unfortunately, Post-Classic Mexican Indian cultures lacked some of the artistic, religious and intellectual spirit that the Classic peoples possessed.

Wars fought over empire building, taxes or tribute imposed on conquered people, slavery, and human sacrifice were practiced in Post-Classic Indian Mexico. By analogy with Europe, the Romans who built their great civilization after the classic Greek era clearly had an advanced culture, lifestyle and society. Their great city of Rome was a wonder. But they lacked the genius in science and art that the classic Greeks possessed. The Romans seem to have been more interested in military victories and empire building than philosophy. Likewise, the Toltecs and later the Aztecs did lead comfortable lives and practiced the scientific innovations of the classic Maya. But both the Toltecs and the Aztecs treated their neighbors with arrogance and superiority. They seemed primarily interested in power rather than art.

6. Quetzalcoatl — Man and God

You remember that Quetzalcoatl, the feathered serpent, was the ruling god of Teotihuacan. The Toltecs built upon this religious figure and enhanced its legend into a powerful myth that came to be known throughout Indian Mexico. The story that follows is probably more fantasy than reality, although in all probability there is some basis in fact. But the reason for the great importance of Quetzalcoatl in Mexican history rests not upon whether the story was true or not. The real importance lies in the story's impact upon future events which greatly affected Mexico and her people.

The legend begins at the time of the Toltecs' first arrival in the Anahuac Valley. Mixcoatl (Cloud Serpent), their king, had led them from what is now Zacatecas to settle at Culhuacan. Mixcoatl was a warrior and a conqueror who, like all such figures, made many enemies along the way. One such enemy was his royal brother who one day killed Mixcoatl and assumed the Tolteca throne. Mixcoatl's pregnant wife escaped, however, and soon gave birth to a son named Ce-Acytl Topilitzin (One Reed our Prince).

Raised in Tepoztlan on religious study, Ce-Acytl Topilitzin came across the records of the great feathered serpent god of the Teotihuacanos, Quetzalcoatl. So impressed was he with this foreign god that he took its name and began to call himself Quetzalcoatl. The young prince Quetzalcoatl then returned to Culhuacan, mounted a revolt against the king, who was his uncle, and killed him. As son of Mixcoatl, Quetzalcoatl now became king of the Toltecs and the capital city of Tula was soon established. Following the legend of the original feathered serpent of Teotihuacan, this Toltec Quetzalcoatl is said to have outlawed human sacrifice from the Toltec religion, asking only for the sacrifice of snakes, butterflies and flowers. He is also said to have taught his people much about the arts, music and agriculture, supposedly even enabling them to grow giant ears of corn in many colors. Other achievements such as a writing system and calendar improvement are attributed to Quetzalcoatl as well. The Toltec wars of conquest were also stopped by the young King Quetzalcoatl. He is said to have preached a message of peace and love rather than of warfare and conquest. What made Quetzalcoatl even more remarkable is the legend of his appearance. He supposedly was very tall, light skinned, fair-haired and bearded. Because of his strange appearance and especially for all the great things he had done, he came to be looked upon with great reverence by his people. He had brought them peace, art, knowledge and great prosperity. Combined with his godly name and unusual appearance he came to be worshiped almost as a god himself. Seemingly, he was loved by all in Tula. But this was not the case.

The Toltec priests of the god Tezcatlipoca (a native Toltec god) hated Quetzalcoatl for his exaltation of the Quetzalcoatl of Teotihuacan (a foreign god to them). They may have also felt rather less influential now that they could no longer decide who should fall to the sacrificial knife. Therefore, these priests began to plot the downfall of their young king. One day Quetzalcoatl fell ill and was offered some "medicine" to drink by one of the priests. The medicine was actually pulque, a strong alcoholic drink which probably had some kind of drug in it. Quetzalcoatl took several cups of the beverage and fell asleep. Awakening the next morning to find himself lying next to his own sister, he was shamed greatly and accused of incest by the priests. Quetzalcoatl was forced into exile. He departed from Tula and headed for Yucatan with some followers.

There seems to be no doubt that he arrived in Yucatan in the year 987 A.D. Clear records of "kukulkan" (feathered serpent in the Mayan language) are found in Mayan writings, as are carvings and statues of serpents' heads ringed with feathers. Finally, the legend concludes with Quetzalcoatl sailing away to the east on the waves of the sea, carried upon a magic raft made of intertwined snakes. He told his followers that although he was leaving, he would return in a "Ce-Acytl," or one-reed year, and that he would reclaim his lost power and glory from those who would practice evil religious rituals such as human sacrifice. The generally accepted date for Quetzalcoatl's departure is 999 A.D.

This legend came to be widely known throughout Indian Mexico. Both the story of the original feathered serpent god of Teotihuacan and that of the Toltec Quetzalcoatl, who was driven from his homeland, were told and re-told throughout Mexico for centuries. And again, whether these events actually occurred or not is not the most important factor. That the myth was widely known and believed is far more important as we will soon see.

Meanwhile, the Toltecs flourished in the Valley of Mexico and maintained their militaristic empire for a while. Soon, however, they too would fade into oblivion, probably the victims of invading tribes of aggressive Indians from the north. Such is the history of Mexican civilizations; they rise, flourish for a time and then pass away, paving the way for newer tribes and peoples. The Toltec Empire is said to have fallen around 1100 A.D. Tradition says that in the year 1215 A.D. a new group of Indians appeared on the scene. At first these new arrivals were merely the latest in a long line of wandering nomadic peoples from the north. Upon their arrival in the Anahuac Valley they were looked down upon as savages and uncivilized people by the highly advanced neighboring tribes who lived there. But this group of less advanced "immigrant" Indians would soon build the greatest city and empire in all of Indian Mexico. They were known then as the Mexica, or Aztecs.

7. The Aztecs

The Aztecs were the last of the major nomadic groups which migrated south into the Anahuac Valley of central Mexico. Legend tells us that they arrived there around 1215 A.D.

The central Valley of Mexico is a high plateau, some 8000 feet above sea level, ringed by even higher mountains and snowcapped volcanoes. At the floor of the valley the Aztecs found a land of lakes, forests, and vegetation which had been settled by various tribes or city-states. The main lake was known as Lake Texcoco. Other smaller lakes such as Xochimilco, Chalco, and Xalcotan made up an area of about fifty by twenty miles that was dominated by water. Some of the lakes were of fresh water and some were of a salty, brackish brine. Much of the lake area was shallow, swampy and marshy. Wildlife of every variety was abundant: water birds such as herons, many varieties of fish, turkeys, chickens, and even larger mammals such as jaguars and mountain lions. In such a fertile area, the people in the city-states were living highly advanced and sophisticated lives.

Texcoco, one of the city-states, had a reputation as a center of culture and learning. There were fine libraries and archives where priests and scholars kept records of important historical, religious and philosophical thought. Other important towns included Xochimilco, an area known even today for the raising of beautiful flowers and plants. There were also the militarily strong tribes such as Atzapotzalco which had control of a hilly area known as Chapultepec, an area where the Aztecs settled in approximately 1270.

Chapultepec had fine natural springs which provided water for drinking.

THE EAGLE AND THE SERPENT. The name Mexico originates from a tribe of Indians known as the Mexica, more commonly known as the Aztecs. Originating from their mythical homeland of Aztlan, the Mexica migrated south, led by their divine leader, Huitzilopochtli. Although he died along the way, he told the Aztecs they should look for an eagle standing on a cactus and devouring a serpent. When they saw this vision, they should build their capital city at that spot. Legend has it that the Aztecs saw just such a sight on a small island in Lake Texcoco, the site of present-day Mexico City. Thus, both the name of the nation (Mexico) and its national flag (with an eagle and a serpent) are based on the Aztecs and their founding of their great city of Tenochtitlan.

At first the Aztecs were treated very badly by the other tribes, who regarded them as savages. But these "savages" could fight. They began to work for the other city-states as mercenaries (hired soldiers). In this way the Mexica grew strong and experienced in war. In 1319 the Aztecs apparently angered the people of Atzapotzalco, who drove them out of Chapultepec. Forced to look for another place to live, the Aztecs finally chose a small marshy island which was not much more than uninhabited swamp land. Besides the necessity to find a home, why did the Aztecs pick this particular spot? The answer lies in the legend of Aztlan.

Aztlan was the mythical homeland of the Aztecs. Historians are unsure as to its exact location, as the Aztecs were a nomadic people at this time. Some speculate that Aztlan was in what is now northern Mexico. Others think it may have been as far north as the present Southwest of the U.S. Aztec tradition has it that centuries before their arrival in the Anahuac Valley, their god-king Huitzilopochtli had told them to go south. While guiding them through their wanderings, he died along the way. But before he died he told them to continue until they would see an eagle devouring a serpent. When they saw this they were to settle and build their home on that spot. Legend also tells us that it was on this swampy, deserted island near the shores of Lake Texcoco that the Aztecs saw such a vision. The Aztecs named their home Tenochtitlan which soon grew to be one of the greatest cities in the ancient world. After defeating the Aztecs in their war of conquest, the Spaniards constructed Mexico City on the ruined and destroyed remains of Tenochtitlan. Mexico City, therefore, is Tenochtitlan and we see an eagle and a serpent on the flag of Mexico to honor the founding of the Aztec capital and Mexico's Indian heritage.

Because of their expertise in warfare, the Aztecs soon earned respect from the other city-states of Lake Texcoco. One of the most important early events in the development of the Aztecs was their conquest of Chapultepec and the natural water supply that went with it. When they had a stable supply of water they could see to it that their city grew. Through great labor that took many, many years, the Aztecs began to reclaim the wetlands for their city. They constructed dikes and dams which blocked off the water and allowed them to drain whole areas of lake land for settlement and building. These lands were then filled in and buildings were constructed. In the 1400s a great system of causeways was built which connected Tenochtitlan to the mainland. Like roads built on foundations which stretched down to the bottom of the shallow lakes, these broad thoroughfares provided easy access to the island city of Tenochtitlan. Upon one of these causeways an aqueduct was built which provided the city with fresh water straight from Chapultepec. The Aztecs then began an extensive program of "chinampa" construction.

Chinampas, or "floating gardens," were probably already in use by the lake dwellers before the Aztecs' arrival. But no one had ever used them so extensively as did the Aztecs. To build these chinampas, Aztec workmen would fashion huge woven baskets of reeds and light branches. These were then filled with good soil and hundreds of men would then drag them to the lake where they would be set out to float. Seeds were planted into the soil and the lake water would gradually seep through to germinate and keep the young plants growing. Eventually, the original basket would wither away but the root systems of the various crops would hold the earth in place. Soon it became difficult to tell the natural island land from the man-made chinampa. Small trees were even planted whose roots would reach down to the lake bottom and anchor the chinampas in place. Today, those who visit Xochimilco can see hundreds-of-years-old chinampas still providing flowers, fresh fruits and vegetables for the population of Mexico City. In the time of the Aztecs, these man-made islands of extremely fertile soil provided the growing population of Tenochtitlan with an additional food supply. Tenochtitlan grew so fast that it came to touch the already existing town of Tlatelolco. Together, by the late 1400s they comprised about five square miles of bustling city life. Like Tenochtitlan, Indian Mexico in general was expanding, communicating and trading among its people as never before, as other sections of the Aztec capital clearly show. See Plates 2 to 4.

One of the most famous aspects of Tenochtitlan was its market place which attracted up to 60,000 people daily. Fernando Horcasitas describes it in his book *The Aztecs, Then and Now:* "The typical market place was divided into seven sections. In the first were sold gold and silver objects, precious stones and feathers. In the second, chocolate and all kinds of spices. In the third, cloth and articles of clothing. In the fourth, food: corn, beans, chiles, tomatoes, amaranth, chia seeds, salt, turkeys, quail, rabbits, hares, deer meat, ducks, maguey honey, and bee hives. Offered in the fifth was a miscellany of avocados, manioc, wild plums, pumpkins, frogs, newts, bark paper, incense, rubber resin, gums, lime, obsidian blades, lumber, skins of animals, sandals and copper instruments. Greens of different sorts and tortillas were sold in the sixth. In the seventh, fine reeds filled with tobacco, and all types of pottery, including pots, plates, bowls and tubs could be purchased." See Plate 5.

As Aztec military power grew the city itself came to shine as "the jewel of the empire." Since the city was set upon water, most transportation was by means of canoes. Tree-lined waterways and paths for those on foot gave the capital a rural atmosphere. Near the market place, in the heart of the city, there was a ceremonial center of the most important state buildings. At the center of this area was the great Aztec pyramid, crowned with twin temples at the top, one dedicated to Tlaloc (the god of rain) and the other for the all-important Huitzilopochtli (the god of war). There was a complex of over thirty public buildings which included palaces of the nobles, temples, schools or academies for the sons of the wealthy, and even a zoo which astounded the Spaniards. As more and more wealth from conquered peoples flowed into Tenochtitlan, the city became spectacular. Because of its canals, the Spanish called it "the Venice of the Americas." Estimates as to how many people actually lived in Tenochtitlan vary, but it is safe to assume that it was one of the largest cities in the world at its height, housing roughly 250,000 people.

Bernal Díaz del Castillo recorded the Spanish reaction to Tenochtitlan: "and ... when we saw all those cities and villages built in the water, and other great towns on the dry land, that straight and level causeway leading to Mexico, we were astounded. The great cities and buildings that were made of stone seemed like images or visions to us. Indeed, some of the soldiers asked whether it was not all a dream. It was all so wonderful that I do not know how to describe the first glimpse of things never heard or seen or dreamed of before."

Not all that the Spaniards found was so wonderful, however. The Aztec religion of sun worship, according to the Spanish priests, had cruel aspects. The Aztecs used human beings as sacrificial victims for their gods. Other Mexican Indian tribes (as well as other civilizations in other cultures) had used human sacrifice, including the Toltecs before Quetzalcoatl did away with the practice. But of the Mexican Indians, the Aztecs are said to have practiced human sacrifice the most. While this practice was supposed to be purely religious there was a practical military side to it as well. Many think that the Aztecs sacrificed to the gods as a means of scaring and intimidating their own people and their neighbors. In most cases it was the captured soldiers who were used as sacrificial victims. After a town or city was conquered by the Aztecs, the vanquished were made to periodically send victims for sacrifice. If they failed to do so, the Aztec armies would march on their lands and lay waste to their settlements.

But the Aztec leadership maintained that human sacrifice was necessary for religious reasons as well. Legend and religious belief had it that there had been four creations and destructions of the earth. There had been darkness upon the earth after the failure of the Fourth Sun. One day the gods gathered at Teotihuacan and one god was able to get the sun to move again by diving into a ceremonial fire. The Aztecs believed that as the god had sacrificed himself in order to get the sun to return and give them light, at least the people (the people of the Fifth Sun) could sacrifice themselves in order to nourish and feed the sun and keep it shining. On certain special ceremonial occasions, or to celebrate a great victory in war, the Aztecs made sacrifices to their gods. Since most of the victims were captured warriors, it is easy to see why the neighboring tribes hated the Aztecs, for the Aztecs preferred to use people from conquered tribes as their victims.

Sentence or Fragment?

DIRECTIONS:

A complete sentence makes sense when read all alone. An incomplete sentence or fragment does not. Some of the following are fragments. Some are perfectly correct, complete sentences. Rewrite the fragments and make them into good sentences. You may add words, get rid of words, or rearrange the words. **Just make sure that each fragment you rewrite is factually correct according to the chapter and makes good sense when you read it alone.** Leave the complete sentences alone.

EXAMPLE: *The land known as Mexico, inhabited by Indians.*

Clearly this does not make sense when read alone. Although there **is no single correct way** to rewrite it, the following is much better:

The land known as Mexico was, and still is, inhabited by Indians.

1. Certain physical characteristics which show that Indians are Asian.
2. Columbus, who landed on an island in the Caribbean Sea in 1492.
3. Asia and America were once joined at the Bering Strait.
4. Nomads, who never stay in one place for very long.
5. Agriculture, which was the key to civilization.
6. The growing of corn, which occurred in Guatemala as early as 8000 B.C.
7. The Mayan civilization was one of the most advanced civilizations of the Americas.
8. Constructing temples, pyramids, aqueducts, and even observatories.
9. The Mayans were the first to use the zero in mathematics.
10. The Mayan calendar which was accurate and helped them in many ways.
11. The Mayans were even able to perform medical operations.
12. Guatemala, which today has a large Mayan population.
13. The pyramids of the Sun and Moon.
14. The "chinampas" or floating gardens.
15. In Teotihuacan there is a temple dedicated to Quetzalcoatl.
16. Tula, which was the capital city of the Toltecs.
17. A great king of the Toltecs, Mixcoatl.
18. Quetzalcoatl who was light skinned and bearded.
19. Human sacrifice, practiced at this time by the Toltecs.
20. Because of many factors, the man Quetzalcoatl became like a god.

21. Tricked by the Toltec priests and forced into exile in 999 A.D.
22. Promising to return in a "ce-acytl" or one-reed year.
23. Many different Indian civilizations lived in Mexico's Anahuac Valley.
24. The Toltec empire which passed from the scene in the 12th century.
25. A small band of wandering nomads from the north.

Short Answer Questions

DIRECTIONS:

Answer the following questions by writing one or two complete sentences for each. Be sure that each sentence you write:

a) Is factually correct and helps to answer the question.
b) Is a complete sentence, which means it makes sense when read alone.
c) Can be understood by someone who has not seen the question.
d) Begins with a capital letter and ends with a period.
e) Is completely in your own words.
f) Uses correct spelling and is neat.

EXAMPLE: *What is another name for the Aztecs?*

The Aztecs were also known as the Mexica. This is the origin of the name Mexico.

1. Who first called Native Americans "Indians"?
2. Define the word "race."
3. From where did the Native Americans migrate?
4. How do we know Native Americans are Asian?
5. What one discovery can make nomadic wanderers become city dwellers?
6. What are the two large pyramids at Teotihuacan?
7. Who was Quetzalcoatl to the Teotihuacanos?
8. What are some of the Mayan civilization's great achievements?
9. Why did the Mayans build observatories?
10. What country today is roughly one half pure Mayan Indian?
11. Who was Quetzalcoatl to the Toltecs?
12. What did Quetzalcoatl promise as he left Tula in 999 A.D.?
13. Briefly describe the Anahuac Valley.
14. What were Texcoco and Xochimilco famous for?
15. What was the homeland of the Aztecs? Where was it?
16. Why did the Aztecs build Texcoco on an island?

17. Briefly describe Tenochtitlan.
18. Explain this statement: "Mexico City is Tenochtitlan."
19. Why was Chapultepec vital to the Aztecs as they built their city?
20. How did the Aztecs make their island city larger?
21. Why did the Aztecs practice human sacrifice?
22. What is the relationship between human sacrifice and the Aztec conquests?

WRITING PARAGRAPHS WITH TOPIC SENTENCES

IMPORTANT DEFINITIONS:

1. <u>Sentence:</u> a group of words beginning with a capital letter and ending with a period. For the purposes of learning to write, a sentence may be understood as a complete thought.

2. <u>Topic Sentence:</u> the first sentence in a paragraph. It tells you what the paragraph is going to be about, so you need to make sure it contains the main idea.

3. <u>Paragraph:</u> a group of sentences divided from others with an indention. It is concerned with the development of a general idea and its details.

SAMPLE PARAGRAPH TOPIC: Describe the Aztec civilization.

SAMPLE PARAGRAPH.

 <u>The Aztec civilization was both beautiful and terrible.</u> Their art was as great as that of any American Indian group. Their science and architecture were complex and highly advanced. Their capital city was perhaps the most impressive city in the world at its height. However, in their religion they sacrificed people to their gods. When the Spanish saw these sacrifices, they were horrified.

PLEASE NOTICE: The topic sentence (underlined) introduces the general idea of the Aztec civilization as being both terrible and beautiful at the same time. The rest of the paragraph gives details and facts that prove the topic sentence to be true. Finally, notice how there is nothing in the paragraph which does not relate directly to the topic sentence.

Paragraph Questions

DIRECTIONS:

Answer the following questions by writing a good paragraph for each. Refer back to the sample paragraph on **page 47** for help. Be sure that each paragraph you write:

a) Is factually correct, helps to answer the question and is in your own words.
b) Looks like a proper paragraph (see sample).
c) Has an <u>underlined</u> topic sentence at the beginning of the paragraph.
d) Contains no fragments.
e) Uses correct spelling and is neat.

1. What is the stereotype that most Mexican Americans have about Indians?
2. How do we know that Native American Indians are really of the Asian race?
3. Describe how farming or agriculture can turn nomads into city dwellers.
4. Describe the city of Teotihuacan.
5. What are some of the technical and scientific achievements of the Maya?
6. What are some of the great Mayan cities? When were they thriving? What are some of their features?
7. Briefly, describe the legend of the Toltec Quetzalcoatl.
8. What is the Aztec legend of Aztlan and the Eagle and Serpent?
9. How did the Aztecs use chinampas?
10. Describe the Aztec capital of Tenochtitlan.
11. How was the Aztec religion connected to their wars for empire?

Clustering, ID Items and ID Paragraphs

DIRECTIONS:

Clustering is a method for bringing together information about any topic. It is helpful to make a cluster before attempting to write. When making a cluster about an identification item (important people, places, and things), write the item in the middle of a piece of paper, then make "satellite bubbles" around it, filling them in with whatever pops into your mind that relates to the item. Ask yourself who or what is this, and why is it important historically?

Keep making bubbles until the ideas stop coming. Look up the item in your book if necessary. Once completed, the cluster is a valuable guide for writing identification paragraphs (ID paragraphs). These paragraphs should be written in acceptable paragraph form (topic sentence, supporting details) and should also answer the two questions mentioned above. Individual ID paragraphs can also be joined together to form the body of effective essays. A sample cluster and paragraph follow.

SAMPLE CLUSTER

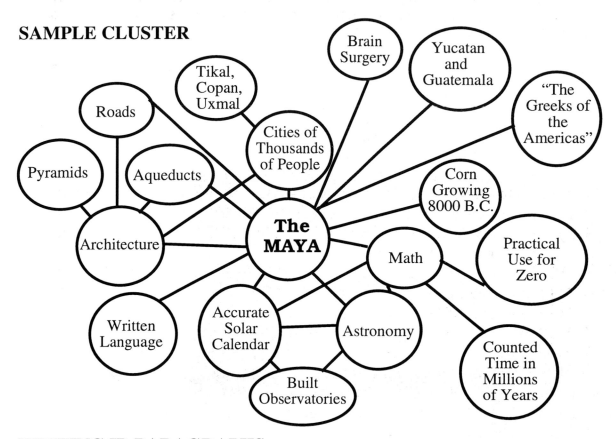

WRITING ID PARAGRAPHS:

Following the sample cluster, it is quite easy to write an effective ID paragraph about the Maya. Notice that not all items in the cluster must be included in the paragraph and that some new ideas that come to mind can be added.

SAMPLE ID PARAGRAPH

The Mayan civilization was one of the most highly advanced in the world. Located in the Yucatan Peninsula of Mexico and Guatemala, from 500 B.C. to approximately 1000 A.D., the Mayans laid the intellectual, scientific and artistic framework for future Mexican Indian civilizations. They pioneered agricultural experimentations which produced bountiful crops that could feed thousands. They counted time in the millions of years and constructed astronomical observatories which still stand. They had a written language and constructed immense cities complete with aqueducts and pyramids. Today, half of the population of Guatemala is pure-blooded Mayan Indian.

Please note: The ID paragraph above not only tells who the Maya were, but also explains their historical importance and significance.

Clustering and ID Items

DIRECTIONS:

Make clusters and/or ID paragraphs for the following identification items. While making your cluster or paragraph, ask yourself who or what the item is and why it is important in the history being studied. Refer to your book if necessary. A sample cluster and ID paragraph can be found on **page 49**.

Bering Strait	the Toltecs
nomad	the Aztecs
agriculture/urbanization	Aztlan
Teotihuacan	Eagle and Serpent
Quetzalcoatl	Tenochtitlan
the Maya	

Essay Questions

DIRECTIONS:

The following are essay questions on the content of this chapter. Before attempting to answer any questions, see **page 187** for directions on how to write an essay and **page 188** for a sample essay.

1. Explain the racial composition of present-day Mexican and Mexican American people.
2. How does the discovery of farming make civilization possible?
3. Discuss the Mayan civilization. What were some of their greatest achievements?

4. Narrate the story or legend of Quetzalcoatl. Begin with the Teotihuacanos, and proceed with the Toltecs.

5. Discuss the Aztecs. Include their migration from Aztlan, their arrival in the Anahuac Valley, their empire building, religion, and their construction of Tenochtitlan.

COUNTER COLÓN-IALISMO Codex

"Counter Colón-ialismo Codex," by the Texas artists Sylvia Orozco and Pío Pulido, is based on the Indigenous codices created by the artists and chroniclers of time in the 16th century following the "conquest." Using individual symbols, the drawing illustrates the impact of the meeting of two hemispheres. A few years before the arrival of the Spaniards in the "New World," a comet was seen by Moctezuma, Emperor of the Mexica nation. For him, it was an omen alerting him that something was about to happen. This work was exhibited at the Centro Cultural de la Raza in San Diego, California during an exhibit curated by Patricio Chávez of the Centro, Liz Lerma of MARS, Movimiento Artistico del Rio Salado in Phoenix, Arizona, and Sylvia Orozco of MEXIC-ARTE Museum, Austin, Texas.

Chapter Two

LA CONQUISTA

1. The Prophecy

The Mexica had become the dominant people in Mexico's central Anahuac Valley. A line of Mexica kings or emperors expanded not only the greatness of their city, but the size of their military empire as well. These emperors feared no one except their many gods. Their power on this earth seemed absolute.

Among the many gods worshiped in the Aztec pantheon of deities, the Mexica kept alive the tradition of the feathered serpent, Quetzalcoatl. The story of the ancient god of Teotihuacan, who had assumed human form as king of the Toltecs, was well-known in Tenochtitlan.

When he left in 999 A.D., the Toltec Quetzalcoatl was said to have predicted that he would return in a "Ce-Acytl," or one-reed year. The Toltec/Aztec calendar was divided into 52 year periods or cycles. Every 52nd year was a Ce-Acytl year; a year when the fair-skinned and bearded Quetzalcoatl might return to claim his lost throne and power.

One such reed year had been 1467. Despite great apprehension on the part of the Aztec rulers, due to an increased use of human sacrifice, nothing unusual or prophetic occurred. The normal end-of-the-cycle rituals were performed and the Aztec rulers breathed easier. Quetzalcoatl had not returned.

By the time of the next reed year, 1519, Moctezuma II had become the emperor of the Aztecs. He presided over an imperial empire at its height. Military victories had enlarged the size of the empire to unprecedented greatness. But Moctezuma II was also the highest Aztec priest. He knew that a reed year held great danger for a culture which used human sacrifice. Would 1519 be the fateful year of the great god Quetzalcoatl's return? Would the prophecy made 500 years earlier by the Toltec king/god be fulfilled? Would Moctezuma, as leader of the Aztecs, be punished for taking the hearts of men in religious ceremony?

Little was Moctezuma to know that this year a light-skinned and bearded man would indeed come to the lands of the Mexica, arriving from exactly the same direction from which Quetzalcoatl was said to have departed. Moctezuma could not possibly have imagined that this man's arrival would mean not only his end, and the end of his glorious empire, but also the end of 25,000 years of Indian Mexico itself.

2. The Aztecs Extend Their Empire

During the rule of the Aztec Emperor Itzcoatl (1428-1440), the power of the Aztecs grew. The first tribes to be conquered were those in the other city-states of Lake Texcoco. Some were conquered by force while others, fearful of the Aztec armies, made treaties and agreed to send tribute and victims to Tenochtitlan. Usually, this tribute was like a tax placed on the conquered people to supply Tenochtitlan with whatever of value these people possessed. The tribe of Cempoalla, located near the eastern Gulf Coast, was conquered and forced to pay such tribute. Moving south the Aztecs extended their conquests, expanding their power to the edges of present day Mexico or as far as the modern states of Oaxaca and Chiapas.

One of the neighboring tribes, however, "enjoyed" a special relationship with Tenochtitlan. The Tlaxcalans, neighbors of the Mexica to the east, were never completely conquered by the Aztecs. Permitted to keep a measure of their independence, Tlaxcala was frequently at war with Tenochtitlan. This guaranteed a steady supply of victims for the Aztecs. In fact, the Aztecs even used the constant Tlaxcalan wars as a battle training ground for their younger military officers. The Tlaxcalans, therefore, were one of the Aztecs' most bitter enemies. They came to hate the Aztecs as greatly as did many of the conquered people. All of these bad feelings toward the people of Tenochtitlan were soon to play a very important role in the downfall of the Aztecs.

3. Strange Omens Appear

As if the gods themselves were trying to warn the Aztecs of some horrible tragedy to come, many bizarre omens (signs which predict the future) were seen in and around Tenochtitlan. Comets flashing fire in the sky, temples of the gods mysteriously bursting into flames, lightning bolts damaging ceremonial buildings, horrible floods from the lake destroying homes and buildings, ghosts' voices heard in the night, a strange bird with a mirror in its head, men with two heads appearing in the city, all these mysterious happenings are described by the Aztec historians. All these came in the ten-year period immediately preceding the Spanish arrival. Modern historians attribute all these strange events to a mass hysteria that was gripping Tenochtitlan, a feeling of approaching doom and disaster that began to grow in the early 1500s in Moctezuma's capital.

Indeed, Moctezuma himself was shaken and worried by these omens. Were the gods trying to tell him something or trying to warn him of some approaching danger? Moctezuma summoned his magicians and religious advisors but none could interpret the signs for him. He grew deeply worried and withdrew into himself, a brooding, puzzled and fearful man. This behavior was in stark contrast to the earlier image of Moctezuma, that of the great warrior and conqueror. But now, in Moctezuma, we can see a weakness of the Aztecs as they faced the invading Spaniards: some of their religious beliefs. Moctezuma, as high priest as well as emperor and ruler, thought of little other than how best to please the many gods of the Aztecs. This tendency to think in religious rather than practical terms would come to play an important role in the demise of Moctezuma and his Aztec Empire.

4. Strange Visitors Arrive

As if to confirm Moctezuma's worst fears, reports began coming in from the Gulf Coast about strange "towers or small mountains floating on the waves of the sea." Another report received a few days later described the strange occupants of these "mountains" as being unfamiliar people who "have very light skin, much lighter than ours. They all have very long beards, and their hair comes only to their ears."

This last report made Moctezuma even more fearful. As soon as he heard about the light skin and beards he immediately began to wonder if it might be Quetzalcoatl or some other gods returning to Mexico to reclaim their past glory. Upon hearing of the strangers' arrival, Moctezuma ordered the entire Gulf Coast watched constantly. Agents of Moctezuma kept a careful watch day and night. Within a short period of time four more ships were sighted. Described as seagoing temples which rested on foundations formed by very large canoes, Moctezuma was now convinced; Quetzalcoatl had indeed returned. Fear and doubt gripped Moctezuma as he spent endless sleepless nights worrying about his future as Aztec Emperor. What would Quetzalcoatl do when he arrived? Would Moctezuma be killed by Quetzalcoatl as he retook his empire? Or would the almighty god allow Moctezuma to live? Moctezuma was sure that he would have to surrender his throne and turn over his kingdom to Quetzalcoatl. But who were these "fair-skinned, bearded men" who had come to the land of the Mexica on "floating pyramids"? Where had they come from and who had sent them?

5. Europeans to America

After the voyage of Columbus in 1492, European nations hungry for riches, power and conquests, all the while full of religious zeal, began launching dozens of voyages of "discovery." Before 1492 the Europeans were totally ignorant of the existence of the continent of America. But now that they knew of a previously unknown land, a "new world," the Europeans wasted no time in setting out to gain riches from it.

One of the most powerful nations in the world at the beginning of the sixteenth century was Spain. For over seven centuries the Spanish had been engaged in a bitter war with the Moors. The Moors were Arabs from the north of Africa who had invaded and conquered Spain in the 800s. Reduced for many years to the status of subject people, the Spanish never gave up trying to drive the Moors out of their country. Warfare became a way of life for the Spanish. Their entire society and culture centered around two things: war against the Moors and devotion to their Roman Catholic religion.

Their one aim in life was to defeat the Moors and drive the hated Moslem religion out of Spain, once and for all. Experienced, efficient and brutal in warfare, the Spanish finally succeeded in defeating the Moors in the same year Columbus sailed (1492). This is not a coincidence. After the defeat of the Moors, the Spanish needed a release for their energies they had previously spent in fighting the Moors. When Columbus returned with stories of gold, non-Christian natives and beautiful lands, the Spanish king and queen soon formulated a plan to send more ships to explore this new world. They were to bring back to Spain whatever gold and treasure they could find and they were to claim as much land as they could for Spain. All the "barbaric savages" they encountered were to have their souls saved by being converted to the Catholic religion.

6. Cuba, a Spanish Port

Further voyages of exploration focused on the Caribbean Sea. The beautiful tropical islands there astounded the Spanish. Soon a naval base was established on the island of Cuba. Cuba provided a perfect rest stop for the Spanish expeditions. After the long Atlantic crossing, the Spanish could rest and repair their ships, if needed, in Cuba. They could then continue their voyages in search of gold and glory.

Many Spaniards who were failures of one sort or another in Spain eagerly headed for the new world in search of fame and fortune. Well educated and capable people came as well. An exciting time was just beginning for all the Europeans who were engaged in exploring America. Spain and the other nations were beginning the European discovery and conquest of the American Continent, a continent wholly Indian. It is no exaggeration to say that the discovery of America probably changed the world more than any other single event. The Europeans changed the culture, religion, language, and even the racial makeup of the American land. The gold and riches that were taken from America financed the European Renaissance and later the Industrial Revolution.

7. Early Voyages to Mexico

An able Spaniard, Diego Velásquez, became the governor of Cuba in the early 1500s. It was his duty to organize and commission further voyages of exploration into the yet unknown lands of America. He was to collect as much gold as possible. The natives were to be taught Christianity.

But in Cuba there was little gold and the time spent cultivating sugar and other cash crops did not fit in with the get-rich-quick dreams of the Spaniards. Among the indigenous people of Cuba there was a persistent rumor of a rich empire which lay far to the west. Supposedly there was a great city that had "streets paved with gold" and where the residents adorned themselves with precious jewels. More enticing, the city was said to "float in the middle of a vast lake", surrounded by high mountains on all sides. Such a tale whetted the Spanish appetite for gold. For these reasons, in 1517, Diego Velásquez commissioned Francisco Hernández de Córdova to see if he could locate this wondrous sounding land. Córdova set sail and headed due west.

He reached the coast of what is today the Yucatan Peninsula and when he landed he came in contact with Mayan Indians living there. Although impressed with their highly civilized ways, it was soon apparent he had not found the fabled city of his search. Soon he left and explored further. But at one stop, still in the lands of the Mayas, a battle broke out between the Spaniards and the Indians. About half of Córdova's men were killed and soon after he returned to Cuba.

Thereafter, Velásquez selected his nephew, Juan de Grijalva, to explore further into this territory. Moving north, hugging the coast, past Yucatan and into the province known today as Tabasco, Grijalva at one point entered a large and promising looking river which today bears his name. He found mangrove swamps and some humble villages, but no mythical floating city. After sailing as far north as the Gulf of Mexico, Grijalva then returned to Cuba, no richer for the effort.

But the Indians in Cuba continued to insist that the mythical and wealthy city was a reality. This time, an increasingly frustrated Diego Velásquez would need to find a far more resourceful and aggressive commander for the next voyage to Mexico. He selected a bold young man of thirty-four years who seemed to fit the bill. His name was Hernan Cortés.

Originally from the Extremadura region of Spain, which also produced other notable conquistadors like Pedro de Alvarado and the Pizarro brothers, Cortés had gained wealth and success in Cuba. But his active and aggressive personality yearned for greater excitement and thrill. So when Governor Velásquez suggested the expedition, Cortés readily accepted. Although Velásquez changed his mind at the last minute, for fear that Cortés would be difficult to control, it was too late. Cortés had slipped out of the Cuban harbor and had even stolen additional ships and also supplies from the Spanish warehouses. The most fateful voyage in Mexican history had begun.

It was the ships of Córdova, Grijalva, and finally Cortés that Moctezuma's lookouts had spotted. And word of these ships was what struck fear into the heart of the Aztec emperor as he sat in his palace and wondered if indeed this was the return of Quetzalcoatl.

8. Cortés

Cortés came to Mexico with an impressive force. He had with him eleven ships of various sizes, with about 700 men: 400 Spanish soldiers, 200 Cuban Indians, and 100 sailors. His weapons included hundreds of Toledo swords, 32 crossbows, 13 harquebuses (large rifle-like guns), ten large and six small cannon. Most important of all, he brought 16 horses. These horses would prove to be a big advantage for Cortés because the Indians had no knowledge of the horse and were initially very afraid of them. In February 1519, Cortés made his first landing on a small island a few miles off the tip of the Yucatan Peninsula. This island is today called Cozumel. It was on this island that Cortés had his first stroke of luck.

While on Cozumel, Cortés had his first contact with the Indians. The Mayans whom he met were friendly to the Spanish. One day, while attempting to communicate with the Indians, Cortés was brought a strange looking White man who cried out in Spanish that he was saved. The man's name was Jerónimo de Aguilar. It turned out that he was a Spaniard who had been shipwrecked and washed ashore in the land of the Maya in 1511. Captured by the Indians, he said that he watched as another Spaniard was killed, cooked and eaten by the Indians. Aguilar had learned the language of the Mayans in his eight years among them. For this reason, he became very valuable to Cortés.

9. La Malinche

Setting sail from Cozumel, the Spanish expedition moved around the tip of Yucatan and landed shortly thereafter on the mainland of Mexico. In an area known today as Tabasco they were attacked soon after their arrival. Mayan Indians swarmed all over the outnumbered Spanish. The Spaniards were nearly defeated in this first battle. The fighting raged on for two days. Finally, Cortés called to his ships and had the horses brought out. The Spanish made a cavalry charge and when the Indians saw this, they turned and ran. Cortés had won his first battle.

A short time later the defeated Indians offered gifts to the Spanish. Many beautiful presents were given. But more valuable than any gift was an Indian woman given to Cortés at this time. She was among a group of twenty slaves given to the Spanish. But she was different. She was a Mexica, an Aztec who had been sold into slavery by her own family. Of noble birth, Marina, as the Spaniards called her, had the bearing of a well educated woman. More importantly, she spoke not only the Aztec language (Nahuatl) but had also learned the Mayan tongue.

Marina also confirmed the existence of the great city they sought. She had seen Tenochtitlan with her own eyes and verified its grandeur. Now Cortés not only had a translator but also a guide who could lead them directly to their destination. And her natural resentment toward her own people for selling her into slavery gave her the motivation to see to it that the Spanish would succeed at the expense of the Aztecs.

Thus, with Aguilar and Marina as translators, Cortés could effectively communicate with many of the Indians he encountered. Making good use of his two translators, Cortés explained to the Mayans about the Christian religion and attempted to convert them. Accompanied by a priest, Cortés would follow this procedure wherever he went in Mexico.

Although the Tabascans had little gold, they, too, confirmed the story of the fabulously rich city far away and high in the mountains. As Cortés's men were pressuring him at all times for the great wealth he had promised them, he now loaded his ships and prepared to move northward towards their goal.

Cortés was not aware that he and his men were being secretly watched by Moctezuma's spies. They had been ordered to observe the strangers' every move and to report back to him. Soon Moctezuma heard that "the strangers are accompanied by a woman from this land who speaks our Nahuatl tongue. She is called La Malinche." Malinche was the closest the Spaniards could come to pronouncing her Indian name, "Malintzin."

10. At Vera Cruz

Cortés and his men landed at what is today Vera Cruz without any problems and established a base camp there. In order to give his voyage more legal authority, Cortés formally established a Spanish settlement on this spot and named it La Villa Rica de la Vera Cruz. He had the priest bless this act and had himself named as governor. One ship was now sent back to Spain with some gifts of gold for the Spanish king. Impressed with the beautiful landscape around Vera Cruz, Cortés and his men attempted to make contact with the Indians there. These Indians turned out to be friendly to the Spanish and exchanged gifts with Cortés and his men. Cortés, with his translators, eagerly asked questions trying to find out more about the great and wealthy empire about which they had heard so much.

After a short time at Vera Cruz a small group of Indians came up to the Spanish camp. At first sight it was clear that these Indians were not from the Vera Cruz area. Dressed in beautifully embroidered clothes adorned with delicate feathers, precious jewels and gold, these Indians proved to be messengers from Moctezuma. When these messengers had left Tenochtitlan, Moctezuma had told them: "Go now without delay. Do reverence to our lord the god. Say to him your deputy Moctezuma has sent us to you. Here are the presents with which he welcomes you home to Mexico." This they said to Cortés as they offered gifts to the Spanish.

In the eyes of the Spaniards, the gifts were fantastic! Fine multicolored woven goods, small gold figurines, turquoise inlaid objects, delicate feather work in brilliant colors, and, most impressive of all, a large flat circular disc covered with hammered gold! The eyes of Cortés's men grew large when they saw these beautiful things. It was for this that they had come so far!

The Aztecs also showed their reverence to Cortés and his men by touching their fingers to the ground and then placing the fingers to their lips. This custom, called "eating dirt" by the Spanish, was a holy sign, reserved only for the highest priests and gods.

When Cortés heard their speech, saw the gifts and the way they greeted him, it was clear to him that the Indians had him confused with one of their gods. This was soon confirmed by Malinche. Immediately he saw this confusion as an advantage he would begin to use in any way he could. He began to act the way a mysterious god would.

He invited the messengers from Moctezuma aboard one of his ships. While there, the ship hoisted anchor and sailed about the harbor. This amazed the Aztecs, for the Indians knew nothing of the sail or its use. Then he ordered the cannons and guns to be fired repeatedly. The noises and smells that came from the weapons horrified the Indians. With no knowledge of gunpowder or iron, these messengers thought surely they were in the presence of gods. Cortés then told them to return to their leader with the message that he (Cortés) had come under the orders of a great lord and king from across the oceans. He also said that he had come to teach them about the true and only God and to show them the falseness of their gods. Needless to say, the messengers wasted no time in returning to Moctezuma.

Meanwhile, Moctezuma was growing even more worried and confused. It is recorded that: "Moctezuma could neither sleep nor eat and no one could speak with him ... He was lost in despair in the greatest gloom and sorrow. He was heard to say 'my heart burns and suffers as if it were drowned in spices.'"

Soon the messengers returned and told him what they had seen. The Aztec Emperor was "astonished and terrified by their report." The messengers told him how all the weapons of the "gods" were made of iron and that "their deer carry them on their backs wherever they wish to go. These deer, our lord, are as tall as the roof of a house."

Moctezuma is said to have received one other piece of information from his spies. He was apparently told that wherever Cortés and the Spanish went the Indian practice of human sacrifice was condemned and the Indians were persuaded to stop this ritual. This further convinced Moctezuma that Cortés must be Quetzalcoatl because Quetzalcoatl had, from the beginning of his reign in Tula, opposed and outlawed human sacrifices.

11. In Cempoalla

After a lengthy stay in Vera Cruz, Cortés decided to move on. He and his men were eager to see the great Aztec capital city they had heard so much about. Loading their ships, they sailed up the coast to the land known as Cempoalla.

Landing in Cempoalla, Cortés was warmly greeted by the chief of the tribe. Soon Cortés learned that these people were bitter enemies of the Aztecs. These Indians hated the Aztecs for the many wars, much tribute, and sacrificial victims they had lost to Tenochtitlan. Their chief told Cortés much of Moctezuma and his empire, and even asked Cortés for protection from the dreaded Aztecs. As Cortés listened, a plan for the conquest of all Mexico began to take shape in his mind. He correctly perceived that the Aztecs ruled Mexico through fear and military strength. They captured people as sacrificial victims and took what tribute they wanted from the tribes they had conquered. In this way they controlled their empire. Cortés reasoned that if he could defeat the Aztecs, perhaps he could gain their empire for himself. Talking to the Cempoallans, he realized that the Aztecs' enemies would make perfect allies against Moctezuma.

In answer to the Cempoallan request for protection from the Aztecs, Cortés agreed only on condition that the Cempoallans stop all sacrifices, allow the Spaniards to destroy all holy idols and statues of their gods, and accept Christianity as the only true religion. Reluctantly, the Indian chief agreed to Cortés's demands. Cortés then quickly ordered his soldiers to climb to the top of the Cempoallan pyramid and throw down the idols. The Indians shook with fear for they expected the Spanish to be struck down immediately by the gods. When nothing happened, Cempoalla fell firmly into Cortés's grasp.

Before leaving Cempoalla and beginning the march to Tenochtitlan, Cortés made a dramatic move. Some of his men were reluctant to leave the coast and begin the march inland. As they numbered only between five and seven hundred, they feared being swallowed up by millions of Indians. The men wanted to take the gold they had found and return to Cuba. To quell the grumbling and prevent an impending mutiny, Cortés ordered that two of the complainers be hanged. Another he had flogged with a lash. He then ordered his ships to be scuttled and run aground so that none of his men would have any more ideas about returning to Cuba. Now there would be no turning back. It was now a matter of success over the Aztecs or death in the attempt.

12. Tlaxcala and Cholula

The Aztecs had abused the Tlaxcalans through the years, but unlike the Cempoallans, the Tlaxcalans did not greet Cortés in friendship. As the Spanish tried to march through their land the Tlaxcalans suddenly attacked. Thousands of Tlaxcalan warriors swarmed over the Spanish. This was the first really large battle the Spanish had experienced. With the help of some of the Cempoallans, the Spanish resisted their attackers for days. Finally the Spanish swords, guns, armor, cannon, and horses, plus the Indian troops, won the victory.

The Tlaxcalans were proud warriors. After the Spanish had defeated them, they agreed to help Cortés fight against the Aztecs. They told Cortés even more about the Aztec empire and exactly how Moctezuma ruled through fear and violence. Cortés now began to hope that if he could gather together a large enough Indian army as he marched toward Tenochtitlan, perhaps Moctezuma would surrender to him when the Spanish arrived. It was a good plan to avoid unnecessary bloodshed. Unfortunately, it was not destined to succeed.

While in Tlaxcala, Cortés learned of a powerful neighboring tribe, the

Cholulans. They were friends of the Aztecs and it would be dangerous to march through their land. Attack was very likely and even with Cempoallan and Tlaxcalan help, victory would not be certain.

Cortés decided, however, that if he could be successful in Cholula, the psychological effect on Moctezuma might be worth the danger. If Moctezuma saw that even the Cholulans were no match for the "gods," perhaps the Aztec emperor might surrender.

So on they marched to Cholula. When they arrived at the outskirts of the city they were greeted in a friendly manner by the Cholulans. Leaving their Tlaxcalan troops outside the city walls, the Spaniards were led inside and treated very well. But Cortés was suspicious. Pretending to be unaware he secretly ordered his men to make preparations for an attack. It was at this time that La Malinche's help was vitally important.

Circulating among the Cholulans, La Malinche soon discovered a Cholulan plot. She hurried to tell Cortés that, just as he had suspected, the Cholulans were secretly planning an attack against the Spanish. Taking the offensive Cortés summoned the Cholulan leaders to his tent. He confronted them with his knowledge of their plot. Angrily he told them of the consequences for plotting against a god such as himself. Without another word the Spanish attacked and killed the Cholulan leaders and began an attack throughout the city. From outside the walls the Tlaxcalans also attacked and soon Cholula was a mass of dead bodies and burned out buildings. Cortés then demanded that the Cholulans become Christians and promise to obey the Spanish from that moment on. The defeated Cholulans had no choice but to agree.

Word spread throughout Indian Mexico of the fall of Cholula. Tribe after tribe began to offer their services to Cortés. The alliances that Cortés was now making with Indians who had been enemies of the Aztecs would prove to be decisive in the conquest. Gathering his forces together Cortés now began his final march through the high mountains to Tenochtitlan.

Moctezuma had also heard of the defeat of Cholula and he made a last desperate attempt to stop the Spanish march. Again he sent messengers, this time with even more gold treasure which he offered to Cortés if he would return to his own land. Of course, these offers served only to make the gold-hungry Spaniards more eager than ever to press ahead and reach Tenochtitlan itself.

13. Enter Quetzalcoatl

As Cortés neared Tenochtitlan, Moctezuma met daily with his highest priests and advisors. His brother Cuitlahuac, among others, warned Moctezuma

Tenochtitlan

not to allow the strangers to enter the city. Arguing that the spies' reports had shown the intruders to be human and not gods, Moctezuma was told that if the strangers were allowed to enter the city they would "cast you out of your house and overthrow your rule and when you try to recover what you have lost, it will be too late." Despite these warnings, Moctezuma had preparations made to greet the strangers formally and in fine style.

On November 8, 1519, Cortés, his Spanish soldiers, and 6,000 Tlaxcalan and other Indian soldiers crossed the main causeway leading to the island city of Tenochtitlan. The first reaction of the Spanish has been mentioned already. You remember that they were amazed by what they saw. As they marched along they wondered when they would come face-to-face with Moctezuma. Would they be attacked or would they be met in peace?

Moctezuma arrived upon a litter, sitting on his golden throne, dressed in his finest clothes with colorful feathers, beautiful jewels and elaborately embroidered decorations. As Moctezuma's procession passed, the assembled people of Tenochtitlan who had turned out to see the "gods" fell to the ground and pressed their faces to the earth. Such was the power of the Aztec emperor that death was the punishment for anyone who looked directly at his face. Moctezuma descended from his platform, and gifts of gold, jewels and beautiful feathers were presented to Cortés and the Spanish. Finally the two men met face-to-face.

Fortunately for students of Mexican history, their exact words have been recorded. After being asked by Cortés if he were indeed Moctezuma, he replied "Yes, I am Moctezuma." Then speaking directly to Cortés, Moctezuma said: "Our lord, you are weary. The journey has tired you but now you have arrived on the earth. You have come to your city ... you have come here to sit on your throne. Now you have come out of the clouds and mists to sit on your throne again. This was foretold by the kings who governed your city and now it has come to pass. You have come back to us. Rest now and take possession of your royal houses. Welcome to your land, my lord."

Malinche translated and then Cortés spoke: "Tell Moctezuma we are his friends, there is nothing to fear. We have wanted to see him for a long time. Tell him we love him well and that our hearts are contented. We have come to your house ... as friends, there is nothing to fear."

The Spaniards were led into the city and given one of the ceremonial buildings in the heart of the city in which to stay. Quickly they turned this palace into a fort and they began to gather all the gold they could find. They stripped the beautiful feathers off the ornamental pieces and melted them all down into gold bars.

The next day Cortés went with Moctezuma to the top of the main Aztec pyramid. Led into the shrine of Huitzilopochtli, Cortés saw what no White man had ever seen before.

Cortés is said to have told Moctezuma: "My lord Moctezuma, I do not understand how a great and wise lord like yourself could fail to perceive that your idols are not gods but evil things called demons." Quickly Cortés realized that if he were to truly conquer the Aztecs, he must replace Huitzilopochtli with the Virgin Mary. But he found that although Moctezuma had offered to give Cortés all that he owned, he refused to consider a substitution of Mary for Huitzilopochtli.

Cortés then decided that Moctezuma himself would have to be captured. Tricked into coming to the Spanish quarters, Moctezuma was surrounded and told he would not be permitted to leave. Cortés was going to rule the city of Tenochtitlan through the Aztec Emperor Moctezuma. Cortés ordered Moctezuma to have the temple of Huitzilopochtli destroyed and to have a Catholic altar built in its place. When Moctezuma refused, Cortés himself rushed to the top of the pyramid. Using a large iron bar he smashed the statue of Huitzilopochtli. Moctezuma followed and begged Cortés to stop before he did any more damage. Cortés then told Moctezuma: "You can see that your gods are merely of stone. Believe in God Almighty who made heaven and earth."

A few days later, all the idols and statues were taken from the top of the Aztec's pyramid. Cortés ordered all the walls washed clean. A Catholic altar and a cross were then constructed on the very spot where Huitzilopochtli once stood. Hoping all the while to conquer and defeat the Aztecs without war, Cortés had actually guaranteed war when he destroyed Huitzilopochtli. Moctezuma and the other Aztec priests now began plotting against Cortés for what he had done to their god.

14. Cortés Leaves Tenochtitlan

Cortés and his men stayed in Tenochtitlan for about six months and learned much about the great capital of the Aztecs. In fact, much of what we know of Tenochtitlan comes from the records left by Cortés and his conquistadores, especially Bernal Díaz del Castillo. Another vital source of first-hand or primary source information about the Aztecs comes from the Spanish priest, Bernardino de Sahagún. After the conquest, Father Sahagún organized Aztec oral historians and artists to produce a twelve volume encyclopedia on Aztec life and history. Many of the direct quotes used in this account come from the Aztec chroniclers who worked with Sahagún.

One day, news reached Cortés that a Spanish expedition of 19 ships and many soldiers had landed at Vera Cruz. Under the command of Pánfilo de Navarez, this force had been ordered by Diego Velásquez to capture and arrest Cortés.

Ever since Cortés had raided the warehouses of Cuba, Velásquez had considered him a criminal. The governor of Cuba was also afraid that, instead of him, Cortés would get all the recognition for the conquest of Mexico. Not wanting to get caught between Navarez and the Aztecs, Cortés decided to leave Tenochtitlan and take a large force of Spanish and Tlaxcalan warriors with him. Hoping to defeat Navarez quickly, and return with added Spanish troops, Cortés left Pedro de Alvarado in command of Tenochtitlan. Alvarado was an able soldier but perhaps too young and hot-tempered to be a good commander, as this incident shows: The Aztecs were celebrating a special religious holiday. On one particular day a large number of Indians gathered in a ceremonial dance. As their numbers increased Alvarado grew nervous. Were the Indians planning something? Were they going to attack his men? At the height of the dance Alvarado ordered an attack. The slaughter is vividly recorded by the Aztec historians: "They (the Spanish) ran in among the dancers, forcing their way to the place where the drums were played. They attacked the man who was drumming and cut off his arms. Then they cut off his head and it rolled across the floor. They attacked all the celebrants, stabbing them, spearing them, striking them with their swords."

The Aztecs soon retaliated and began to attack the Spanish. Alvarado was forced to order his men to retreat inside the palace for safety. The spell had now been broken — these white-skinned strangers were not gods but enemy invaders who had to be killed.

Meanwhile, Cortés had won a quick victory over Navarez and was headed back to Tenochtitlan with extra Spanish soldiers and horses. When he entered the palace, met with Alvarado and was told what had happened, he was furious. Disgusted at Alvarado's stupidity, he shouted to him that he had ruined everything. Meanwhile, the Aztecs had stepped up the attack against the Spanish and Tlaxcalans. Cut off without food and water, and being attacked continuously, Cortés wondered how long his men could hold out. In a last attempt to save his men Cortés ordered Moctezuma to call down to his people from atop the palace. Moctezuma was to ask his people not to attack the Spanish. He reluctantly climbed to the top of the palace. He raised his arms to quiet the crowd of Indians that had gathered but, before he could utter a word, he was attacked by his people. Calling him a coward and a traitor they threw many stones at him. Struck on the head by a rock, Moctezuma was dragged inside the palace by the Spaniards. He died a few days later.

The cause of Moctezuma's death is not certain. Some claim the Spanish murdered him because he was no longer of any use to them. Others say he died from his wounds. Still others maintain that he died of a "broken heart," that he had no will left to live because he had realized that he had been wrong all along. He had allowed the enemy to enter Tenochtitlan without a fight.

15. La Noche Triste

The Aztecs had anticipated a Spanish retreat and had torn a huge hole in the causeway leading out of Tenochtitlan. Cortés, therefore, ordered that a large wooden platform be made to throw over the gap in the causeway. Slipping out of the palace under the cover of darkness and a light rain, the Spanish and Tlaxcalans made their way out of the city. All Aztec sentries encountered along the way were silently murdered. It seemed that the Spanish would be able to escape safely. Placing the wooden platform over the roadway, they began to cross it. But as the horses went over the wood their hooves made a loud noise. In minutes the Spanish were surrounded and attacked by hundreds of warriors.

Canoes filled with Aztecs came at them from all sides. Hundreds of Tlaxcalans and all of the horses were killed. Many Spanish who had stuffed their clothing full of gold sank to the bottom of the lake and drowned because of their greed. It is said that the waters of the lake turned red from the slaughter there on the causeway. The Spanish grouped together and continued hacking and slashing their way through a mass of Aztec warriors.See Plate 6. Finally, the Spanish broke through and managed to escape. Cortés and the small number of his men who had survived made it safely out of the city. Cortés is said to have cried for his lost comrades under a cypress tree outside of Tenochtitlan. This tree, by the way, can still be seen in Mexico City today. At this moment the Spanish could have been completely wiped out by the Aztecs. But for some reason, the Spaniards were not followed out of Tenochtitlan. This proved to be a very costly mistake for the Aztecs.

Cortés and his men were helped by the remaining Tlaxcalans. Although bruised, bleeding and wounded, Cortés was already planning the total conquest of Tenochtitlan.

16. The Siege of Tenochtitlan

In Tlaxcala, Cortés and his men nursed their wounds and mourned their dead. But ever confident, Cortés began planning the final attack against the Aztecs. He would attack the city by water and cut off all entry to and exit from the city. He would starve them out, cut off their food and water supply and defeat the Aztecs. Unknown to him, however, he was soon to receive unexpected help.

On the Navarez expedition there had been a Black slave infected with smallpox. From him the disease spread quickly throughout Mexico. Soon people by the thousands were sick and dying even within Tenochtitlan itself. As the Indians had no immunities to European diseases they died by hundreds and thousands. They wrote: "Sores erupted on our faces, our bodies, our bellies. We were covered with agonizing sores from head to foot." Even the new Emperor Cuitlahuac died of the disease. As a result, his son, the 19-year-old Cuauhtemoc, became the final emperor of the Aztecs.

Meanwhile in Tlaxcala, Cortés put out a call for warriors from all the tribes of Mexico for one great battle against Tenochtitlan. His call was answered as Indians by the thousands came to Tlaxcala to help. The years of conquest and of taking victims from the other Indians of Mexico were now coming back to haunt the Aztecs. Moving from Tlaxcala, Cortés set up a base camp in the city of Texcoco. Cortés instructed the Indians to dig a canal that would connect Texcoco to the lake. For two months 8000 Indians worked. They finished the canal and constructed thirteen sailing vessels like large rafts with sails. Cannon were mounted upon these ships. With no knowledge of the sail, the Aztecs could not maneuver their canoes against the Spanish. Cortés now used these rafts to surround Tenochtitlan. The Aztec canoes trying to leave the city were sunk, as all the causeways leading out of the city were cut and heavily guarded by the Spanish and their Indian allies. The Aztecs could not get to their main food supply, the corn fields located on the mainland.

What Cortés essentially did was to organize and lead a revolution of Indians against their hated masters, the Aztecs. Those subject people whom the Aztecs had abused for years now eagerly sought an opportunity for revenge. The Spanish fired their cannon from the boats and their allies attacked on foot. The Aztecs answered with swarms of arrows. It went on like this for weeks and weeks. But slowly the Aztecs were weakened by disease and lack of food and water. Cortés sent repeated requests for a surrender but was refused every time by Cuauhtemoc.

The Spanish left their boats and attacked on land in the heart of the city. Building after building was set on fire. Other structures were blown to pieces by the Spanish cannon. As the pieces of the destroyed houses filled up the canals, the Spanish were able to march in more easily. Some Spaniards were captured and were said to have been sacrificed in full view of their friends.

But the Aztecs could not hold out: "The only food was lizards, birds, corncobs, and the salt grasses of the lake. They ate the bitterest weeds and even dirt. Nothing can compare with the horrors of that siege and the agonies of the starving. We were so weakened by hunger that, little by little, the enemy forced us to retreat." Many buildings were set on fire and soon a cloud of black smoke hung low over the once proud and beautiful city of Tenochtitlan.

Another appeal was made to Cuauhtemoc for surrender and again it was refused.

Cortés now realized that the city would have to be completely destroyed if he were to defeat Cuauhtemoc. So the Spaniards and their Indian allies destroyed everything in their path. Within two weeks 75% of the city had been leveled. As he described the final assault, it is clear that even Cortés was affected by the brutality as he himself wrote: "Our friends accompanied us armed with swords and shields and such was the slaughter done that day on water and on land that with prisoners taken the survivors numbered no more than 40,000. And such were the shrieks and weeping of the women and children that there were none whose heart did not break."

Finally the war chiefs decided that the city had to surrender. Cuauhtemoc was put in a war canoe and went personally to surrender to Cortés. When the people saw him go they cried and with tears in their eyes they shouted: "Our young prince is leaving us! He is going to surrender to the gods." The words spoken by Cuauhtemoc to Cortés have been recorded by the Aztec historians: "I have done everything in my power to save my kingdom from your hands. Since fortune has been against me, I now beg you to take my life. This would put an end to the Kingship of the Mexica and it would be just and right for you have already destroyed my city and killed my people."

17. The End and the Beginning

The siege of Tenochtitlan lasted eighty days. The Aztec warriors had numbered several hundred thousand. Of these, only about 40,000 survived. No one will ever know how many died of smallpox, hunger and thirst. As the Aztecs left their burning and destroyed city, Spanish soldiers were stationed along the roads, searching everyone for gold. Cuauhtemoc was tortured and had his feet burned by Cortés when he would not reveal the location of his uncle Moctezuma's treasure. The Spanish even began selecting some of the still-fit and strong-looking Aztecs for their own personal slaves. Some of these were branded on the spot with the initials of their Spanish master.See Plate 7. The three hundred years of slavery that the Indians of Mexico were to spend under their Spanish rulers had begun. Perhaps the cruelest twist of fate came to the Tlaxcalans and other Indians who had helped the Spanish in hopes of gaining their freedom from the hated Aztecs. These Indians were treated no differently from the others who now were conquered peoples. Cortés's Indian allies now merely exchanged one set of masters for another.

The Aztecs were forced to give up any last trace of pride they once might have had for their city and empire. A poem written in Nahuatl in the year 1528 by an unknown poet says:

{}/**```

*Broken spears lie in the roads
we have torn our hair with grief.
The houses are roofless now, and their walls
are red with blood.*

*Worms are swarming in the streets and plazas
and the walls are spattered with gore.
The water has turned red as if it were dyed
and when we drink it
it has the taste of brine.*

*We have pounded our hands in despair
against the adobe walls
for our inheritance, our city, is lost and dead.
The shields of our warriors were its defense
but they could not save it.*

*We are crushed to the ground
we lie in ruins.
There is nothing but grief and suffering
in Mexico where we saw beauty and valor.*

Today in Mexico City, at Tlatelolco, in the Plaza of the Three Cultures, an inscription is written on a wall. It sums up what must be said as we look back on the conquest of Mexico by Spain. It states:

*"On this spot on August 13, 1521,
the Aztec forces,
    bravely led by Cuauhtemoc,
fell to the power of Hernan Cortés
and the Spanish army.
    It was neither a defeat nor a victory,
but rather
the painful birth of the mestizo people
    who are Mexico."*

Indian Mexico had come to an end. With the Aztec Empire destroyed, all of Mexico would never be the same again. But out of the ashes of Tenochtitlan came a new culture, a new country and a new people: the Mestizos.

18. Identity

It is crucial for Mexicans, Mexican Americans and Latin Americans to understand the concept of the Mestizo. The word literally means part Indian and part Spanish. During the conquest of Mexico, the Spanish soldiers were struck by the beauty of the Mexican Indian women. La Malinche herself bore Cortés a son, a young boy who, symbolically, represents the beginning of the Mexican Mestizo people.See Plate 7. After the conquest, intermarriage (and other unions not necessarily by consent) between Spanish and Indian produced more and more Mestizo offspring. Official Mexican government census figures into the 1980s estimate Mexico's population as being as high as 80% Mestizo. But how do these facts help Mexican Americans determine their identity?

Identity, inevitably, entails understanding of our racial background. Remember that we defined race as one's genetic or biological heritage. In the case of Mexican Americans, history has played the key role in shaping our racial composition. Previously we determined that the Native American is Asian or Oriental. Obviously, this would be true of the Aztecs and other Mexican Indians who joined with the Spanish and produced Mestizos. Racially, the Spanish are White, Caucasian or European. But the Spanish also include the Moors, Arabs from the north of Africa, who lived in Spain and intermarried with the Spanish for centuries. After the conquest, when Indians began to die by the hundreds of thousands due to European diseases and Spanish cruelty, Black slaves from Africa were imported to Mexico for their labor. In fact, during the colonial era of 1521-1821, there were actually more Black people than Spanish in Mexico. Through the centuries, the Blacks have also mixed into this new Mexican "raza."

Therefore, both Mexicans and Mexican Americans have a variety of racial combinations. Some are pure Indian or, essentially, Asian. Some are pure Spanish or White. The majority are Mestizos, or combinations of both White and Asian. This explains the tremendous variety in the physical appearance of Mexican and Mexican American people today. What many of us do not realize is that this mixed race of Mexicans did not even exist five hundred years ago. Clearly, the Mexican people are direct products of their history.

But race alone does not define identity. To know that a people's history has produced many possible racial combinations tells only half the story. Identity

MEXICO CITY'S CATHEDRAL.   In Mexico City's central plaza, or "Zocalo," stands this immense Catholic Church, or cathedral. This plaza is in exactly the same spot as was the ceremonial center of the Aztec capital city, Tenochtitlan. After the Spanish had defeated the Aztecs they wanted to eliminate the Aztec religion and substitute Catholicism in its place. Therefore, the main Aztec pyramid was destroyed. Many of the stones from this pyramid were used in the construction of the cathedral. Within a short walk from this cathedral one can see the remains of the "Templo Mayor" (or Great Aztec Pyramid). An exquisite museum has been built to house all the beautiful Aztec artifacts discovered along with the remains of the pyramid itself. Mexico City was thus constructed on top of the remains of the capital city of the Aztecs. In other words, Mexico City **is** Tenochtitlan.

must also entail culture or way of life. The history of Indian Mexico and La Conquista have shaped the culture of the Mexican as well.

Some of the most basic components of the Mexican American's identity derive directly from the Spanish conquest of the Indians. For example, how many Mexican or Mexican Americans today have Indian last names? It is extremely rare to see a Mexican person with an Indian last name. Spanish last names such as Cortés, Alvarado, Castillo, Cervantez, López and González account for almost all of our surnames. What many Mexican Americans do not realize is that these are essentially "slave names" given to the Indians, Mestizos and Blacks who worked as slaves and peones on the Spanish-owned haciendas after the conquest. The workers were the property of the patrón or *hacendado* under the system of *encomiendas* in Mexico during the Colonial Era. And the Indians who worked for a particular owner were given his surname. Like the African Americans, we too have had our surnames imposed upon us. But how many Mexican Americans reject their names as slave names? Muhammad Ali (Cassius Clay) and Kareem Abdul Jabbar (Lewis Alcindor) are two well-known examples of African Americans who have chosen African names as more fitting for their self-image.

The language and religion of the Mexican are also a direct result of the conquest. The Spanish language became the official language of Mexico in 1521, as did the Roman Catholic religion. In 1531 the Spanish authorities in Mexico received a boost in their attempt to convert the Indians to their religion. On a hill outside of Mexico City, a brown-skinned Virgin Mary is said to have appeared to an Indian boy named Juan Diego and asked him to build a church in her honor on that spot. When news of this "miraculous" appearance of "La Virgen de Guadalupe" began to spread throughout Mexico, Indian conversion to Catholicism accelerated. The fact that there was no separation of church and state in Mexico at this time, that Roman Catholicism was the official state religion, and those practicing other faiths were subject to death at the hands of the Spanish Inquisitors may have also contributed to the growth of the Catholic faith in Mexico. Approximately eighty to ninety percent of Mexicans and Mexican Americans are Roman Catholic to this day. In this manner, history has made us what we are.

Mexican foods show Indian influences in Mestizo culture. The tortilla, the tamale, chiles, mole sauce and many other popular Mexican foods are thousands of years old, all dating back to ancient Indian Mexico. Popular Mexican holidays such as the Day of the Dead also date back to Indian times. Also, the traditional "quinceañera" celebration for fifteen-year-old Mexican girls is derived from an Aztec "coming of age" ceremony for Indian women. Even mural wall painting originated with the Indians. Aztec and other Indian medical practices such as the use of natural herbs and roots are still practiced by Mexican "curanderas." Indeed, in most mercados and pharmacies in Mexico and the U.S. Southwest, herbs and plants for particular ailments are sold alongside more "modern" medicines. "Yerba buena" and "manzanilla" for the stomach, "tila" to calm the nerves, and "boldo" for the liver, are only a few of the most common herbal remedies used by Mexicans and Mexican Americans today.

Thus, both in race and in culture, we Mexican Americans are a people of many influences. The history of our people is stamped on our faces, is in our language, our names, our foods and our religion. It might have been very different. What if Quetzalcoatl had not been driven out of Tula, promising to return as he did? What if his legendary appearance had been different? What if Cortés had arrived on a year other than 1519, which was Ce-Acytl to the Aztecs? In short, would Spain have been able to conquer the mighty Aztecs without the help of the Quetzalcoatl legend and Moctezuma's confusion? If the Spanish had been driven out of Mexico, what if the French, the Dutch or the English had become the European conquerors of Mexico instead? Pirates and explorers from these nations were all active in the same years as Cortés's voyage. We, the Mexican Americans, would not even be here, looking and speaking as we do, if the conquest of Mexico by Spain had not taken place in 1521.

Knowing that we are symbolically part Aztec, part of the greatest and most powerful Indian civilization of the Americas, and part Spanish, part of the largest and richest colonial empire of the modern era, does give many Mexican Americans a sense of pride.

Knowing one's identity is the first step toward realizing one's fullest potential. Having a clear sense of who we are, and why, will prevent us from trying to be something we are not. Knowing one's identity and the history behind it can give one the confidence and pride to look to the future with optimism and hope.

19. The Colonial Era

After the defeat of the Aztecs by Cortés and his Indian allies, the face of Mexico began to change. Spaniards, and later Blacks (brought in as slaves), arrived in the land that was to be called "Nueva España" (New Spain). Further conquests and expeditions were undertaken as far north as California and as far south as Central America. Spain's American colonial empire was born and soon Nueva España was one of its most important components.

For the Indians of Mexico, this was to be the beginning of a dark period of slavery, extermination and exploitation that was to last a full 300 years. Indian labor was vital for the production of gold and silver from Mexico's rich mines. Agricultural products could not be harvested without the native labor force. Poor diet, subhuman living conditions and disease reduced the indigenous population drasti-

Sor Juana Inez de la Cruz

Sor Juana was the greatest Mexican writer of the Colonial Era of Mexico. She was also an early champion for the rights of women in Mexican society. A gifted poet from a very early age, she combined feminism and romance in her poetry. At the age of eighteen she entered a convent where she would spend the rest of her days in intellectual study and poetic writing. Sor Juana assembled one of the most impressive collections of books in Mexico in her day, an astounding four thousand volumes! Today, most Mexican historians consider her "the first great poet of the New World."

cally and the new Mestizo race soon appeared in ever increasing numbers. These first Mestizos were most often out-of-wedlock children of Spanish fathers and Indian mothers. They soon found themselves caught between two cultures and often isolated from both.

Spanish society looked down upon the Mestizos as an "impure" mixed race that was no better than the "inferior" Indian. The Indians themselves tended to reject the Mestizos as symbols of their conquest and enslavement. The society of New Spain thus consisted of several distinct classes: The viceroy and the other royal and military officers who ran the colony at the command of the Spanish crown enjoyed all the benefits of being at the top of the social ladder. Next in line came the Catholic Church hierarchy and the priests. The large hacendados or land owners competed with the Church for ownership of the best lands. Often, the largest land owners were also military officials. The Mestizos and the Indians were at the bottom of the social ladder. They soon began converting to Catholicism, a change which made them easier to control by the state, the Church, and the slave owners of the haciendas and mines.

Untold wealth, luxury and privilege characterized the ruling classes of Nueva España — in sharp contrast with the abject poverty of the Indians. The finest schools were available to those who could afford to pay for them. But for the Indians, knowledge of only the rudiments of the Spanish language and resultant illiteracy doomed them to permanent misery, for they were cut off from any upward mobility.

This period of Mexican history is grim and bleak to recount, but its importance should not be minimized. The Colonial Era lasted for nearly twice as long (300 years) as has Mexico's current independent period. Many of Mexico's current problems (illiteracy, corruption, imperfect democracy) can be traced directly back to the exploitation of the Colonial Era.

But out of the degradation of the Colonial Era came also the birth of modern Mexico as we know it. Mexico would gain independence from Spain in 1821, due in great part to the Indians' and Mestizos' desire to put an end to their misery. Mexico, as an independent country, was born of the independence movement that came in the 19th century.

Mexico was thus to escape Spanish control only to fall victim to a threat from another foreign country, the United States of America. The next chapter will investigate how Mexico lost over one half of its national territory after gaining independence from Spain. The territory they lost is today part of the U.S. and has come to be called Aztlan.

Chapter Two

LA CONQUISTA:

WRITING EXERCISES

On the following pages you will find the writing exercises for this chapter. For additional explanations, please see "To the Teacher" or "A Note to the Student" on **pages 21 and 26**. Teachers are urged to select the writing exercises most appropriate for their particular classes. Below are the writing exercises for Chapter Two:

1. Sentence or Fragment?

This exercise is designed to help students learn how to recognize incomplete sentences (fragments) and then rewrite them as complete sentences. The most important idea here is that a complete sentence makes sense when read alone. When rewriting the fragments, the students must make sure not to change history!

2. Short Answer Questions

Once a student knows what a sentence is (and is not!), he or she can answer brief questions with one or two sentence answers of their own. This list of questions also makes a good study or review sheet when preparing for a test.

3. Paragraph Questions

These questions require slightly longer answers which are to be written in paragraphs. A sample paragraph along with definitions of such terms as "topic sentence" is included in the writing exercises of **Chapter One**.

4. Clustering and Identification (ID) Items

ID Items refer to and identify important people, places and things. Clustering is a way of brainstorming ideas based on these ID Items. Once the cluster has been made, use it as a guide and write an ID Paragraph. A sample cluster and a sample ID Paragraph can be found in the writing exercises section of **Chapter One**.

5. Essay Questions

Very broad or complicated questions require essays or compositions as answers. A sample essay and instructions on how to write essays, both as homework and during in-class essay exams, are provided in the writing exercises section of **Chapter Five**.

Sentence or Fragment?

DIRECTIONS:

A complete sentence makes sense when read all alone. An incomplete sentence or fragment does not. Some of the following are fragments. Some are perfectly correct, complete sentences. Rewrite the fragments and make them into good sentences. You may add words, get rid of words, or rearrange the words. **Just make sure that each fragment you rewrite is factually correct according to the chapter and makes good sense when you read it alone.** Leave the complete sentences alone.

EXAMPLE: *Moctezuma, who was sure Cortés was Quetzalcoatl.*

Clearly this does not make sense when read alone. Although there is **no single correct way** to rewrite it, the following is much better:

Moctezuma was convinced Cortés was Quetzalcoatl because the Spaniards arrived during a reed year and were light skinned.

1. The Aztecs, or Mexica, who settled in the Anahuac Valley.
2. Tenochtitlan, the capital city of the Aztecs.
3. The Aztecs knew of the prophecy by the Toltec, Quetzalcoatl, that he would return in a reed year.
4. Moctezuma, the Aztec Emperor in 1519.
5. The Tlaxcalans, the bitter enemies of the Aztecs.
6. Strange omens or signs which predict the future.
7. Moctezuma's lookouts who were stationed on the Gulf Coast.
8. The Moors of northern Africa had ruled southern Spain for 800 years.
9. Diego Velásquez, the Spanish governor of Cuba in the 1500's.
10. Hernan Cortés's voyage to Mexico.
11. La Malinche became very valuable to Cortés as his translator.
12. The arrival of Aztec messengers from Moctezuma at Vera Cruz.
13. The Cempoallans told Cortés much about the hated rule of the Aztecs.
14. A vicious three-week-long war between the Spanish and the Tlaxcalans.
15. The meeting between Cortés and Moctezuma.
16. The arrival of Panfilo de Navarez, with orders to arrest Cortés.
17. Pedro de Alvarado's horrible mistake while in command during Cortés's absence from Tenochtitlan.
18. Nearly all of Moctezuma's treasure was lost during the Spanish retreat on La Noche Triste.

19. The siege of Tenochtitlan led to the defeat of the Aztecs.
20. The role of diseases brought to Mexico by the Spanish.
21. The Indians were to spend 300 years as slaves to the Spanish.
22. Indian, Spanish and the concept of the Mestizo.
23. Mexican Americans' last names.
24. The appearance of La Virgen de Guadalupe.
25. Mexico was known as Nueva España during the Colonial Period.

Short Answer Questions

DIRECTIONS:

Answer the following questions by writing one or two complete sentences for each. Be sure that each sentence you write:

a) Is factually correct and helps answer the question.
b) Is a complete sentence, which means it makes sense when read alone.
c) Can be understood by someone who has not seen the question.
d) Begins with a capital letter and ends with a period.
e) Is completely in your own words.
f) Uses correct spelling and is neat.

EXAMPLE: *What is the importance of the Quetzalcoatl legend?*

Moctezuma thought Cortés was the god Quetzalcoatl returning to Mexico, and did not attack. This is one of the keys to the conquest of Mexico.

1. Why was the year 1519 important to the Aztecs?
2. Who was Moctezuma II ?
3. How large was the Aztec empire?
4. What was the relationship between the Aztecs and the Tlaxcalans?
5. Why was Moctezuma's religion a weakness when faced with the Spanish?
6. How were the Spanish and their ships first described to Moctezuma?
7. Who did Moctezuma think the Spanish were? Why?
8. Who were the Moors?
9. What main orders were given to the Spanish explorers who went to the new world?
10. How was the island of Cuba used by the Spanish?
11. Why was Diego Velásquez important?

12. Who were the two Spanish explorers to Mexico before Cortés?
13. How many men and ships did Cortés bring to Mexico?
14. How did Cortés gain La Malinche as his translator?
15. What important people arrived to see Cortés at Vera Cruz?
16. Why were the Cempoallans and Tlaxcalans important to Cortés?
17. How did Moctezuma greet Cortés?
18. Why was Cortés forced to leave Tenochtitlan and go to Vera Cruz?
19. What was Alvarado's big mistake while Cortés was gone?
20. How did Moctezuma die?
21. Why was La Noche Triste sad for the Spanish?
22. For how long did Cortés surround and attack Tenochtitlan?
23. Define Mestizo race.
24. Define Mestizo culture.
25. When did many Mexican Indians begin to convert to Catholicism?

Paragraph Questions

DIRECTIONS:

Answer the following questions by writing a good paragraph for each. Refer back to the sample paragraph on **page 47** for help. Be sure that each paragraph you write:

   a) Is factually correct, helps to answer the question and is in your own words.
   b) Looks like a proper paragraph (see sample).
   c) Has an underlined topic sentence at the beginning of the paragraph.
   d) Contains no fragments.
   e) Uses correct spelling and is neat.

1. Briefly describe Cortés's equipment. Why did it give the Spanish a big advantage over the Indians?
2. How did Jerónimo de Aguilar and La Malinche help Cortés?
3. Why did Cortés take Moctezuma's messengers aboard his ships while in Vera Cruz?
4. What was going through the mind of Moctezuma as he received the reports of his spies about Cortés and the Spanish? Why?
5. What important move did Cortés make before leaving Cempoalla? Why did he do it? What does this tell us about Cortés?

6. How and why was Cortés able to gather such a large and effective Indian army? Why did Indians such as the Tlaxcalans join Cortés?
7. Why did Cortés capture Moctezuma?
8. How did Pedro de Alvarado change the future of the conquest?
9. Describe "La Noche Triste."
10. Why is Cuauhtemoc considered a hero in Mexican history?
11. Describe the siege of Tenochtitlan.
12. What happened to the Indian allies of the Spanish after the completion of the conquest?
13. How should we view men like Hernan Cortés? Was he a hero or a mass murderer? (Support your opinion with facts.)
14. How does knowing the history of the conquest of Mexico help Mexican Americans to understand who they are?
15. How might the conquest of Mexico have turned out differently? What are some of the more interesting "ifs" of the story?
16. Describe the Spanish elements of Mestizo culture.
17. Describe the Indian elements of Mestizo culture.
18. How did Mexican people initially come to have Spanish last names?
19. Why do Mexicans tend to be of the Catholic religion?

Clustering and ID Items

DIRECTIONS:

Make clusters and/or ID paragraphs for the following identification items. While making your cluster or paragraph, ask yourself who or what the item is and why it is important in the history being studied. Refer to your book if necessary. A sample cluster and ID paragraph can be found on **page 49**.

Tlaxcala
Moctezuma II
Jerónimo de Aguilar
La Malinche
Sor Juana Inez de la Cruz

Noche Triste
the Siege of Tenochtitlan
the Mestizo (race and culture)
Pedro de Alvarado

Essay Questions

DIRECTIONS:

The following are essay questions on the content of this chapter. Before attempting to answer any questions, see **page 187** for directions on how to write an essay and **page 188** for a sample essay.

1. Some historians have called Cortés one of the luckiest conquerors in history. What advantages did Cortés have and how did he use them?
2. How and why is the concept of the Mestizo so important to Mexicans and Mexican Americans as they try to understand their identity? Describe the Spanish and Indian elements of Mestizo culture.
3. How did the European discovery and conquest of America change this continent? Compare it before and after the European's arrival. Include such things as racial change, language, religion, culture, way of life, food, etc.
4. Is it correct to say that Cortés organized a revolution of Indians against the Aztec Empire? Why? Explain.

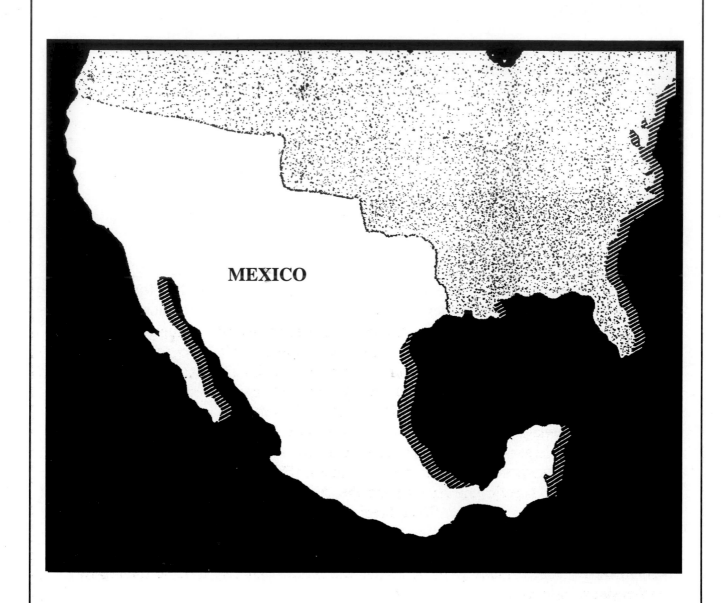

Chapter Three

THE LOSS OF AZTLAN

1. Aztlan Redefined

Aztlan is the name of the Aztecs' mythical homeland. Although we are certain it must have been located far to the north of their capital city of Tenochtitlan, the exact location of Aztlan is something about which historians disagree. Was Aztlan located in what is today northern Mexico? Or could it have been as far north as the current Southwest of the United States? In the 1960s, in the U.S., Aztlan referred to that part of the United States that once had belonged to Mexico.

Aztlan is a colorful and legendary land with a unique and majestic geography that has been home to many distinct peoples. First it was the Native Americans such as the Navajo, the Apache and the Comanche. Then came Spanish padres, explorers and rancheros. Soon, Mexican settlers established some of the first cities in the Southwest. Next came the clash between the Mexicans and the Anglo American cowboys and cattle barons who have come to symbolize the myth of the Southwest. Today, many parts of Aztlan are more ethnically diverse than most other places on earth.

Traditionally, the history of this land has been taught to students in the United States from the perspective of what is called "Manifest Destiny." That point of view, briefly, describes the rapidly growing and young democratic United States of the 19th century. It was believed to be destined to move its borders all the way to the Pacific coast, spreading the blessings of "liberty, justice and the American way" to all in its expanding path. In the teaching of this history, military events such as the Battle of the Alamo and the Mexican War, along with American heroes such as Davy Crockett, Jim Bowie and Sam Houston, have been depicted as instrumental in making this American vision come to pass.

Recently, however, important social, economic and political factors have forced a re-examination of this view of history. We have seen a tremendous surge in the Mexican and Mexican American population of the U.S. Southwest. We have also seen the Chicano activists make demands that the Latino population utilize its increased numbers to mobilize itself politically and thus gain better control of their own destinies. Similarly, it has been hoped that bilingual and multicultural education would reflect more than just one point of view.

Now, in the 1990s, a proposal for a free trade agreement between the United States and Mexico promises to tie these two countries' futures together more closely than ever before. Some Mexican and Mexican American intellectuals have argued that if Mexico is to allow the U.S. to invest in Mexico and send American products freely into the land to the south, then Mexico should, in turn, be allowed to "freely export" one of its most marketable commodities to the United States; Mexican labor. Obviously this would mean a re-evaluation of the border between the two countries as we know it today.

It would seem that now, more than ever, the accurate facts regarding the history of the American Southwest must be recounted and set free from the persistent myths and stereotypes that are so hard to put to rest. All who live here should know exactly how the United States acquired this land, how the current border was drawn, and what this all means for both countries and the people who live on both sides of the border.

2. *El Grito*

The story of Mexico's loss of Aztlan must begin with Mexico gaining something first, namely its independence from Spain. In the early 1800s, a Mexican priest by the name of Miguel Hidalgo y Costilla had been banished to the relatively backwater pueblo of Dolores, Guanajuato, for his "unconventional ideas." Hidalgo questioned the notion of priestly celibacy and he saw no reason why priests should not marry. The priest read books that were officially banned by the Catholic Church; he challenged the absolute authority of the Popes in Rome; he questioned the idea of Christ's virgin birth; and on occasion, it is said, he even enjoyed gambling and dancing!

In Dolores, he met Ignacio Allende and his wife Doña Josefa Ortíz de Domínguez. This illustrious couple had organized a "literary club" which was actually much more interested in plotting Mexican independence and the overthrow of the Spanish than in reading novels or poetry. They had even gone so far as to begin stockpiling ammunition and weapons for the eventual explosion for indepen-

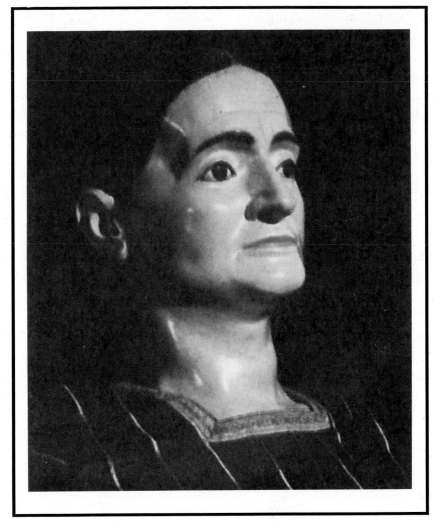

Doña Josefa Ortíz de Domínguez
ceramic; anonymous; ca. 1810
Museo Nacional de Historia,
Chapultepec Castle, Mexico City

Doña Josefa Ortíz de Domínguez was the wife of Ignacio Allende and a member of the "literary club" which, along with Miguel Hidalgo, was primarily responsible for the beginning of the Mexican Revolution for independence from Spain. Doña Josefa was not only very well educated and well read on the democratic currents of her day, she was also intensely involved in the actual military preparations made by her husband and Hidalgo for the uprising against Spain. In fact, it was Doña Josefa who personally warned Miguel Hidalgo of the arrest of her husband, which led to Hidalgo's famous "El Grito de Dolores."

Miguel Hidalgo y Costilla was the parish priest in the small Mexican town of Dolores, Guanajuato. He, along with other Mexican intellectuals, felt that by the 1800s Spanish colonial rule of Mexico had to end. Thus, on September 16th, 1810, Hidalgo summoned the members of his church by ringing its bell and delivered the most famous speech in Mexican history. His *Grito de Dolores* was the spark for the revolution that would eventually gain independence for Mexico from Spain. Today, of course, September 16th is Mexican Independence Day.

dence that they were sure would come. Before long, Hidalgo became an important member of the circle.

When word reached Hidalgo through Doña Josefa that Allende had been arrested for plotting against the state, Hidalgo, on September 16, 1810, rang the bells of his church, calling together the mostly Indian and Mestizo members of his parish.

Assembling them together, he gave the most famous speech in Mexican history: "El Grito de Dolores." He denounced the Spanish rulers for their three hundred year domination and pillage of Mexico and he called upon his followers to regain their homeland for themselves. From this one speech an incredible chain of events resulted. Hidalgo personally led his followers out of the church and, along with the prisoners he freed from the local jail, began to march toward the neighboring towns, picking up supporters along the way. Soon this poorly armed and equipped band of Indians and Mestizos, led by Hidalgo and the now-freed Allende, swelled to such size that they were able to challenge Spanish authority over the entire nation.

Although Hidalgo, Allende, José María Morelos, and the other great leaders of this rebellion were killed by the Spanish before the war ended, by 1821 Mexico had gained its independence from Spain. Nueva España would be no more.

Drawing on the real name of the Aztecs, the Mexica, Mexico was born. Also in honor of the Aztecs, this time for their founding of their capital city, Tenochtitlan, the Eagle and the Serpent became the symbol of Mexico. The symbol was placed on her new national flag. And September 16, the date of Hidalgo's "Grito," became Mexican Independence Day.

But the revolution against Spain was not as successful as Hidalgo would have wanted. There were many more serious problems for Mexico on the horizon.

3. Mexico's Infancy

The young Mexican nation was soon to find that her dependence on Spain as the "mother country" had not in the least prepared Mexico to manage her affairs as an independent state. For one thing, the untimely death of Hidalgo had produced an "unfinished" revolution. The power in Mexico, basically, remained where it had always been during colonial times. The military, the Catholic Church, the wealthy Mexicans and foreigners witnessed the departure of Spanish authority, but not a reduction in their power and influence. The poor of Mexico, the Indians and Mestizos, were to remain poor and uneducated. The names and titles of those in power had changed, but little else had.

The first major problem at this time was financial. As Spain had been driven out, the money had gone with her. Combined with the expenses and devastation of the recently completed war, Mexico was now independent but totally broke. Mexico's other problems stemmed from an absence of a strong government.

In the early years power in Mexico rested principally in two institutions: the Catholic Church and the military. The Church had acquired large land holdings during the Colonial Era. There had never been a separation of church and state, so the Church influenced Spanish royal policy. Even stronger after independence, the Church enjoyed many privileges along with its huge land holdings. In addition, its political influence continued. As for the army, one basic rule of thumb would prove true for most of the 19th century in Mexico: whoever controlled the army could rule the nation. Both churchmen and military men had the advantage of special courts which were their own separate legal systems. Ordinary policemen or judges could do nothing to control the behavior of the Church or the military. In addition, due to the lack of democratic institutions such as voting and self-government in Spain and Nueva España, Mexico was left with no tradition of democracy. As a result, the men who dominated Mexican affairs in the early years could hardly be called innovative political leaders. Indeed, the first presidents of Mexico were all military men who achieved control of the nation through their control of the army. At this time one man stands out as the dominant figure. His name was Antonio López de Santa Anna.

4. Antonio López de Santa Anna

Santa Anna was born in Vera Cruz, Mexico, in 1794. As a teenager he joined the Spanish king's royalist army. A youth of sixteen, he saw his first action in 1810 in the battles against Hidalgo's forces. By 1812, however, he had turned against Spain and joined the Mexicans fighting for independence. Having distinguished himself in the final days of the war, he was awarded important commands in the new Mexican army.

In 1823 all of Mexico's leaders gathered in Mexico City to form a new government. A constitution was written that was modeled after the Constitution of the United States. Among other things, the Mexican Constitution of 1823 called for full democratic voting privileges, a federalist system whereby the states of Mexico would maintain certain powers and independence, and a method of electing a president and vice-president through votes in all the state legislatures. The first presidential election was scheduled for 1824. General Guadalupe Victoria became Mexico's first president with Nicholás Bravo as vice-president.

Victoria proved, however, to be an ineffective president. The financial

Antonio López de Santa Anna, the man who, unfortunately, dominated Mexican political and military affairs from the 1830s until the 1850s. President or dictator of Mexico on numerous occasions, Santa Anna not only "signed away" Texas to Sam Houston in 1836, he also surrendered to Winfield Scott in 1848 which gave the U.S. approximately one half of Mexico's northern territory.

problems continued. Soon it became clear that although Mexico had constitutional democracy, real democracy and the advances that go with it would be hard to come by. Mexico's population at this time was mostly uneducated and even illiterate. These people had had no opportunity for an education under Spanish colonial rule. There were also several million Indians who still spoke no Spanish whatsoever. Local and state elections thus became cruel jokes whereby Indians and illiterates by the hundreds were led to the voting booths by crooked politicians and promised pulque or aguardiente (native alcoholic drinks) in return for their votes for a particular candidate. The early Mexican government was a powerful dictatorship in control of the army rather than of the people.

The national governmental leadership in Mexico City soon entered an extremely unstable period. Mexican presidents and vice-presidents would come and go as if through revolving doors. For example, in the 22 years between May 1833 and August 1855, the government of Mexico changed hands 36 times! As will soon become clear, this chaotic leadership was to play a vital role in Mexico's loss of her northwest territories to the U.S.

5. Caudillos, Pronunciamientos and Cuartelazos

Faced with the horrible economic problems, and an army that would revolt if not treated with special favor, no Mexican president of this period ever served his entire term. When a president began to be unpopular the various military generals would criticize the president and plot his downfall. When a general thought he had the support of the army he would make a formal "pronunciamiento" which was like a speech or formal pronouncement against the president. This general would then organize a "cuartelazo" which is like an uprising of the army or, literally, a barracks revolt. The general would then lead this revolt as the "caudillo," or commander. More often than not during this turbulent period it was Santa Anna who led the cuartelazo. Santa Anna was made dictator of Mexico four different times, and four different times he was overthrown. All in all, he served as president of Mexico on 11 different occasions.

By 1829 Mexico seemed again on the verge of civil war. The infighting between the jealous generals was reaching a crisis. But just when it seemed that things could not get any worse, they did. President Vicente Guerrero, Mexico's second president, received word that Spain was launching an invasion of Mexico to reconquer her lost colony. Landing in Tampico in 1829 the Spanish began their attack. Guerrero placed Santa Anna in charge of the Mexican forces and he soon began a siege of Tampico, surrounding and attacking the Spanish. As yellow fever and starvation began to wear down the Spanish soldiers, Santa Anna was soon able to force a surrender. Thus by 1830 Santa Anna was perhaps the most popular hero of Mexico as he had saved the republic from the Spanish.

After the war with the Spanish, Mexican politics returned to their chaotic and violent ways. Several cuartelazos and minor military encounters rocked the capital, Mexico City. But by 1833 things had quieted down enough to hold an election. When the results of the 1833 election for president were announced, few were surprised that Antonio López de Santa Anna had been chosen as president. The vice-president was Valentín Gomez Farias. Santa Anna, however, quickly grew tired and bored with the day-to-day duties and administrative demands of the presidency. He was a general, after all, and not a scholar or a politician. Santa Anna clearly enjoyed the thrill of gaining heroism and power but could not settle into the routine of governing. He decided to retire as president and return to his home in Vera Cruz. Farias would become president.

Farias and Santa Anna had been known in Mexico as political liberals, that is, people who favored reforms or changes that would supposedly benefit the common people. As president, Farias began to carry out some of these reforms. But when he began to heavily tax the Church, eliminate the Church courts, and attempt to limit the power of the Church as well, the powerful clergy grew furious. Farias also attempted to reduce the size of the army, eliminate the special military courts, and lower the pay given to military men. All of these moves were designed to help get Mexico out of the horrible financial mess she was in. But Farias made powerful enemies of the Catholic Church and the military by his actions.

Mexican conservatives, people who wanted Church and military privileges untouched, now began looking for some strong military leader or caudillo who would overthrow Farias and restore the Church and military to their accustomed positions of high privilege. Whom do you suppose they found? None other than Santa Anna! He was now more than willing to march in, as the strong man on the white horse, to save Mexico from disaster. It made no difference that Farias had been Santa Anna's own vice-president or that Santa Anna was himself supposedly a supporter of liberal ideas. It seems that Santa Anna could just never resist the lure of heroism and worship by the masses as Mexico's savior. With the support of the Mexican army, Santa Anna was soon back in the president's chair after, of course, some minor violence.

Once president, he went about undoing all that Farias had done. The Church and the military retained their special privileges. Santa Anna even went so far as to abolish the Federalist Constitution of 1824. He replaced it with what is known as a "centralist" constitution which basically centered all political power in Mexico City and the central government of the country. This abolition of federalism amounted to a blatant move toward personal dictatorship. In so doing, Santa Anna set in motion a chain of events which would soon result in Mexico's loss of

Aztlan to the United States.

6. Mexico's First Thirty Years

Mexico's independence from Spain, therefore, did not alter her situation for the better. The poor people stayed poor, foreign countries continued to dominate the economy through loans, and the rich Mexicans continued to run the country's government for their own benefit rather than for the benefit of the Mexican people. Santa Anna was the perfect example of this type of leader.

The revolution for independence against Spain had not been a true revolution, for the foreigners, the Church and the military maintained the control over the country that the Spanish had previously held. The poor people, the Indians and the Mestizos who had fought to gain independence, did not really benefit. Mexico's leaders were too concerned with their own power and privilege to be truly effective.

Throughout these early years of Mexican independence Santa Anna continued to dominate Mexican politics. Whether actually in office as president or not, Santa Anna was usually in control of Mexico's military establishment. Whoever controlled the army could control Mexico. Santa Anna seemed to know just the right moment to pronounce against a president, raise an army and march in as the conquering hero. Then, so that he would get none of the blame for Mexico's impossible problems, he would retire to his hacienda and allow someone else to be blamed for unpopular decisions. When the time was right he would repeat the process over again.

Actually, Mexico would have been much better off in its infancy without a man such as Santa Anna. But the Mexicans, in their early days of independence, were the products of three centuries of Spanish rule. Indeed, Santa Anna would seem to be a parody of the Spanish military man. The Mexicans, with no tradition of democracy or self-government, only knew how to run a country based on control by the military, the Church, and the wealthy. It would have been unrealistic to have expected them to do otherwise.

As a result, for the first thirty years of Mexico's independence, Mexico did not progress, but went backward. Political instability nearly became civil war several times, and Mexico's finances were in a state of ruin. Mexico's highways were not maintained, her rich mines were mostly abandoned or flooded, excellent farmland lay vacant, and industry grew at a snail's pace for want of sound management and investment. There was little or no foreign trade and the continual threat of foreign invasion hung over Mexico's head.

But these misfortunes are minor when compared to the loss of one half of

Mexico's national territory; territory that, today, could have made Mexico a world power.

7. "Manifest Destiny"

Before we look at the uprising for independence in Texas, we must quickly review U.S. history leading up to this dispute.

The 13 original English colonies located on the east coast of the U.S. became independent of England in 1783. In 1787 the famous U.S. Constitution was written. Blessed with a relatively well-educated population, sound leadership, a tradition of democracy, and rich lands, the new nation soon began to grow. In 1803 the U.S. government purchased the Louisiana Territory from France. This moved the American boundaries far beyond the Mississippi River. In 1819 Florida was acquired. In fewer than 40 years the new nation had greatly increased its territory.

The busy Protestants and other English and European settlers wasted no time in settling and populating these new lands. It seemed to many in the U.S. that it was the fate or destiny of the White North American people to settle, populate, civilize and develop the American continent, perhaps even beyond the present boundary of the nation. The annexation of Canada had even been seriously debated several times in the U.S. Congress. When the Americans gazed at the vast rich lands of Mexico's northwest territories, it seemed to them that these lands were going to waste.

Indeed, Spain and then Mexico had done relatively little to develop or colonize these territories. The long distance from the center of power in Mexico City made administration difficult. We have already seen that in the early days of independence the Mexican nation was not capable of running its own government smoothly, let alone developing or adequately policing her most distant territories such as Texas and California.

There was much talk in the U.S. of an American nation that would one day stretch from "sea to shining sea." This was said to be America's holy mission, her fate, her "Manifest Destiny." Discussed in these terms, it seemed an unpardonable sin to allow Mexico to retain and do "nothing" with rich territories like Texas and California. It seemed almost inevitable that the new American nation would take advantage of Mexico's political instability, and the relative power vacuum in Mexico's northwest territories, to take and eventually rule over the legendary Aztec homeland of Aztlan.

8. The Texas Revolt

During the colonial period, while Texas was still a part of Nueva España, Texas had been thinly populated by Spanish and Mexican colonists. The aggressive Comanches who lived in the mountains of the Texas interior had discouraged extensive settlement. Spanish government administration was almost absent due to the long distance between Texas and Mexico City.

Spain sought to populate the territory of Texas in 1821. Just before Mexico's independence, an American by the name of Moses Austin was given permission to bring 300 American families to Texas. After Austin's death and Mexico's independence, Stephen Austin took up his father's task and brought the Anglos to Texas. Many other similar arrangements were made by the new Mexican government. Land was cheap (ten cents an acre). By 1835 there were 30,000 American citizens living in Texas compared to only 7,800 Mexicans.

The new Mexican government had realized from the beginning that the U.S. might be a threat to Texas. Therefore they made these new U.S. settlers promise to learn Spanish, become Catholics and to take an oath of allegiance to obey the laws of Mexico. Although they had hoped that these new settlers would become Mexicans and would serve as a barrier to further American settlement, the Mexican government soon found it had been wrong.

One of the early problems involved the use of Black slaves from Africa. In the southern United States the use of such slaves for agriculture was considered essential. Many of the early Anglo settlers to Texas brought slaves with them.

In 1829 the government of Mexican President Vicente Guerrero passed an anti-slave law. Since there was virtually no slavery at all in the other Mexican states, this law was clearly aimed directly at the Mexican territory of Texas. The Mexicans hoped to discourage further U.S. immigration into Texas by means of this law. The Mexicans had by now realized that the North Americans were greatly outnumbering the Mexicans and could cause Mexico great harm if this continued.

In 1830 the Mexican government took another step to stop the immigration of Anglo Americans into Texas. A colonization law was passed which outlawed any further entry of U.S. settlers into Texas. The law attempted to encourage more Mexican settlement in Texas. Unfortunately for Mexico, neither part of this new plan worked. Settlers from the U.S. poured into Texas, often bringing slaves with them. Sometimes the slaves escaped into Mexico. When the slave owners had difficulty getting their human property back from Mexican officials, relations worsened even more.

Additionally, there were many other things the Anglo settlers disliked. In Texas, and subject to Mexican law, the "Anglo-Tejanos" did not enjoy all the same legal rights given them by the U.S. Constitution. Notably absent was the right to

In Guatemala's mountainous interior the vast majority of the population is pure-blooded Mayan Indian. Note the colorful clothing of these Mayan children. Do you see any Asian features or characteristics in their faces?

PLATE 9

A Mayan Indian family pauses to rest by the shores of Guatemala's beautiful Lake Atitlan. Notice the similar clothing of the family. Usually, all the members of a particular village will dress in virtually identical clothing.

PLATE 10

A Mayan gentleman stands outside a small store in Solola, Guatemala. The warm woolen blanket around his waist is for the cold weather which often hits the Guatemalan highlands.

PLATE **11**

Mayan Indian women on a market day in Chichicastenango, home of the largest Indian market in Guatemala. Their *huipiles* (blouses) have incredibly vivid colors. All of their clothing is hand-woven and colored with natural plant dyes.

PLATE **12**

The great pyramid at Uxmal, on Mexico's Yucatan Peninsula, is one of the most important archaeological sites of the Classic Mayan period. This pyramid is over 200 feet tall and has exactly 365 steps leading up to the top. Notice the rounded sides of the pyramid. To get an idea of the size of the pyramid, also note the tourists climbing the steps.

PLATE **13**

Detail of carvings done on one of the structures at Uxmal. The sculptured face here is of Chac, the Mayan Sun God. Note the perfectly square building blocks on the left as well as the intricate carving into the solid stone. Many have wondered how the Mayans could have created such exquisite carvings while using only stone knives and chisels.

PLATE **14**

Tulum: the Mayan fortress on the shore of the Caribbean Sea. Of all the Indian ruins in Mexico, Tulum is one of the most popular destinations for tourists.

PLATE **15**

One of the most beautiful pyramids in all of Indian Mexico can be found at Chichen-Itza on Mexico's Yucatan Peninsula. Built during the Post-Classic period by the Mayans of this region, Chichen-Itza reveals many Toltec influences.

PLATE **16**

trial by jury. Legal arguments came up often over disputed land claims. The old Spanish and Mexican land grants often had poorly defined boundaries. When the Anglos moved in, they naturally wanted as much of the best land as they could get.

But trials to settle the conflicting land claims between the Anglos and the Mexicans were difficult to arrange. The territory of Texas, at this time, was a part of the Mexican state of Coahuila. The nearest legal court was located in Saltillo, far away from Texas. The Anglos were thus often frustrated by the Mexican legal system. Additionally, it was soon clear that the Anglos had not bothered to become Catholics, learn Spanish, obey Mexican law and adopt the culture of Mexico. They had essentially broken the terms of the original agreement for settlement. But there was little or nothing the Mexican government could do. The Anglos began to resent Mexican authority and violent outbursts between Mexican soldiers and the Anglo settlers became more and more frequent.

One of the worst aspects of this coming together of people from the U.S. and those from Mexico was the attitude of superiority many of the U.S. Americans carried with them. Because they were a people who had been raised on wars with the North American Indians and the use of Blacks as slaves, they came to view the Mexicans also as "inferiors" who were obstacles to "progress." This was another aspect of "Manifest Destiny" and U.S. expansion at that time. Because the U.S. settlers viewed the Mexicans as backward and obstructing advancement, the North Americans thought they had the right to break Mexican laws and react with violence.

The final break occurred in 1833. Remember that it was in 1833 that Santa Anna pronounced against Farias and abolished the Federalist Mexican Constitution. Under the new Centralist Constitution, all power and legal authority now rested in Mexico City. To the Anglo-Tejanos, this meant that all their desires for more independence and power over their own affairs were doomed. The Texans declared their independence from Mexico by proclaiming their land the "Lone Star Republic." David Burnet was chosen president and a Mexican who opposed Santa Anna's abolition of federalism, Lorenzo Zavala, was made vice-president.

The stage was now set for Santa Anna to again ride off at the head of an army, this time to maintain the territorial integrity of Mexico and restore his country's honor. He raised an army. Many of his soldiers were Mayan Indians who were forcibly drafted. Untrained in warfare, this reluctant army began the long march northward to Texas.

In March, 1836, Santa Anna reached present-day San Antonio, Texas. He soon learned that a small band of Texans had barricaded themselves in an old Franciscan mission, ready to do battle with the Mexicans. This old mission is known as the Alamo.

9. Remember the Alamo!

Santa Anna thought that his army could defeat the Texans and force them to rejoin the Mexican nation. However, there were Mexicans as well as Anglo Americans living in Texas who opposed Santa Anna's leadership and who felt that Texas independence was their best path. Mexicans like Lorenzo Zavala and Juan Seguin joined with the Americans at this time.

At the Alamo, approximately 200 troops were under the command of William Barrett Travis. Legendary western heroes Davy Crockett and Jim Bowie were also there. Many Americans from other states such as Kentucky and Tennessee also had volunteered to help Texas fight against Mexico. Captain Juan Seguin and a force of Mexican "Tejanos" were also in the Alamo. Since the days of the Austins' first invitation to the Anglo settlers, these Mexicans had believed that Americans and Mexicans could live together in peace in Texas. Unfortunately, men such as Juan Seguin did not see their dreams become reality.

In March of 1836 Santa Anna's troops arrived at the Alamo. Travis and his men were well equipped with cannon and long rifles and were protected by the thick walls of the mission. As the fighting began, Santa Anna's army was unable to penetrate the mission. Although the Mexicans had many more troops, the Texans enjoyed a good defensive position.

Travis soon realized that while his men could hold out for some time, without reinforcements they would eventually run out of ammunition and be killed. Therefore he sent Seguin to try to get word to Sam Houston to send reinforcements. Seguin did not return in time. After approximately two weeks of battle, Santa Anna signaled for an attack. His men stormed the fort, running directly into rifle and cannon fire. Many Mexican soldiers died. But such were their numbers that they were able to climb the walls and enter the fort. Going down fighting, all those inside the Alamo were killed or later executed by Santa Anna.

Although not the decisive battle of the Texas War, the Alamo provoked hatred toward Mexico throughout the other United States. Many Americans now came to Texas to help in the defeat of Mexico. More importantly, this battle also sowed the seeds of Texan hatred of Mexicans that has lasted to this day among many.

The story of the Alamo is legendary in the history of Texas. Those who died inside were immortalized as having gone down fighting for freedom and independence. Most history books do not mention, however, that one of the freedoms these Texans sought was the freedom to own slaves. What is always mentioned is the cruelty of Santa Anna and the Mexicans. Santa Anna's decision to kill all those inside the Alamo was said to prove the violent and bloodthirsty nature of Mexicans.

The legacy of this battle was hatred and bitter feelings. Soon another battle of the Texas War increased the bad feelings among American Texans towards Mexico.

10. Goliad and San Jacinto

Near the small Texas town of Goliad, a squad of Texans under the command of Colonel James W. Fannin was forced to surrender to a Mexican army under General José Urrea. Fannin and about three hundred of his men were captured and held. Urrea wrote to Santa Anna requesting that the Americans' lives be spared. Santa Anna wrote back ordering that the prisoners be executed. Reluctantly, Lieutenant Colonel Nicholás de la Portilla carried out Santa Anna's order.

Meanwhile, Santa Anna's army had been chasing Sam Houston's smaller army all over the state. Some early victories over Houston made Santa Anna overconfident. At the crucial battle of San Jacinto, Houston caught Santa Anna off guard with a surprise attack. The Mexicans were routed and over seven hundred Mexicans were killed. Barely escaping with his life, Santa Anna was captured a day later while hiding in some bushes, alone. Thus ended the Texas War for independence.

While a prisoner, Santa Anna signed agreements with President David Burnet to end all fighting and to withdraw all Mexican troops across the Rio Grande. Santa Anna also agreed that a future commission from Texas would be received in Mexico City to grant Texas its independence. Back in Mexico, Santa Anna's actions were declared illegal by the Mexican government, stating that the president did not have the authority to sign away part of Mexico's territory. But these actions by the Mexican government were useless. Texas would never again be a part of Mexico.

For ten years Texas was known as the "Lone Star Republic," an independent nation. At first it seemed that perhaps Americans and Mexicans could live together in peace, as Mexicans like Juan Seguin had hoped. But this dream soon proved to be impossible.

Juan Seguin was elected the first mayor of San Antonio under the new Lone Star Republic. But soon he found himself virtually powerless because of the immigration of new Anglo residents who considered Mexicans unwelcome or even still "the enemy" in Texas. Although Seguin and his family had been among the original Mexican settlers of Texas and had also worked with Stephen Austin to invite in the first Americans, they received death threats and were once almost hanged by a lynch mob. Forced to flee to Mexico to meet an uncertain fate, Seguin, like thousands of Mexicans, became a man without a country, caught in the middle of two cultures, two nations, and all the hostilities and bitterness between them.

Even without active support from the U.S., Texas was able to maintain her independence as the Lone Star Republic from 1836 until 1845. This was due in great part to Mexico's continuing political problems and the "revolving door" presidency. Mexico was also invaded, this time by France, in the "Pastry War" of 1838; so-called because of a brief occupation by the French which occurred after Mexican soldiers smashed a French citizen's pastry shop. Mexico's internal problems and poor leadership had cost her the territory of Texas, but the loss of Texas was only the beginning.

11. The U.S.- Mexico War

In 1845, after much debate between the pro- and anti-slavery sides, Texas was admitted to the U.S. as a slave state. Mexico, of course, protested this annexation (gaining of territory) by the U.S., but there was little Mexico could do. The new U.S. president, James K. Polk, was quick to seize any opportunity to gain additional Mexican territory for the U.S.

At this time there was a bitter argument between Mexico and the U.S. over the new border between Texas and Mexico. The Mexicans claimed that the Rio Nueces had been the southern border of Texas since the time of the Spanish. Polk and the Texans disagreed, claiming the Rio Grande as the real border. Although only 150 miles separated the two rivers, if the line of the Rio Grande were followed west it would mean several thousand square miles of additional territory for the U.S.

Mexico's General Mariano Paredes was given an army to enforce the Rio Nueces as the true border. But in keeping with the sorry state of Mexican politics, Paredes used the army for a cuartelazo and had himself declared president of Mexico.

President Polk ordered General Zachary Taylor to enter the disputed area between the two rivers. It seems clear today that Polk sent Taylor into the disputed area as a provocation to start a fight with Mexico that would give him an excuse to take more Mexican territory, especially California and Santa Fé, New Mexico. There is even evidence that Polk's war message to Congress was written in advance of Taylor's adventure.

A brief exchange of shots resulted between Taylor's troops and those of General Mariano Arista. On May 9, 1846, Taylor reported to Polk that sixteen of his men had been killed or wounded by the Mexicans. Polk wasted no time in acting. Going before the U.S. Congress, Polk declared that Mexico had invaded the

United States of America and had "shed American blood on American soil." Apparently the American soil he was referring to was the disputed area between the two rivers. Polk also stated that Mexico had "proclaimed that hostilities exist and that the two nations are now at war." A declaration of war against Mexico was hurried through Congress. Despite the objections of men like Congressman Abraham Lincoln, the U.S. now found herself at war with Mexico.

Michael C. Meyer wrote in his book, *The Course of Mexican History:* "He (Polk) went before Congress and delivered a war message that bore little resemblance to the truth ... How different things looked from Mexico City! Not only had the Americans taken Texas, but they had changed the traditional boundary to double its size. When the Mexicans sought to defend themselves against the additional encroachment, the Yankees cried that Mexico had invaded the U.S.!" But, whether it was right or wrong, Mexico now faced the real threat of an invasion by the U.S. As one might have guessed, the Mexican army rose up and ousted Paredes. Santa Anna was called back yet another time to save the nation.

12. The American Invasion

The Americans mounted a triple invasion against Mexico, striking in three directions at once. The Army of the West, under General Stephen Kearny, proceeded into New Mexico and California. The Army of the Center led by Zachary Taylor invaded northern Mexico. The Army of Occupation, led by Winfield Scott, struck directly at Mexico City.

The invasion by General Winfield Scott was the major U.S. offensive. Scott came in several warships and had 10,000 men with him. Landing at Vera Cruz, Scott mounted an artillery attack on the city with his warships. For several days the Americans carried out a heavy mortar attack against the heart of the city. Civilian casualties were high. On March 27, 1847, Vera Cruz surrendered to Scott. Approximately 2,000 Mexicans died in the attack, with civilian deaths outnumbering military losses two to one.

Santa Anna now attempted to block Scott who was, by now, on his way to Mexico City. Scott took Puebla without a fight. At this point, when Scott's army was only hours away from the Mexican capital, one would think that the Mexicans would band together, forget the arguing and power struggles and attempt to save their country. Unfortunately for Mexico, the infighting and arguing continued as it had since Mexico's independence. The final defense of Mexico City was disorganized and insufficient. Distrusting the supposedly crooked federal politicians of Mexico City, the various Mexican states had refused to contribute money for Mexico's last defense.

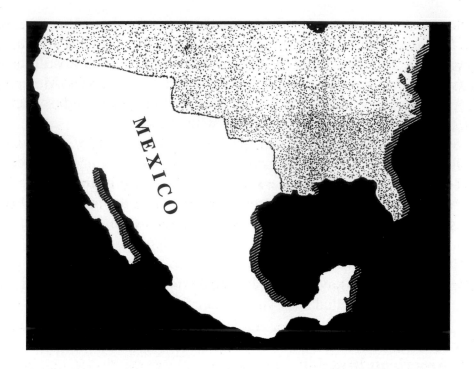

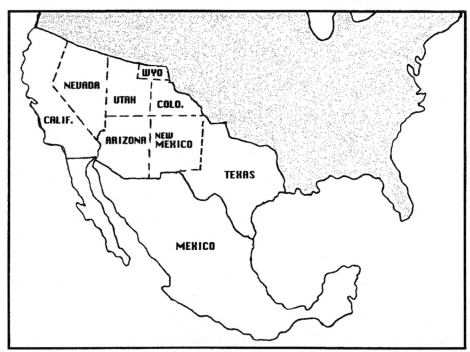

Mexico and the U.S. 1821-1836
The areas of California, Arizona, New Mexico, Texas, Nevada and parts of Wyoming and Colorado still belonged to Mexico until 1836. "Manifest Destiny," the Texas War and the U.S.-Mexico War changed all that.

Winning battles at Contreras and Churubusco, Scott proceeded toward Mexico City. Superior weapons, military tactics and leadership made the U.S. Army victorious, although at Churubusco the Mexicans made a valiant stand. On September 7, 1847, the bloodiest battle of the war took place as the Americans attacked at Molino del Rey. The Mexican casualties were over 2,000 and the Americans lost about 700.

The last remaining Mexican position was the Castle of Chapultepec. A squad of Mexican soldiers and military school cadets defended the castle to the death. These young cadets have gone down in Mexican history as "Los Niños Heroes" as they refused to surrender to the Americans. But they were killed and the army of Scott had won the final battle. Now it occupied Mexico City.

13. The Treaty of Guadalupe Hidalgo

After long and difficult negotiations the treaty that was to end the war was signed in the town of Guadalupe Hidalgo, just outside of Mexico City, on February 2, 1848. These were the terms: All of present-day Texas, California, New Mexico, Arizona, Utah and Nevada became part of the U.S. Parts of Colorado and Wyoming were also involved. The Mexicans were to keep everything south of the Rio Grande. The U.S. was to pay $18,250,000 for the land.

A more controversial part of the treaty involved the treatment of Mexican citizens who were living in the areas just acquired by the U.S. In part the treaty reads: "The Mexicans ... shall be incorporated into the union of the United States and admitted as soon as possible, according to the principles of the federal constitution, to the enjoyment of all rights of citizens of the U.S. In the meantime, they shall be maintained and protected in the enjoyment of their liberty, their property, and civil rights now vested in them according to the Mexican laws."

In other words, the earliest Mexican Americans, approximately 100,000 of them, were promised that they could keep their land and other property in accordance with the laws of Mexico and the U.S. Unfortunately, as in the case of the treaties signed with the American Indians, the U.S did not live up to the terms of this treaty. Mexicans were not able to keep their lands, often because of violence or the threat of violence. Especially after gold was discovered in California in 1849, lawsuits filed in local U.S. courts began to take the best lands away from the Mexicans. Conducted in English, these legal cases over land ownership were difficult for the Mexicans to understand. Many Mexican families had owned large areas of land since the days of the Spanish. But the old Spanish land grants had sometimes described vague boundaries. All these facts worked against the Mexicans. Soon, few Mexicans remained in Aztlan as tens of thousands of Americans poured into the newly acquired territory. An international boundary line had been re-drawn and the Mexicans now found themselves unwelcome in a land their ances-tors had helped to settle and develop. As in the case of Juan Seguin, many Mexi-cans even faced the hangman's noose as their punishment for attempting to defend homes that were guaranteed to them under the Treaty of Guadalupe Hidalgo. Is it any wonder that this treaty, the border and the treatment of Mexicans within the new boundaries of the United States are still so controversial today?

14. Why Aztlan was Lost

An independent country for fewer than thirty years, Mexico had managed to lose over one half of her national territory. As we have seen, the cause for this rests equally on Mexico's lack of organized and effective leadership and on the land hunger and aggressive actions of the United States. Attempting to sort out all these facts and to lay blame or responsibility for them is a risky business at best. But interesting questions do suggest themselves: How eager was President Polk to find an excuse to make war on Mexico and seize her territory? His reasoning that Mexico had invaded America and shed blood on American soil may have seemed true to him at the time. If the reason for going to war was the 16 casualties suffered by Taylor in the disputed area, was it justice to take several hundred thousand square miles of territory from Mexico as punishment? It would seem that Polk and the U.S. Congress could not resist taking advantage of Mexico's lack of effective control over her northwest territories.

If Mexicans want to find someone to blame for their misfortunes in the early days of independence, why not blame Spain? After all, it was Spain that plundered Mexico and dominated her people for three hundred years. The Mexi-cans had no choice but to drive out Spain when they were able. But once indepen-dent, Mexico found herself without any of the advantages that make an indepen-dent country able to govern itself effectively. Her population was largely illiterate and uneducated and thus was easily taken advantage of by power-hungry generals and politicians. Soon Mexico's national leadership had begun a game of "musical chairs" for the presidency. How could one expect the U.S. not to take advantage of Mexico? The taking of Aztlan also fit with the principles of "Manifest Destiny" popular in the U.S. If it was "God's will" that the U.S. would stretch from "sea to shining sea," then how could another nation's national territory stand in the way? But the facts that the land was taken under such questionable circumstances and that the Mexican people involved were not treated humanely, as required by a le-gal treaty, should be taken into consideration when discussing the future of Aztlan.

15. The Southwest Look

As mentioned previously, the American Southwest is a legendary land that has fired the imagination of generations worldwide. Primarily due to the American film industry, the land the Aztecs called Aztlan is one of the most famous on earth. What is little realized, however, is that the Mexicans have left their imprint on this land in an indelible way. Much of what we associate as typically American or Southwestern was first brought to Aztlan by the Spanish and the Mexicans.

The Spanish were the first horsemen of the American continent. They brought the horse to what is now the United States. Spanish noblemen, known as *caballeros*, brought their horse culture to central Mexico, and later it moved north with the Mexicans. Cowboy hats were first *sombreros*, which the Mexicans wore to keep the sun off their necks during their long hours on horseback. The ropes, or lariats, which cowboys use to rope steer were *las reatas*, used for the same purpose by the Spanish and Mexicans. Spurs were first called *Espuelas*. Chaps, those leather riding pants, were originally called *chapas*. The words *rodeo* and *corral* are spelled and mean the same in Spanish and English. Even cowboy boots (*botas*) and guitars (*guitarras*) were originally Spanish or Mexican.

The same can be said about other vital aspects of survival in the arid lands of the Southwest. Productive agriculture through the use of irrigation was pioneered by the first Mexican colonizers in places like Tejas (before it was Texas). Since there isn't much wood for building homes on the prairie, as in the arid valleys of Spain, the Spaniards and Mexicans developed adobe homes with ceramic tiled roofs which stayed relatively cool in the summer and warm in the winter. It would be an understatement to say that this thick-walled and tile-roofed architectural style is still with us today. One can see this in hundreds of fashionable housing projects in the American Southwest, places which always seem to be called something like "Rancho Del Sol." Southwestern furniture, Mexican food, all these things lend a distinctive flavor to the American Southwest which many Mexican American teenagers probably do not even realize is a part of their cultural heritage.

16. The Future of Aztlan

In Los Angeles today there are more people of Mexican descent than in any other city except Mexico City. Other large cities in the U.S. Southwest are currently undergoing similar population changes. Many of the Mexicans living in the U.S. today are the so-called "illegal aliens" who have come to the U.S. seeking jobs, hope for the future and a better life. Of all the immigrants who have come to the U.S., these Mexican immigrants are different in one important way: they are immigrating into a land which was once part of their nation.

The density of the Mexican and Mexican American population in the U.S. Southwest is evident. Indeed, in many Mexican "barrios," day-to-day life looks, sounds and feels more like life in Mexico than in the United States. Some would argue that Aztlan is merely reverting to its original character.

As we saw in the first chapter, Mexican Indians and the new race of Mexican Mestizos are indigenous or native to what is now the U.S. Southwest. After the last of the Mexicans were driven out of Aztlan, people of the United States felt that their "Manifest Destiny" had come true and that this land was now completely and forever theirs.

But the years since the Mexican Revolution of 1910 have witnessed a new migration, an economic migration northward by literally millions of Mexicans back into what was once Mexico. Decades ago, when the border was less closely watched, this migration was relatively easy. Now it is an odyssey full of peril for those brave enough to attempt it. In 1983 the U.S. Department of Immigration and Naturalization (informally known as the "Migra") reported that over 1,000,000 "illegal aliens" were apprehended while attempting to cross the U.S./Mexico border. No one knows how many made it safely across.

In 1986, the number of undocumented immigrants apprehended reached an all-time high of 1.6 million. Today we cannot accurately count the number of "illegal aliens" in the United States but it is surely in the millions. Indeed, by 1991 over 1.6 million undocumented immigrants in California alone had completed the first phase of the new "amnesty" immigration plan and had gained legal permanent residence in the U.S. Over 30% of these new American residents are Mexican.

Still, the number of Mexicans and Central Americans who are crossing into the United States without visas or passports is increasing even more dramatically. Population explosions and civil wars in Latin America are two reasons. But there is another reason, the simple law of supply and demand. In the United States there are many jobs that a large number of American citizens just will not do: farm laborer, factory worker, car wash attendant, housekeeper, parking lot attendant, day laborer, house painter, construction worker, live-in maid, or babysitter; the list grows longer each day. No matter the size of fines employers face for violating the latest immigration law, there will continue to be a massive demand for Mexican labor in the United States. And certainly there is no shortage of unemployed Mexicans in Mexico eager to try their luck at a better life in "El Norte."

There must be a better way to handle the situation as it now exists whereby undocumented workers are prone to exploitation and horrific living and working conditions. Frank Del Olmo, in a column for the *Los Angeles Times,* once suggested that where a job market exists for Mexican workers, protection should be provided by U.S. labor laws and the Mexicans allowed to form or join labor unions in order to diminish their vulnerability to exploitation. Until now, however, Mexican labor has been treated as the unprotected "free trade" of one of Mexico's most valuable exports: its hard-working people.

Whatever the case may be in the present, it is projected that by the year 2000 the Mexican, Mexican American and the other Latino populations of Aztlan will become the majority population of this area. Apparently the U.S. is having as little success in keeping the Mexicans out of Aztlan as Mexico had when they tried to keep the North Americans out of Texas in 1830. It seems that Mexicans and Americans are fated to live together in this land whether both sides want to or not. That Aztlan is now, and will probably forever be, part of the United States none can deny. But it is likewise hard to deny that the Mexican *raza* (race) was here originally, is still here in great numbers, and will probably always be here. History is difficult to change. The real question is how well Americans and Mexicans will learn to live together in Aztlan.

What bothers many Mexicans and Mexican Americans is the discrimination at the border. Every attempt is made to lure U.S. residents and their dollars into Mexico. Indeed, Americans do not even need a passport to enter Mexico. But the exact opposite is true for Mexicans. One reason why so many Mexicans cross the border illegally is the extreme difficulty of obtaining legal papers necessary to enter the U.S. Based on the history of Aztlan, this is hard for many to accept.

The surge in population among Mexicans and Mexican Americans in Aztlan may yet bring many changes other than the obvious cultural ones already mentioned. Since the U.S. is a democratic country, the Latinos are now realizing that the power to control Aztlan may once again be in their hands. Effective voter registration and turnout could make great changes in the political leadership and life here in the U.S. Southwest. Already more and more Mexican American representatives, mayors, congressmen and even governors are appearing in the American Southwest. Soon, perhaps, we may see an Aztlan that reflects its history even more than it does now.

Whatever is done or attempted as a solution to the border and "illegal alien" situations, for example, must take into account the unique and shared history of Aztlan. Important decisions on these matters would seem to be more logically made in consultation between the United States and Mexico and not just by the U.S. alone. The new voices of the Mexican Americans and their leadership are already pushing for an equitable resolution more in keeping with the history of this area.

For the young Mexican American people of today, even those born in the U.S., it is important to realize their brotherhood with the people of Mexico. We who live here in the U.S. must not let the historically recent border divide us as a people. Many young Chicanos often look with disdain on the Mexican immigrants who have recently arrived here. We must realize that on both sides of the border we are people native to Aztlan. Although we may find ourselves now on different sides of this new border, culturally and ethnically we are one people.

In the larger picture, the increasingly multi-ethnic and multi-racial character of Aztlan truly makes it a unique place. Nowhere else in the world do so many different kinds of people live together. Someday Aztlan could become a model for the world as a place where different kinds of people can accomplish much if they but take the time to learn about each other and to listen to different points of view. In this context, perhaps it is not too late to begin to treat Mexico as a true partner of the United States in the important decisions about immigration, trade, economics, pollution and the politics that affect both countries.

Chapter Three

THE LOSS OF AZTLAN:

WRITING EXERCISES

On the following pages you will find the writing exercises for this chapter. For additional explanations, please see "To the Teacher" or "A Note to the Student" on **pages 21 and 26**. Teachers are urged to select the writing exercises most appropriate for their particular classes. Below are the writing exercises for Chapter Three:

1. Sentence or Fragment?

This exercise is designed to help students learn how to recognize incomplete sentences (fragments) and then rewrite them as complete sentences. The most important idea here is that a complete sentence makes sense when read alone. When rewriting the fragments, the students must make sure not to change history!

2. Short Answer Questions

Once a student knows what a sentence is (and is not!), he or she can answer brief questions with one or two sentence answers of their own. This list of questions also makes a good study or review sheet when preparing for a test.

3. Paragraph Questions

These questions require slightly longer answers which are to be written in paragraphs. A sample paragraph along with definitions of such terms as "topic sentence" is included in the writing exercises of **Chapter One**.

4. Clustering and Identification (ID) Items

ID Items refer to and identify important people, places and things. Clustering is a way of brainstorming ideas based on these ID Items. Once the cluster has been made, use it as a guide and write an ID Paragraph. A sample cluster and a sample ID Paragraph can be found in the writing exercises of **Chapter One**.

5. Essay Questions

Very broad or complicated questions require essays or compositions as answers. A sample essay and instructions on how to write essays, both as homework and during in-class essay exams, are provided in the writing exercises section of **Chapter Five**.

Sentence or Fragment?

DIRECTIONS:

A complete sentence makes sense when read all alone. An incomplete sentence or fragment does not. Some of the following are fragments. Some are perfectly correct, complete sentences. Rewrite the fragments and make them into good sentences. You may add words, get rid of words, or rearrange the words. **Just make sure that each fragment you rewrite is factually correct according to the chapter and makes good sense when you read it alone.** Leave the complete sentences alone.

EXAMPLE: *Aztlan which is another name for the U.S. Southwest.*

Clearly this does not make sense when read alone. Although there is **no single correct way** to rewrite it, the following is much better:

Aztlan is another name for the U.S. Southwest.

1. Mexico, a colony of Spain for three hundred years.
2. Miguel Hidalgo who started Mexico's war for independence from Spain.
3. Hidalgo is like the George Washington of Mexico.
4. A lack of money which resulted when Spain was driven out.
5. Two powerful institutions in Mexico, the Catholic Church and the Mexican military.
6. Whoever controlled the army could rule Mexico.
7. Antonio López de Santa Anna who was one of the most important men in Mexico's early years of independence.
8. Mexico's Constitution of 1823 and the U.S. Constitution of 1787.
9. Federalism or shared power between the states and the central government.
10. An educated population is one of the basic ingredients of democracy.
11. Democracy which is defined as the rule of the people through their votes.
12. Several million Indians who not only were uneducated but also spoke little or no Spanish.
13. A cuartelazo was when the military would overthrow the government.
14. After Santa Anna overthrew Farias and abolished federalism.
15. Mexico's first thirty years of independence.
16. "Manifest Destiny," a feeling or belief by North Americans.
17. Moses and Stephen Austin and three hundred American families.
18. In 1829 the Mexican government passed an anti-slave law.

19. The colonization law of 1830.
20. As Americans came to outnumber the Mexicans in Texas.
21. Texas or the "Lone Star Republic."
22. An old Franciscan mission, the Alamo.
23. All those who fought inside the Alamo were killed by Santa Anna.
24. Another important battle, Goliad.
25. After the battle of San Jacinto.
26. General Zachary Taylor's report to President James Polk.
27. Winfield Scott and the bombing of Vera Cruz.
28. The promises made in the Treaty of Guadalupe Hidalgo.
29. Violence was used to get the Mexicans off their lands.
30. The question of Mexican "illegal aliens."
31. The present border between Mexico and the U.S.

Short Answer Questions

DIRECTIONS:

Answer the following questions by writing one or two complete sentences for each. Be sure that each sentence you write:

a) Is factually correct and helps to answer the question.
b) Is a complete sentence, which means it makes sense when read alone.
c) Could be understood by someone who has not seen the question.
d) Begins with a capital letter and ends with a period.
e) Is completely in your own words.
f) Uses correct spelling and is neat.

EXAMPLE: *What does the name Aztlan stand for?*

Aztlan was said to be the homeland of the Aztecs. It is also another word for the U.S. Southwest.

1. For how long was Mexico a colony of Spain?
2. What privileges and resources did the Catholic Church have in Mexico at this time?
3. What was Mexico's military known for at this time?
4. Define democracy.
5. After whose constitution did Mexico model hers?

6. What prevented Mexico from having real democracy as called for by her constitution?
7. Define "cuartelazo."
8. Who was the most prominent caudillo in Mexico's early years of independence?
9. Why did Spain invade Mexico in 1829?
10. Why did Santa Anna overthrow Farias in 1833?
11. What change in Mexico's government did Santa Anna make in 1833?
12. What does it mean when we say that Mexican politicians and generals lacked political maturity?
13. Why did Americans feel Aztlan was going to waste?
14. Why did Americans feel they had a right to take Aztlan?
15. What was the importance of the Austin family in Texas?
16. Was slavery a problem in the Mexican territory of Texas? Why?
17. What promises did American colonists have to make to Texas? Did they keep them?
18. Why did Americans and Mexicans get into disputes in Texas?
19. Why did Santa Anna's abolition of federalism anger the Texans?
20. Why did the battle of the Alamo anger Americans so much?
21. What happened at the end of the battle of San Jacinto?
22. Why were Mexico and the U.S. arguing over two rivers?
23. What was Polk's reason for war against Mexico?
24. Why was Mexico not able to fight an effective war against the U.S.?
25. What territory or states did the U.S. take after the U.S.-Mexico War?
26. What did the Treaty of Guadalupe Hidalgo say about Mexicans who owned land in Aztlan?
27. Why was violence used against Mexicans after the U.S.-Mexico War?
28. How has Aztlan changed recently?

Paragraph Questions

DIRECTIONS:

Answer the following questions by writing a good paragraph for each. Refer back to the sample paragraph on **page 47** for help. Be sure that each paragraph you write:

a) Is factually correct, helps to answer the question and is in your own words.
b) Looks like a proper paragraph (see sample).
c) Has an <u>underlined</u> topic sentence at the beginning of the paragraph.
d) Contains no fragments.
e) Uses correct spelling and is neat.

1. Describe Mexico's problems with money and the military in her early years of independence.
2. What prevented Mexico from having real democracy as called for by her constitution?
3. What does the overthrow of Farias by Santa Anna tell us about Santa Anna and his leadership qualities?
4. Summarize Mexico's problems in her first thirty years of nationhood.
5. Define and fully explain "Manifest Destiny." Give examples.
6. What role did slavery play in the history of Texas and Mexico?
7. What were the main reasons for the Americans' decision to secede from Mexico?
8. Why is the battle of the Alamo so famous?
9. Why is the story of Juan Seguin particularly sad?
10. What were President Polk's public reasons for going to war with Mexico? What do you think were the real reasons?
11. Why do Mexicans remember the invasion by Winfield Scott with as much anger as Texans remember the Alamo?
12. How was land taken from Mexicans after the U.S.-Mexico War?
13. Why is the Treaty of Guadalupe Hidalgo so controversial today?
14. What are the most important causes of Mexico's loss of Aztlan?
15. What have Mexicans and Spaniards contributed to the culture of the Southwest?
16. What does the growth of the Mexican American population tell us about the border between Mexico and the U.S.?
17. Why does the present border situation and the treatment of "illegal aliens" make some Chicanos angry?
18. Should Mexican Americans feel a sense of brotherhood with the people of Mexico? Why or why not?

Clustering and ID Items

DIRECTIONS:

Make clusters and/or ID paragraphs for the following identification items. While making your cluster or paragraph, ask yourself who or what the item is and why it is important in the history being studied. Refer to your book if necessary. A sample cluster and ID paragraph can be found on **page 49.**

Miguel Hidalgo

the U.S.-Mexico War

Doña Josefa Ortíz de Domínguez

Antonio López de Santa Anna

cuartelazo

"Manifest Destiny"

the Alamo

battle of San Jacinto

James K. Polk

Winfield Scott

Treaty of Guadalupe Hidalgo

Mexico/U.S. border today

Chicano voting power in Aztlan

Lone Star Republic

Essay Questions

DIRECTIONS:

The following are essay questions on the content of this chapter. Before attempting to answer any questions, see **page 187** for directions on how to write an essay and **page 188** for a sample essay.

1. Who was Miguel Hidalgo? What were his beliefs? What did he accomplish? And what role did Doña Josefa Ortíz de Domínguez play in his life?
2. Review the career of Antonio López de Santa Anna and the effect he had upon Mexico. Include the various cuartelazos until the Texas War. What is your opinion of his effect on Mexico?
3. Review the first thirty years of Mexico's independence in terms of her financial problems, political instability, inability to achieve democracy, and the resultant inability to effectively protect her territory from the U.S.
4. Summarize the Texas War. Include early American settlement in Texas, slavery, land disputes, Santa Anna's abolition of federalism and then the war itself.

5. Discuss the U.S.-Mexico War. Include the disputed area between the rivers; Polk's war message to Congress and his public reasons for war; the U.S. invasion of Mexico; Mexico's lack of an effective defense; the Treaty of Guadalupe Hidalgo; and the taking of land from Mexicans in Aztlan.

6. Given the history of Aztlan, what do you think about the following issues: Mexican "illegal aliens" who come to the U.S.; the border itself and its "one way only" nature; the growth of the Mexican American population in Aztlan; brotherhood between Mexicans and Mexican Americans?

7. How can Chicanos who know both Aztlan's history and the U.S. system of democracy make changes in Aztlan? What changes do you think should be made?

Benito Juárez was Mexico's first great president. A full-blooded Zapotec Indian from Oaxaca, Juárez was orphaned as a boy and could not even speak Spanish as a youth. From these humble beginnings Juárez went on to graduate from law school, become Governor of Oaxaca, Secretary of Justice, Chief Justice of the Mexican Supreme Court, and finally President of Mexico.

Chapter Four

THE MEXICAN REVOLUTION: PART I
The Era of Porfirio Díaz

1. Introduction

Most Mexican American students may know in some vague sense that the Mexican Revolution was an important event in Mexico's history. They may also be familiar with some of the great figures of the revolution such as Pancho Villa and Emiliano Zapata. But few Mexican Americans are informed about the actual events which took place during this revolution.

To study the Mexican Revolution is not an easy task. Many students and even history teachers have become confused amid the rush of the many battles, generals, presidents, and related events. But if time is invested in learning about what really happened during Mexico's Revolution of 1910, the results can be well worth the effort.

The great heroes of Mexico's recent past, men such as Villa, Zapata, Francisco Madero and Lázaro Cárdenas, all earned their reputations during the tumultuous Mexican Revolution. And if we follow the revolutionary changes through to the 1940s, then we will be more fully equipped to understand the Mexico we see today in the 1990s.

Let us now begin our investigation of the Mexican Revolution or, as it has come to be called, "the wind that swept Mexico."

2. Benito Juárez

The new Mexican nation had suffered greatly in her early days of independence from Spain. Her colonial dependence upon the Spanish had not prepared Mexico or her people to be an effective independent nation. As a result, Mexico experienced a period of severe political instability which culminated in 1848 with the loss of one half of her territory to the United States.

Subsequently, Mexico would finally gain effective leadership in the person of Benito Juárez. The story of "Don Benito" is one of the most stirring in Mexican history. Born a pure-blooded Zapotec Indian in the Mexican state of Oaxaca, Benito was orphaned at the age of three and could not even speak Spanish as a boy.

Eager for an education, Benito walked over forty miles from his village to the state capital, Oaxaca City. There he lived with an older sister who found the boy a job with a Franciscan order. His pay would be his school tuition. He not only learned Spanish quickly but was soon a top student. The only question was whether Benito should enter the priesthood or study law. He chose the legal profession and was soon admitted to the bar of his home state.

The same year Juárez graduated from law school he also became an alderman (like a city councilman) in Oaxaca City. Soon he was elected to the state legislature. But he did not forget his legal career. As a lawyer he championed the cause of the native Zapotec people who were fighting ongoing problems with the Catholic Church and the wealthy landowners. In 1848, Juárez was elected governor of the state of Oaxaca.

Juárez came to be involved with a group of reformers who sought to rid Mexico of the dictatorship of Santa Anna. This movement, known as the Revolution of Ayutla, led to the resignation of Santa Anna in 1855 and a new constitution for Mexico, written in 1857, of which Benito Juárez played a very important role in drafting. Ultimately, Juárez became the Secretary of Justice and later Chief Justice of the Supreme Court of Mexico.

At this time he was also responsible for the important "Ley Juárez," a new national law which would begin the process of officially separating the Mexican government from the Catholic Church. The Ley Juárez and other reform laws were bitterly opposed by the Church and Mexican conservatives. Things became so chaotic that another rebellion shook the nation: the War of the Reform.

The reform elements of Mexico, under the leadership of Benito Juárez and men such as Sebastian Lerdo de Tejada, eventually prevailed and in 1861 Benito Juárez was elected president of Mexico. What President Juarez and his nation now needed most desperately was a period of calm so that the new constitution and the reform laws could be put into effect. Unfortunately, Mexico received exactly what it did not need: another invasion by a foreign power.

The Catholic Church and Mexican conservatives who opposed President Juárez and the proposed reforms began a search for alternatives to the elected presidential government of Mexico. They reasoned, "Why not a foreign colonial power and a Catholic emperor?" All that was needed was a European nation in search of a colony and a willingness to send its military to conquer Mexico.

France, under the leadership of Napoleon III, fit the bill. Soon French troops landed in Mexico and installed Maximilian of Austria as Emperor of Mexico! The French authorities felt that it would be relatively easy to defeat the rag tag Mexican military and the Indian president, Benito Juárez. But Juárez became a guerrilla fighter who had to travel about the nation to avoid capture. The Mexicanos fought bravely against the French occupation.

One of the most important battles of the war with France came on the 5th of May, 1862. On that occasion, a much smaller, poorly equipped Mexican army led by Ignacio Zaragoza and a young commander named Porfirio Díaz defeated a much larger and better equipped French force. Although it was not to be the decisive battle of the war, it has been commemorated by the important Mexican holiday "Cinco de Mayo" as the beginning of the end for the French.

Five years later, in May of 1867, Maximilian formally surrendered. Juárez decreed that Maximilian be tried for his offenses against the nation. On June 19th, Maximilian was executed so that Mexico could send a message of independence to the rest of the world.

Benito Juárez resumed his interrupted presidency and was re-elected once more. He remained as the nation's president until 1872 when he suffered a coronary seizure and died in office. Mexico's first truly great president had died without having fully realized his dream of a reformed and modernized Mexico.

The stage was now set for the amazing rise to power of Porfirio Díaz, the man who would rule Mexico for thirty-four years and whose regime is generally credited with having sparked the Mexican Revolution of 1910.

3. Mexico in 1876

Mexico in 1876 was a nation almost totally backward and underdeveloped. The years of political turmoil, combined with the foreign invasions by Spain, the United States and France, had made it virtually impossible for Mexico to modernize. She also had an empty treasury. She lacked the money to pay her government workers or to invest in large industrial projects. She was faced with a huge foreign debt owed to several different countries. Unable to pay off her loans, Mexico had the reputation in Europe of being extremely irresponsible, financially. As a result of these financial problems, few Mexicans or foreigners would take the chance of investing large sums of money to improve the country.

Mexico's public services were totally inadequate to meet the needs of the people. Many of these problems were caused by corruption and dishonesty in government, or by simple mismanagement due to lack of governmental experience. Mexico's rich mines had still not been restored to good working order. Many were still flooded and inactive. Railroads for public transportation were few and far between. Juárez had begun the construction of rail lines but not enough had been built. As a result, the concept of "patria chica" (small nation) persisted, which means that most Mexicans never ventured out of the small pueblos or villages in which they were born. There were few telegraph lines and the important docks in the harbor cities were outdated and insufficient. Throughout Mexico, law and order was virtually unknown. Mexico's people suffered from severe health problems due to a lack of doctors, hospitals and medicine. There was a high infant mortality rate and, in general, health and sanitation projects were limited.

Mexico found herself not much better off 55 years after she overthrew Spanish colonial domination. What would the future hold? Unfortunately for Mexico and her long-suffering people, things were to get much worse for many years before they were to get any better.

4. Don Porfirio

Porfirio Díaz first gained national recognition in Mexico during the war against Maximilian and the French army. As a young brigadier general, Díaz, along with General Ignacio Zaragoza, masterminded the startling defeat of the French on May 5th, 1862.

Díaz had been an important fighter with Benito Juárez. His military career had been heroic. Born in Oaxaca in 1830, a Mixtec Indian with some Spanish blood, Díaz had originally considered a career in the priesthood but it was soon clear that his future lay with the military. After his defeat of French forces at Puebla, he continued as a guerrilla chief, fighting with Juárez. After the defeat of the French, Díaz served as a military commander under President Juárez. In 1871, when Juárez announced that he would seek a third term as president, Díaz decided to run against him. In a close election, Juárez was re-elected. Díaz then declared himself in revolt against Juárez but this attempt to gain the presidency soon failed.

After Juárez had suffered a stroke while in office and died in October 1872, Lerdo de Tejada ran against and defeated Díaz for the vacant presidency. Lerdo's presidency turned out to be a relatively good one and he announced that he would seek re-election in 1876. Again claiming that the re-election of presidents was wrong, Díaz staged another army revolt, this time against Lerdo. Reinforced by his

Porfirio Díaz was initially a military leader and ally of Benito Juarez. Díaz fought for the victorious Mexican army in the famous battle of Puebla on May 5th, 1862. After becoming president in 1876, Díaz went on to construct a dictatorial machine that would rule Mexico for the next 34 years. Díaz's presidency provided some modernization for the nation, but the corruption in his regime is generally credited with sparking the disastrous Mexican Revolution of 1910.

friend Manuel González, Díaz defeated the troops of Lerdo and took control of the presidency of Mexico for the next 34 years.

5. The Díaz Dictatorship

The first challenge to President Díaz came in the form of the usual revolts led by dissatisfied or power-hungry caudillos. Díaz realized early in his first term that this political instability had to end if Mexico were ever to progress. He thus began to strengthen his federal army as well as the *Rurales*, which were the troops keeping the peace in the countryside areas of Mexico. It has been claimed by many of Díaz's opponents that he filled the ranks of the Rurales with men who were former bandidos.

Successfully putting down the early revolts against him, Díaz formulated a strategy to prevent any more of these revolts from taking place. He made it clear that any military man who supported him would be richly rewarded. Often these rewards came in the form of appointments to be state governors or other high government officials. Díaz also made it clear, however, that anyone caught plotting against him would be quickly executed or exiled. Under Díaz the caudillos were more or less in competition among themselves for the favors that Díaz handed out. State governors and other high officials could be as dishonest and crooked as they pleased as long as they did not plot against Díaz.

Díaz had seen to it that there would be relative political stability under him. Now he desired to impose law and order upon the nation. He believed that political stability and law and order in Mexico would eventually attract wealthy foreign investors. Díaz thought that foreign money was essential for Mexico's modernization. In order to gain this law and order Díaz greatly increased the size of the Rurales. Over 800 new officers were added. By 1910 the Rurales numbered over 2,700 well-equipped men. The common people of Mexico soon learned that the Díaz police, army, and Rurales were not to be taken lightly. Some have said that these "peace-keeping" forces of Díaz used extreme force. It became common to hear of prisoners who had been shot "while attempting to escape," or of prisoners who had "committed suicide." Soon it was clear that it was not a good idea to fall into the hands of the Díaz forces. As a result, banditry was reduced and relative law and order prevailed throughout most of Mexico. Díaz spent approximately 25% of the nation's money on funding for the military and for the Rurales.

Thus, by the end of Díaz's first term in office (1880) Mexico was a more stable country although many would say that the stability was produced through fear. But as Díaz had hoped, this stability meant the re-appearance of foreign investors ready to try their luck in making fortunes in Mexico. Díaz had also begun to pay off Mexico's huge foreign debt, especially to the U.S. Mexico was now moving toward financial well-being for the first time. As Díaz's first term ended, many pleaded with him to run again. But Díaz preferred to step down so as to follow the no re-election clause in Mexico's constitution. This further improved his reputation in Mexico. As his successor, Díaz chose his secretary of war, Manuel González. His voluntary stepping down was not really such a sacrifice for Díaz as it appears. He knew that, if he wished, González would be easy to control and he also knew that he would soon be back in the president's chair.

In 1880 Manuel González took over as president. With Díaz directing things from the background, the modernization of Mexico began in the form of railroad and telegraph construction. Foreign capital was beginning to flow into the country. Things seemed to be looking up. But soon a corruption scandal rocked the González administration. Many think that the González regime was corrupt and dishonest. Others say González simply overspent. For whatever reason, González's reputation was ruined. Riots broke out in Mexico City. They were violently put down by the Federales. Many Mexicans felt relieved when, in 1884, Porfirio Díaz swept to an overwhelming victory and became president again. From now on Díaz would not bother to resign after each four-year term. He would hold onto his power in a virtual dictatorship that lasted until 1911.

Soon the new Díaz administration took shape and it was possible to see the direction in which Mexico would develop. A Mexican of French ancestry, José Ives Limantour, was appointed by Díaz to be minister of the treasury. Next to Díaz, Limantour seemed the most powerful man in Mexico. He represented a group known as the "Científicos" who had certain ideas about what was best for Mexico. Díaz clearly agreed with them and thus Limantour began to transform Mexico completely. See Plate 23.

The Científicos believed that the native Indian population would never become a productive part of Mexico's economy. Therefore it was useless to spend vast amounts of money on attempting to educate the Indians. The only thing the Indians were good for was their labor. The Científicos believed that Mexico should be ruled by White men and it should be civilized by the importation of foreign capital. Francisco Bulnes, one of Díaz's chief administrators, even stated once that "5,000,000 Argentines (Whites) are worth more than 14,000,000 Mexicans." Thus, almost all of the schools built during the Díaz era were constructed in the larger cities, away from the Indians.

But the Indians of Mexico were not simply to be left alone under the Díaz regime. They were to suffer further. As we have seen, Díaz held out the rewards of high political office to generals and other important friends of his. It soon became clear that Díaz was manipulating state and local elections to see to it that men chosen by him would become the governors of the Mexican states. As governors,

José Ives Limantour, a Mexican of French ancestry, was secretary of the treasury under President Diaz and leader of the so-called "Científicos" who ruled Mexico. Limantour masterminded the economic strategy for Mexico that involved selling off Mexico's rich raw materials to foreigners and allowed the seizure of Mexican agricultural lands for use by large corporations and haciendas. Limantour and Diaz managed to balance Mexico's budget but soon the revolutionary explosion would destroy all that the Científicos had achieved.

these men began the practice of taking the traditional *ejido* lands away from the Indians.

In most Indian and Mestizo pueblos and villages, ejido lands were the public lands where the Indians raised their crops and grazed their animals. These lands were owned in common by the residents of entire villages. Many of these small pueblos with their ejidos had existed as stable towns since before the conquest of Mexico by Spain. The ejido lands were vital to the economic survival of rural villages. But under Díaz these lands were seized and gathered together under the Hacienda System.

6. Los Hacendados

Many of Díaz's state governors used their control of the state police and the Rurales to take the best ejido lands away from the Indian pueblos. Foreign companies were invited in by Díaz to survey and mark the boundaries of these lands. Under Díaz's laws, once a foreigner had surveyed the land and planned to improve it, he won the right to purchase it. If the Indians could not prove legal title to the land it was available for others to seize. But how could the Indians legally prove that the lands were theirs? They had lived on these lands since before the Spanish conquest of Mexico. Where could they get the legal deeds necessary to prove ownership? Thus began the brutal seizure of millions of acres of ejido lands.

Large and wealthy haciendas began to emerge throughout Mexico. Ordinarily it was the state governors of Díaz or foreigners who owned the largest haciendas. Soon, fewer and fewer people owned more and more of Mexico's best land. By 1900 most Indian villages had lost their public lands. A few hundred families owned 134 million acres of the best land in Mexico. Haciendas of forty to fifty thousand acres were common. Some had up to one-half million acres. Some of the richest hacendados even owned as many as fifty different haciendas. Entire states were thus dominated by one or a few wealthy families.

The state of Chihuahua offers a good example. Don Luis Terrazas was the founder of the extended family that came to dominate the state. In the 1870s, 1880s and 1890s Don Luis was in and out of the state governor's chair in Chihuahua. He acquired more and more land and haciendas through his control of the Mexican troops. He soon became the largest hacendado in all of Mexico. By the early 20th century his land holdings amounted to 7,000,000 acres. He owned over 50 haciendas in Chihuahua. He owned 500,000 head of cattle, 225,000 sheep, 25,000 horses, and some of the finest fighting bulls in Latin America. During the Díaz era, Terrazas or members of his extended family held offices in the state's legislature for 66 terms and 22 terms in the national legislature.

When the wealthy haciendas had no more ejido land to occupy, they began encircling the pueblos and villages. This soon killed off many of the small towns for they were cut off from the outside world and had no more land on which to support themselves. Indian and Mestizo residents of these small pueblos had for centuries supported themselves through their farming on the ejido lands. Now, faced with starvation, they hired themselves out as workers on the large haciendas. They soon came to be, literally, tied to these haciendas by means of the system of debt-peonage. See Plate 22.

7. Los Pobres de la Tierra

Indian or Mestizo workers (peones) often had to move onto the hacienda lands. They would be given a rude one-room adobe hut. Water often had to be carried great distances. The peones were charged rent on these houses. They then went to work plowing, planting and harvesting for the hacendado. Often the peones were not paid in money. They received chips or coupons that could only be exchanged for food at the hacienda's store, the "tienda de raya." More often than not, a peon's wages were not enough to feed one's family. The tienda de raya would then freely grant credit to the workers. But soon the peon found himself hopelessly in debt to the "patrón" (owner).

Under the laws of Díaz, once a debt had been established the peon was forbidden to leave the hacienda. He had to remain and work until the debt was repaid, which was usually impossible. Food and rent costs always seemed to be more than the wages. Dishonest record keeping in the tiendas was common. When the peon died, the debt was passed on to his children, who were likewise forbidden to leave the hacienda until the debt was paid.

On the hacienda grounds the "mayordomo," or foreman, was legally responsible for law and order. He was the sheriff, judge and jury for the peones. If he "accidentally" killed an Indian there was no legal way to protest. The hacienda was thus a closed, completely self-sufficient society from which there was no justice and no escape for the Indian peones. Stories of beatings, lynchings and rapes were common as there was no police involvement to protect the poor.

On the haciendas the infant mortality rate was often as high as 25%. The diet of the Indians was nearly always the same: corn, beans and chile, but with virtually no meat at all. As Michael Meyer writes in his book, *The Course of Mexican History:* "The millions of rural Mexicans who found themselves in dying villages or subsisting as peones on the nation's haciendas were worse off financially than their rural ancestors of a century before."

Ramón Corral was the governor of Sonora under President Porfirio Díaz. Corral used the dreaded *Rurales* to seize the rich valley lands of Sonora's Yaqui Indians. Then Corral personally sold the captured Indians as slaves to the plantation owners in Yucatan. He was later chosen by President Díaz to be his vice-president in 1910. Some feel this was a sort of "life insurance" policy for Díaz, as Corral was such a hated figure in Mexico that none would dare kill President Díaz for fear that Corral would assume the presidency.

The plantations of Yucatan and Quintana Roo were reputed to be the worst of all. Indians who had resisted the haciendas were often shipped to these plantations and worked, chained together, under the blazing tropical sun. One such group of Indians who fought for their ejido lands were the Yaquis of Sonora. Their fertile valley lands were seized by Governor Ramón Corral because the Indians "weren't using the lands efficiently enough." Under the Indian Jefe (Chief) Cajame, the Yaquis rose up and fought against the Rurales and Federales in defense of their lands. The Indians defeated several army squadrons sent to capture them. When the Indians were finally defeated, Governor Corral had Cajame shot. Corral then made a deal with the plantation owners of Quintana Roo. He would sell the Yaquis to them. Then Indians would labor on the plantations in chain-gangs to prevent escape. Corral received 75 pesos a head for the Yaquis and thus became a rich man. In Sonora the wealthy landowners grew their rice and cotton on the land of the Yaquis while, in Quintana Roo, the Yaquis died like flies on the plantations. Such was "justice" for the Indians under Díaz.

8. The Modernization of Mexico

To the foreigners of Europe and the U.S., the cruelty of the hacienda system was invisible. Foreign investors were courted by Díaz. He wanted them to invest their money in Mexico. This was Díaz's and Limantour's strategy for the modernization of Mexico. They hoped to show the foreigners that Mexico was now a nation of political stability and law and order. They sought to reassure the foreigner that he and his money would be safe in Mexico. Indeed, throughout the Díaz era, the foreign visitor to Mexico actually enjoyed better legal protection than did the average Mexican. By 1910 over one half of all rural Mexicans lived and worked in haciendas and we have already seen what Díaz's "law and order" meant to them.

For foreigners, however, everything was done to ensure their well-being. In the Mexican courts, foreigners, especially Americans, were given preferred treatment. Favorable verdicts over disputed Indian ejido lands, for example, almost always went to the foreigner or to the wealthy Mexican hacendado. For the Mexican peones there was no justice at all.

But despite the tremendous cost to Mexico's own people, the modernization of Mexico had begun. Under Limantour's tenure as minister of the treasury, Mexico's national budget was balanced in 1894. This was the first time in Mexico's independence that her debts were not larger than her profits. New treaties and trade agreements were now entered into with many foreign countries. Once diplomatic relations had been firmly established, Limantour began to make deals for

Teresa Urrea

Born in Sinaloa, Mexico, of a wealthy rancher-patrón and a Yaqui girl of fourteen, her parents were not married. Around the age of sixteen, Teresa went into an unexplained trance and, in that state, she cured a servant woman of paralysis by a laying on of the hands. Following this, she was said to have cured many people and her fame spread. Thousands of people came to see "The Saint of Cabora," as people called her. From Mexico City, the local priests were told to denounce her from the pulpit as a heretic. Then the Church convinced Porfirio Díaz to arrest her. But Teresa had a faithful following of Yaqui Indians. To protect her, they ambushed the federal troops near Cabora. Thus began the "Tomachic War," or, the Revolt of the Ya-

La Santa de Cabora

quis. The Yaquis went into battle shouting her name.

Teresa was finally arrested and imprisoned. But the government was forced to release her when the Yaquis continued their revolt.

The Church finally prevailed upon the authorities to deport her. She was deported to the United States in 1893. In Tomacacori and El Paso, the Church continued its denunciations of her, forcing her to move to Clifton, Arizona in 1897. Teresa Urrea was loved by the Mexicans, and especially by the Yaqui Indians. She married a Yaqui Indian, causing an uproar among the Christians.

In Clifton, Teresa Urrea healed the daughter of a local Anglo American banker. In gratitude he took her to Los Angeles. There, her fame was immediate and money was raised to send her on a tour of the United States and Europe.

In 1904 she returned to Clifton, Arizona where she had a 2-story hospital built. Eighteen months after her return, Teresa Urrea died. As Carey McWilliams has said, "Although the doctors said that she died of tuberculosis, the Mexicans of Clifton insisted that she had worn out her spirit in the service of her people; to them she is still the Saint of Cabora."

With Porfirio Díaz as president, 15,000 miles of railroad track were constructed in Mexico between 1876 and 1910. Unfortunately, U.S. and English corporations owned and planned the construction of the railroads so
that Mexican raw materials could more easily be shipped out of Mexico.
The railroads became a focal point for Díaz's critics. Later, they became
one of the most important means of transportation for rebel troops which
were seeking to overthrow President Díaz.

Mexico's improvement.

One of the biggest of Díaz's projects was a new railroad system for Mexico. Railroads were seen as the only way to link together the various parts of Mexico because of the difficult mountain terrain that covers much of the country. Foreign money, experts, technicians and railroad professionals poured into Mexico to begin the laying of the rails. American, French and British money and technical knowledge were primarily responsible for the railroad system. The progress of the building was truly amazing. In 1876 Mexico had 400 miles of railroad track. By 1911 she had over 15,000 miles.

In mining, foreign money and technical experts again did wonders with Mexico's slumbering mines. The vast wealth that lay beneath the ground soon began to pour out. Foreign companies were lured into Mexican investment by the promise of low taxes. The foreigners could also keep large quantities of what they mined. Modern machinery dramatically increased the production of Mexico's mines. In 1877 Mexican gold production was 1.5 million pesos. In 1908 it was 40 million pesos. In silver, it went from 24.8 million pesos in 1877 to 85 million pesos in 1908.

Mexico's rich oil deposits were also tapped by advanced foreign technology. Mexico soon became one of the world's leaders in oil production. American and British money was primarily responsible for the jump in oil production. Additionally, the fishing industry, agriculture, textiles and harbor facilities were improved dramatically during the Díaz years. Mexico's total foreign trade shows clearly the jump in economic activity that took place during the Díaz years. In 1876 Mexico's foreign trade was worth 50 million pesos. In 1910 the figure was 488 million! Could anyone doubt that Díaz and Limantour had worked an economic miracle in Mexico?

9. The Costs of Mexico's Modernization

Unfortunately, as we have seen, the common Mexican did not benefit at all from these profits. Díaz's corrupt state governors, the hacendados, Limantour and his Científicos always seemed to make huge profits for themselves in the sale of lands to foreign investors. But the average Mexicans, the Mestizos and the Indian peones, were in fact worse off than they had been a hundred years earlier. Food costs had risen sixfold yet the wages had not gone up in a century.

The brutal force and violence used by Díaz's Rurales and Federales was making Díaz-haters out of the common people. The Indians wanted their ejido lands back. Those in the press who dared to criticize Díaz were arrested or shot. Elections became a joke at all levels. Díaz was even successful in making the

Mexican Congress nothing more than a group of his friends and associates who would pass whatever laws Díaz needed to maintain his dictatorship. Every four years Díaz would run for president again and every four years he would be overwhelmingly re-elected. The fact that any who dared oppose him faced possible death may have accounted for Díaz's electoral success.

Even the economic miracles had hidden sides to them. Most of the oil and mineral wealth of Mexico was taken out of the country and used in foreign countries. The foreign investors owned the oil wells and the mines. Mexican workers were given the lowest jobs and were not trained to be able to take over the higher paying technical jobs later. Often, foreign workers were paid more for doing the same job as the Mexicans. Even the railroads, the proudest achievement of the Díaz regime, had a negative aspect. Americans had been primarily in charge of selecting the routes the trains would follow. Often, these routes were designed so as to bring Mexican oil and minerals out of Mexico and into the U.S. Thus there were many rail lines that connected different parts of Mexico with the U.S. However, in certain parts of central and southern Mexico, the only way for the Mexican people to get from one town to another was by mule or burro.

During the 34-year reign of Porfirio Díaz, Mexico came to look like a modern country. Modern buildings, factories, oil wells, harbors, hydro-electric plants and railroads made Mexico seem prosperous. But it was a false prosperity. Mexico was clearly enjoying the most stable political period of her independence, but the economic development of Díaz and the political stability were created at too great a cost. For, unknowingly, Díaz had created the conditions for the Mexican Revolution; a revolution that would last for some thirty years and would see Mexican fight against Mexican in some of the bloodiest and most destructive warfare that has ever been seen on the American continent.

Chapter Four

THE MEXICAN REVOLUTION, PART I:

WRITING EXERCISES

On the following pages you will find the writing exercises for this chapter. For additional explanations, please see "To the Teacher" or "A Note to the Student" on **pages 21 and 26**. Teachers are urged to select the writing exercises most appropriate for their particular classes. Below are the writing exercises for Chapter Four:

1. Sentence or Fragment?

This exercise is designed to help students learn how to recognize incomplete sentences (fragments) and then rewrite them as complete sentences. The most important idea here is that a complete sentence makes sense when read alone. When rewriting the fragments, the students must make sure not to change history!

2. Short Answer Questions

Once a student knows what a sentence is (and is not!), he or she can answer brief questions with one or two sentence answers of their own. This list of questions also makes a good study or review sheet when preparing for a test.

3. Paragraph Questions

These questions require slightly longer answers which are to be written in paragraphs. A sample paragraph along with definitions of such terms as "topic sentence" is included in the writing exercises of **Chapter One**.

4. Clustering and Identification (ID) Items

ID Items refer to and identify important people, places and things. Clustering is a way of brainstorming ideas based on these ID Items. Once the cluster has been made, use it as a guide and write an ID Paragraph. A sample cluster and a sample ID Paragraph can be found in the writing exercises of **Chapter One**.

5. Essay Questions

Very broad or complicated questions require essays or compositions as answers. A sample essay and instructions on how to write essays, both as homework and during in-class essay exams, are provided in the writing exercises section of **Chapter Five**.

Sentence or Fragment?

DIRECTIONS:

A complete sentence makes sense when read all alone. An incomplete sentence or fragment does not. Some of the following are fragments. Some are perfectly correct, complete sentences. Rewrite the fragments and make them into good sentences. You may add words, get rid of words, or rearrange the words. **Just make sure that each fragment you rewrite is factually correct according to the chapter and makes good sense when you read it alone.** Leave the complete sentences alone.

EXAMPLE: *Porfirio Díaz, dictator of Mexico for 34 years.*

Clearly this does not make sense when read alone. Although there is **no single correct way** to rewrite it, the following is much better:

Porfirio Díaz was the dictator of Mexico for 34 years.

1. Benito Juárez, a Zapotec Indian.
2. The "Ley Juárez."
3. The French invasion of Mexico and Maximilian.
4. Benito Juárez was Mexico's first great president.
5. Porfirio Díaz and the battle of Puebla.
6. Underdeveloped, economically and politically unstable.
7. Mexico had serious problems in 1876.
8. A huge foreign debt and a reputation for financial irresponsibility.
9. The heritage of political instability.
10. Public services such as medical attention and medicine.
11. The mining industry in general in 19th century Mexico.
12. Although the U.S. had, by this time, a transcontinental railroad.
13. Law and order in the Mexican cities.
14. Banditry in the more rural areas.
15. Díaz's successful cuartelazo.
16. The Rurales were the Díaz police forces in the countryside of Mexico.
17. Political corruption by the state governors.
18. Anyone caught plotting against Díaz.
19. Law and order and justice for the average Mexicans.
20. José Ives Limantour and the Científicos.
21. Mexican Indian education during the Díaz years.

22. The return of investment by foreigners in Mexico.
23. Indian public lands or ejidos.
24. Seizure of ejido land under the hacienda system.
25. Don Luis Terraza of Chihuahua.
26. Debt-peonage was the economic system of the haciendas.
27. Paid in coupons while receiving credit from the hacienda store.
28. Debt owed to the haciendas.
29. Conditions for rural Mexicans were worse in 1900 than in 1800.
30. Governor Ramón Corral and the Yaquis of Sonora.
31. Modernization of Mexico by means of foreign capital.
32. Statistically, Mexico seemed a prosperous nation in 1910.
33. The apparent law and order lured the foreign investor.
34. Mexico's economic advances in gold, silver, oil and railroads.
35. The force used by the Rurales.

Short Answer Questions

DIRECTIONS:

Answer the following questions by writing one or two complete sentences for each. Be sure that each sentence you write:

a) Is factually correct and helps answer the question.
b) Is a complete sentence, which means it makes sense when read alone.
c) Could be understood by someone who has not seen the question.
d) Begins with a capital letter and ends with a period.
e) Is completely in your own words.
f) Uses correct spelling and is neat.

EXAMPLE: *When did Mexico drive out the French and who was their leader?*

Mexico successfully ended French attempts at colonization under the leadership of Benito Juárez in 1867.

1. Why did Benito Juárez walk to Oaxaca as a boy?
2. What were some important governmental positions held by Benito Juárez?
3. Give some examples of Mexico's underdevelopment in 1876.
4. What was Mexico's financial condition in 1876?
5. What is meant by corruption in government?
6. Was foreign investment lacking in Mexico in 1876? Why?

7. What natural resources were not being developed by Mexico at this time?
8. What was the situation with Mexico's railroads and harbors in 1876?
9. Describe Mexico's condition regarding law and order in 1876.
10. Where and how did Porfirio Díaz first become famous in Mexico?
11. How did Díaz actually assume the presidency?
12. Briefly, how did Díaz make sure there would be no military revolts against him as president?
13. What form of bribery was most often used by Díaz to pacify his rivals?
14. Briefly describe the Rurales.
15. Who was José Ives Limantour?
16. What did the Científicos believe about the Indians of Mexico?
17. Define Indian ejido.
18. Why was it difficult for the Indians to prove they owned their land?
19. What were the haciendas? Who were the hacendados?
20. Tell a little about Don Luis Terrazas.
21. Briefly explain how debt-peonage worked.
22. What were the tiendas de raya?
23. Why was it so hard for peones to get out of debt?
24. How are the Yaquis connected with Governor Corral of Sonora?
25. Describe how foreigners received better treatment than some Mexicans.
26. What was good about Mexico's mineral production under Díaz? What was bad about it?
27. Why was Mexico's prosperity under Díaz a false prosperity?
28. Why was Díaz becoming unpopular in Mexico by 1900?
29. In general, what was the problem with Díaz's modernization of Mexico?

Paragraph Questions

DIRECTIONS:

Answer the following questions by writing a good paragraph for each. Refer back to the sample paragraph on **page 47** for help. Be sure that each paragraph you write:

    a) Is factually correct, helps to answer the question and is in your own words.
    b) Looks like a proper paragraph (see sample).
    c) Has an <u>underlined</u> topic sentence at the beginning of the paragraph.
    d) Contains no fragments.
    e) Uses correct spelling and is neat.

1. Describe the career of Benito Juárez.
2. Why did the French invade Mexico? What part did "Cinco de Mayo" play?
3. Describe Porfirio Díaz's early military career and how he first became president of Mexico.
4. How did Díaz make sure there would be no military revolts against him?
5. What role did the Rurales play in Díaz's dictatorship?
6. What was Limantour's plan for attracting foreign investment into Mexico?
7. How did the peones of Mexico come to be tied to the haciendas through the system of debt peonage?
8. Who was Ramón Corral? How is his experience with the Yaquis typical of what happened to the Indians under Díaz?
9. Give some specific examples of the apparent modernization of Mexico under Díaz.
10. Why did the average Mexican people not benefit from Díaz's modernization of the country? Cite statistics.
11. Why was Teresa Urrea called "La Santa de Cabora?"

Clustering and ID Items

DIRECTIONS:

Make clusters and/or ID paragraphs for the following identification items. While making your cluster or paragraph, ask yourself who or what the item is and why it is important in the history being studied. Refer to your book if necessary. A sample cluster and ID paragraph can be found on **page 49.**

Benito Juárez
Porfirio Díaz
the Rurales
José Ives Limantour
Teresa Urrea ("La Santa de Cabora")

ejidos
Don Luis Terraza
hacienda system / debt peonage
Ramón Corral / the Yaquis

Essay Questions

DIRECTIONS:

The following are essay questions on the content of this chapter. Before attempting to answer any questions, see **page 187** for directions on how to write an essay and **page 188** for a sample essay.

1. Write a biographical essay about Benito Juárez. Be sure to include all the major stages of his life and career.
2. Describe the various components of Porfirio Díaz's strategy to ensure that his dictatorship would not be overthrown.
3. How was the hacienda system of Díaz created from the ejido lands of Mexico's Indians? Be sure to include debt-peonage, the tienda de raya, Ramón Corral and Don Luis Terrazas.
4. Describe the modernization of Mexico that occurred during the Díaz era. What were the hidden negatives of this modernization? Be sure to include foreign privilege and the control of natural resources.

Chapter Five

THE MEXICAN REVOLUTION: PART II
Revolutionary decade — 1910-1920 — and beyond

1. Prelude to Revolution

At the beginning of the 20th century, Mexico seemed a nation on the rise. Political leaders and financial tycoons in Europe and the U.S. believed that Mexico's advances were due to the brilliant leadership of Díaz and Limantour. What these foreigners saw in Mexico meant nothing to the vast majority of Mexicans. The image of Mexico as a prosperous and growing nation was false, and soon its falseness would become dramatically clear. The carefully constructed dictatorial political system of Porfirio Díaz and the Científicos would come crashing down. Mexico was on the verge of a fiery holocaust that would sweep the nation for thirty years.

As Díaz had gone about the business of fixing elections, installing crooked state governors, selling Mexico's wealth to foreigners and seeing to it that the Indians were reduced to slavery, he was also creating many enemies. At the beginning of the 20th century voices of protest and complaint against Díaz grew louder. To his enemies Díaz had become "Don Perpetuo." He was in his late seventies and still gave no indication that he would ever step down or even allow a fair and open election to take place.

Mexican intellectuals began to criticize Díaz more openly than before. Wistano Luis Orozco, a noted judge, criticized the Díaz policy of allowing large parcels of land to fall into the hands of a wealthy few. Camilo Arriaga openly objected to the preferential treatment given to the Catholic Church. The Church had been permitted to own large areas of land without paying tax on them. In return, the churchmen preached obedience to the Díaz regime. Arriaga thought that the Church openly directed the peones not to protest the seizure of their lands by the haciendas. Arriaga called for a National Liberal Convention in 1901 to discuss solutions to Mexico's social problems.

By far the most vocal and aggressive attackers of Díaz were the Flores-Magón brothers: Jesus, Ricardo and Enrique. Together they published and wrote articles in a Mexico City weekly newspaper entitled *Regeneración*. Criticizing Díaz, they also called for a liberal movement to select new leaders for Mexico. For their efforts the brothers were jailed by Díaz. Soon Arriaga was also in jail for speaking out against Díaz. Twice more the Flores-Magón brothers printed attacks against Díaz and twice they were jailed again. Finally, they decided to escape to the U.S. where they could freely write against Díaz. In 1904 they settled in San Antonio, Texas and began printing *Regeneración* and smuggling thousands of copies into Mexico. One of their main financial supporters was the son of a wealthy Coahuila hacendado. His name was Francisco I. Madero.

2. Madero

Francisco Madero certainly did not look the part of a national hero. He was a short, thin, meek-looking man whom many dismissed as a dreamer or even a mystic. Educated in Europe and the U.S., Madero had amazed his wealthy family by seeing to it that the peones who worked on his family's hacienda were well fed and had proper medical attention. He is said to have fed 50 children of Indian families in his own home. Few would have guessed in 1904 that this unassuming country gentleman would be the one to bring the "Porfiriato" to an end.

From Texas, the Flores-Magón brothers, with Madero's encouragement, kept up the pressure on Díaz. A 1904 issue of *Regeneración* read in part: "Forever — for as long as Mexico can remember — today's slavery will be identified with the name of the devil that made it all possible. His name is Porfirio Díaz, and his bestiality is being carried out in Mexico ... The jefes politicos do not send thieves and other criminals to jail, rather they sell them as slaves. You may say that Díaz does not benefit directly from this human commerce ... But what about the governors of Vera Cruz, Oaxaca, Hidalgo, and other states and their cronies who do benefit? Who appointed these governors? Porfirio Díaz. But the day of liberation *is* coming. Prepare yourselves, my fellow Mexicans."

The brothers Flores-Magón may have been wrong about the day of liberation soon to come but they were right about the approaching end of Porfirio Díaz.

After Díaz had sent an assassin to San Antonio to be rid of the Flores-

Francisco Madero was the most prominent of the opponents of Porfirio Díaz. Educated in Paris, France and at the University of California at Berkeley, Madero believed passionately that Mexico's problems could be solved with honest democracy and no re-elections of presidents. After Díaz's fraudulent re-election in 1910, Madero organized a mass uprising which would eventually topple Díaz from power. But as president, Madero proved to be tragically indecisive and failed to unite with his natural allies such as Villa and, especially, Zapata. The assassination of Madero in 1913 plunged the country into its bloody civil war.

Magón brothers, they moved their paper to St. Louis, Missouri. In 1906 they published the "Liberal Plan." This was a list of demands for improvements that should be put into effect immediately. They called for freedom of speech and of the press; less power for the jefes politicos and state governors; no more church schools; public ownership of church properties; better schools for the poor; no more tiendas de raya; cash for the peones' labor; a redistribution of rural lands; and a return of the Indian ejido lands. Thousands of copies of this issue of *Regeneración* found their way into Mexico. Soon the beginnings of active dissent occurred.

In the state of Sonora, near Nogales and the American border, there is a town called Cananea. Colonel William Greene (an American) owned the Cananea Consolidated Copper Co. By the early 1900s this was one of the largest copper mines in the world and Greene was typical of the foreign businessmen who owned rich properties in Mexico. In 1906 the Mexican workers in Greene's mines went on strike. They complained that U.S. workers were paid more money for doing the same job Mexicans did. They also said that the best jobs always went to the Americans. The strike became violent and soon the Rurales arrived. The Rurales asked to speak to the leaders of the strike. When the leaders stepped forward they were seized and hung on the spot by the Rurales.

Other strikes followed. Vera Cruz, Puebla, Orizaba and Tlaxcala saw similar labor unrest. In each case, Díaz Federales or Rurales were called in to put down the uprising by force. In 1907 at a textile plant in Río Blanco workers went on strike. They were protesting horrible working conditions that included long hours, low pay and child labor. Federales were called in once again, this time firing directly into the strikers, killing and injuring even women and children. A climax was approaching.

In 1908 Madero published a book called *La Sucesión Presidencial en 1910* (The Presidential Succession in 1910). In the book Madero called for a more honest election than in the past. He also called for an opposition political party to be formed. He came out against the re-election of Díaz, but said that if Díaz were to continue as president, at least the people should freely elect a vice-president. Here we see an example of what would prove to be Madero's fatal weakness. Madero believed that Díaz's dictatorship and the lack of effective democracy were Mexico's worst problems. Once the people could use their voting powers fairly, with no re-elections, the other problems of the country would then be solved. In other words, Madero was more concerned with a political revolution than a social one. Indeed, when Madero began to tour Mexico, speaking out against Díaz, he was asked why he did not give the lands of his family's haciendas back to the poor. His answer: "The Mexican people do not want land, they want liberty." Unfortunately, events would prove Madero wrong and he would pay with his life for this mistake.

Nevertheless, in 1909 Madero toured Mexico making speeches against

Díaz. He created an anti-re-election political party and offered himself as a candidate for president. He was soon officially nominated for president by the Anti-Re-election Party. At this time, however, Díaz announced that he would indeed seek re-election in 1910 and that his vice-president would be Ramón Corral. Liberal and anti-Díaz elements were angered by this because Corral had been the state governor of Sonora who personally sold the Yaquis into slavery.

The dream of Madero for a fair election was shattered when he was suddenly arrested by Díaz. Election day, June 21, 1910, saw Madero securely locked up in the San Luis Potosí jail. Throughout Mexico anti-re-election leaders had also been jailed. When the election results were announced, Díaz and Corral had been re-elected, winning several million votes to a few hundred for Madero. Few believe today that the results were fair or accurate.

In September 1910, President Díaz organized a fantastic birthday celebration, known as the "Centenario," for Mexico. The nation was one hundred years old, and the old dictator would soon turn eighty. A gala celebration was held in Mexico City. Foreign leaders from all over the world were invited to see the new Mexico, an advanced and modern nation that owed everything to the leadership of Díaz. As foreign dignitaries and the wealthy Científicos and hacendados sipped French champagne, the streets of the capital were cleared of Indians and the other poor people. Díaz did not want any of his guests to think that Mexico had problems. For that one fiesta, Díaz spent over 20,000,000 pesos, more than double the government's yearly budget for education. The lavish ceremony of that night, however, was the last gasp of a dying regime, for within a month the armed rebellion that would topple Díaz was to explode.

3. Revolts in the North

In October 1910, Madero published his *Plan de San Luis Potosí*. In it he called for armed revolt against Díaz and declared himself the provisional (temporary) president of Mexico until real elections could be held. He further set the date of November 20, 1910, as the day the rebellion was to begin. Madero escaped from the jail in San Luis Potosí and went to the United States. On November 20th he slipped across the border into Mexico but failed to meet with his supporters. He returned, discouraged, to Texas. But the next day proved more successful and soon Madero began to hear of successful uprisings throughout Mexico.

The most important of the early battles were in the state of Chihuahua. Under the leadership of Pascual Orozco, the rebels began fighting the Federales and capturing several important small towns. Soon all segments of Mexican society were joining up with the rebels. All who joined had their own personal reasons for

Pancho Villa is one of Mexico's mythic figures of the Mexican Revolution. Shown here with his famous *Dorados* (the Golden Cavalry) in action, Villa operated mostly in the north, in states such as Chihuahua and Durango, where he was born. A brilliant military leader, there are endless corridos (ballads) which sing the praises of the colorful exploits of Villa and his forces.

Soldadera

Soldadera

The Mexican Revolution of 1910

Known as soldaderas, women played a crucial role in the Mexican Revolution. Many women accompanied their husbands into battle, often joining in the fighting when necessary. Indeed, as in all guerrilla style wars, women often played a key role in the unexpected attacks against which the regular armies often were unprepared to defend themselves. This was especially true with Villa's forces in the north, and with Zapata's followers in Morelos. It was common to see women take up arms alongside the men.

fighting, but in those early days of 1910 they were united against Díaz and the hated Federales and Rurales. Poorly armed and equipped, with no uniforms, bands of guerrilleros sprang up everywhere. These groups would make surprise hit-and-run attacks against the government forces. One of the top assistants to Orozco in Chihuahua was a young man named Doroteo Arango. Formerly a peon, he had escaped from an hacienda in Durango and became a bandido. He was soon a famous cattle rustler who would boldly steal thousands of cattle from the wealthy Terrazas family. He became a hero to the peones of Chihuahua because he was never caught by the Terrazas. In 1910 this young rebel joined forces with Orozco. Today he is known as one of the legendary fighters of the revolution. He went by his nickname — Pancho Villa.

Along with the forces of Orozco and Villa in Chihuahua, rebel bands began to win victory after victory against the forces of Díaz. In Sonora, Coahuila, Sinaloa, Vera Cruz, Zacatecas, Puebla, Guerrero and Morelos, the rebellion spread. Rebel guerrilla units lived off the land and struck where least expected. In this way they kept the government forces continually off balance. Crucial to the success of these guerrilla bands was the support of the common people, the peones who fed, hid and protected the rebels.

On May 10, 1911, under the leadership of Pascual Orozco, the rebel troops managed to capture the important border town of Ciudad Juárez. Villa also played a role in this battle. It was a major defeat for Díaz and a great victory for Madero. Soon, other important towns fell throughout Mexico. On the 12th of May the town of Cuautla, in the state of Morelos, fell to the rebel forces under Emiliano Zapata.

Many of the federal generals were in their sixties and they did not provide aggressive or intelligent leadership in the final days of the Díaz regime. Other important towns soon fell to the rebels, among them Durango, Hermosillo and Cananea. In the chaos of revolution business activity began to decline. The press began to openly attack Díaz and federal troops began to desert.

On the 25th of May, 1911, Díaz met with Madero in Ciudad Juárez and formally resigned; so did Limantour. Francisco de la Barra, Díaz's secretary of foreign relations, became interim president. Díaz was put on a ship headed for France. All assumed that soon Madero would be president. Joy spread throughout Mexico. The worst was over, people thought. Now the business of creating a Mexico for the Mexicans would begin and conditions would improve. Madero went by train to Mexico City and was accorded a hero's welcome.

But the optimism of those days was to prove premature. At the time, few realized that Mexico was about to enter the bloodiest decade in her history.

4. The Madero Presidency

Before elections could be held the interim presidency of de la Barra gave a preview of the problems to come. De la Barra had kept all of the old Díaz governors and government officials. Soon it became clear that little real change was going to happen immediately. But giving the new government the benefit of the doubt, the guerrilla chiefs (Orozco, Villa and Zapata) waited to see what would happen.

Emiliano Zapata, in Morelos, was especially suspicious of de la Barra and Madero. Zapata and his guerrilla army had battled the sugar plantation owners of Morelos and had succeeded in regaining lost ejido lands. Zapata had even begun redistributing the land to the peasants. He met with Madero and explained that the redistribution had to proceed immediately if the revolution against Díaz was to have true meaning. Madero hesitated and explained that things must be done carefully, legally and officially, especially when it came to land. Madero further demanded that Zapata disarm his men to show good faith in the new Madero government. Zapata returned to Morelos and began, reluctantly, to disarm his men.

De la Barra, however, was not satisfied with Zapata's actions. He claimed that Zapata was not laying down his arms fast enough. De la Barra sent federal troops into Morelos under the command of General Victoriano Huerta. Fighting soon broke out and the uneasy peace was ruined. Huerta became more aggressive, Zapata responded, and soon Morelos was on fire again. Zapata then declared himself to be in revolt against Madero. For nine years this was to be Zapata's pattern. He cared not who happened to be the president of Mexico. What he wanted was land for his people. When he did not get it, he fought. We will be looking more closely at Emiliano Zapata later. But at this point remember that from 1910 until 1919 Zapata continued to fight against every president of Mexico.

On November 6, 1911, Madero and his vice-president, José María Pino Suarez, took office, after easily winning the election. Now Madero would have the opportunity to see if democracy would truly solve Mexico's problems. His main goals were to reduce foreign privilege and to create democracy. But he was soon to find that the revolution meant different things to different people. He was quickly bombarded by demands coming at him from all sides.

The common people of Mexico, represented by Zapata and Villa, wanted to be rid of the domination of those whom they saw as the descendants of the Spanish conquistadores. Further, the average Mexicans wanted the foreigners, the "gringos," out of Mexico. They saw them as the newest conquistadores. Madero seemed never to understand the depth of these feelings. While the masses were pleading for the lands to be restored, Madero moved slowly, too slowly. Madero may have been blinded by his own roots. As a member of Mexico's wealthy upper class, he could see the wrongs of the Díaz regime, but he could not act against the interests of his own wealthy Mexican hacendado class.

His government proposed to buy back only a few haciendas and distribute the ejido lands back to the people. But the prices asked for the haciendas were outrageous. Proof of legal ownership of the land fell to the Indian pueblos who ran into legal difficulties with the lawyers of the hacendados. The Madero administration actually restored few lands to the people. Similarly there was no real labor reform. As troops were sent by Madero to put down strikes, more strikes broke out which hurt the economy. There were few of the promised reforms in education. Madero's government did not really increase the amount of money spent on schools.

However, Madero did begin social programs, enough programs to worry the rich hacendados. But he did not do enough to satisfy men like Zapata. As a result, Madero was caught in the middle with revolts breaking out against him from all sides. The armed revolt began, as we have seen, with Zapata in Morelos. It spread to Guerrero, Tlaxcala, Puebla and the state of Mexico. Conservative critics of Madero began to complain that he was becoming like Díaz and was appointing his friends and relatives to important governmental positions.

Soon a series of important generals began to declare themselves in open revolt against Madero. Even Pascual Orozco, the hero of Ciudad Juárez, came out against Madero. To silence Orozco, Madero was forced to turn to Victoriano Huerta. Huerta was successful in defeating Orozco and returned to Mexico City. But soon Huerta began to plot with Félix Díaz (Porfirio's nephew) and Bernardo Reyes for the downfall of Madero.

Huerta had been an important general under Díaz and today appears in Mexican history as a man famous for betrayal and treachery. And betray Madero he did. Soon the forces of Huerta and Félix Díaz staged a phony artillery battle in Mexico City. The violent shelling lasted for ten days and resulted in horrible civilian injuries and deaths. These ten days of fighting, known as the *Decena Trágica,* were meant to demonstrate to the people of Mexico City that Madero's government could not keep order. Madero and Pino Suarez were forced to resign. Huerta soon betrayed Félix Díaz as well when he had himself named president of Mexico. On February 22, 1913, Madero and Pino Suarez were shot and killed. Most historians assume that Huerta was responsible.

5. The Huerta Dictatorship

Madero's presidency and the high hopes he raised were thus destroyed. With another military dictator in the president's chair, Mexico's pressing social

General Victoriano Huerta is, along with Porfirio Díaz, one of the real villains of the Mexican Revolution. Huerta took advantage of the situation, while Madero was president, and plotted the downfall of Madero. He purposely caused chaos in Mexico City (known as the "Decena Trágica") in order to discredit Madero. Then he had Madero shot in order to assume the presidency for himself. Huerta was also reputedly an alcoholic and a heroin addict. In modern terms, "he was an easy guy to hate."

General Alvaro Obregón had a long and influential career before, during and after Mexico's revolution. He was governor of Sonora under Madero; he fought against Huerta after Madero's death and he joined with the Zapatistas to overthrow Carranza. As president he began the land re-distribution program under the National Agrarian Commission which finally led to an end of the fighting in 1920.

problems did not seem likely to be solved. Indeed, the presidency of Huerta was to be characterized by military maneuvers rather than by social programs.

As soon as word spread that Huerta had overthrown Madero, rebellions broke out once again all across Mexico. In Coahuila, Chihuahua and Sonora the revolutionary fires spread. This time, however, the warfare took the form of a civil war as so often happens following revolutions. The bloodshed from this civil war was to go on for another seven years.

In Mexico's northeast, in the state of Coahuila, the governor was a man named Venustiano Carranza. Carranza had been a firm supporter of Madero. Carranza immediately announced that he would not support Huerta. Carranza formed a Constitutionalist Party to defend the Mexican Constitution of 1857. Villa, in control of Chihuahua, and Alvaro Obregón in Sonora, soon joined with Carranza. Carranza declared their forces to be a Constitutionalist Army, with himself as the "First Chief" of this army. He stated that he would become the interim president of Mexico when Huerta was defeated.

In Morelos, Zapata opposed Huerta when it became clear that Huerta would do nothing to settle the land question. But Zapata would not join forces with Carranza either, for he distrusted Carranza's background as an hacendado. Zapata's continued warfare against Huerta in Morelos, however, prevented Huerta from concentrating on Villa and Obregón in the north. As a result, the Constitutionalist forces began winning victories against the Federales in Sonora and Chihuahua. Huerta decided to fully arm Mexico, raising the size of the army to 250,000 men through a forced draft, beginning the bloody civil war of 1913-1914.

In Chihuahua, Villa now ruled supreme and began a progressive reform of the state. He distributed land to the peasants, cleaned the streets, built schools, set up health clinics and even printed his own money. Zapata was engaged in similar activities in Morelos.

Overall, the Mexican Revolution took a horrible toll on the common people of Mexico. The various armies had to live off the land, finding food wherever they could. Cattle rustling and looting became common. Although the forces of Carranza, Villa and Obregón may have spoken of their desire to free the people, they burned, looted and ravaged just as horribly as did the forces of Huerta. Obregón was perhaps the most civilized of the three. Zapata, if violent, always had the aim of returning land to the peasants. But nonetheless, Mexico suffered as she had never suffered before. It has been estimated that over 1,000,000 Mexicans lost their lives in the Mexican Revolution. A sizable portion of the dead were innocent civilians. Approximately 10% of the Mexican population came to the U.S. to escape the bloodshed.

As the fighting continued the United States became directly involved. Woodrow Wilson, the president of the United States, had been closely following the progress of the fighting. He was also influenced by events overseas as Germany seemed to be sympathetic to Huerta. Later, in 1917, Germany would actually try to get Mexico to enter World War I by promising Mexico her lost northwestern territories from the United States in return for a Mexican attack on the U.S. from the south!

In 1914, however, attention focused on a German ship heading toward the important harbor of Vera Cruz. This ship was said to be carrying heavy ammunition and weapons for Huerta. Wilson decided to send the U.S. Marines into Vera Cruz harbor to block the arrival of the German ship. But soon a dispute broke out between the Mexican officials and the American forces. The Marines eventually took control of the port but not without some bloody fighting and the loss of many innocent lives. This U.S. occupation of Vera Cruz did indeed hurt Huerta as munitions and other supplies, which would have arrived, were blocked by the Americans.

Anti-U.S. sentiment in Mexico City now became very strong. To many Mexicans it appeared that the U.S. was trying to control the course of the revolution for its own benefit. Indeed, when Madero had appeared to threaten U.S. business interests, Huerta had been encouraged by the U.S. Ambassador to Mexico, Henry Lane Wilson, to overthrow Madero. When Huerta became too dictatorial for U.S. tastes, support was shifted to other contenders such as Villa. Some observers of U.S. policy viewed American actions at this time as the continuation of a pattern that characterizes U.S. policy in Latin America. The U.S. seemed consistently to demonstrate a desire to manipulate and control events in Latin America for the benefit of the U.S. Meanwhile, Huerta put out a call to Carranza, Villa, Obregón and Zapata to join him in the fight against the U.S. troops. But these enemies of Huerta preferred to take advantage of the situation instead.

Villa now began his most successful operations of the war. With his famous "Dorados" (the "Golden Ones") as cavalry he took Torreón, Coahuila and then Zacatecas. Obregón defeated Huerta's troops in Sinaloa and Jalisco. Zapata was on the move in Morelos, as always. But the unity of the Constitutionalists did not hold as Villa and Carranza began arguing over the direction of the revolution. Soon Villa broke relations with Carranza and headed for Mexico City to occupy the capital. Huerta was surrounded and surrendered on July 8, 1914, blaming Wilson for his downfall.

On the 10th of August, the federal troops of Huerta surrendered their arms in Mexico City, thus creating a power vacuum (absence of power). On August 15 Obregón entered the capital in triumph for the Constitutionalist forces. Under the terms of the original agreement, Carranza was now supposedly Mexico's leader until an election could be held. Obregón continued to support Carranza, but Villa and Zapata did not.

Villa and his men marched to Mexico City. Carranza realized that it would be a mistake to make a stand against Villa in the capital. Carranza and Obregón therefore withdrew to Vera Cruz. American troops still in occupation of the city turned it over to Carranza and departed. At this point Mexico was without any real government or leadership. Chaos ruled and no one could be sure of what was in store for the future.

6. Villa and Zapata Meet

With Carranza in Vera Cruz, Zapata decided to take his men into Mexico City and press his demands for immediate and permanent land reform now that Huerta had been defeated. Arriving before Villa, the Zapatistas were orderly and polite, almost shy, as they moved about the capital. In comparison, the troops of Villa made a rowdy and raucous entry, taking over hotels and refusing to pay for meals in restaurants. The meeting of the two great guerrilla chieftains of the revolution took place in Xochimilco, on the outskirts of Mexico City. The American historian, Robert E. Quirk, has reconstructed the face-to-face meeting of Villa and Zapata and describes it as follows:

"Villa and Zapata were a study in contrasts. Villa was tall and robust, weighing at least 180 pounds, and with a florid complexion. He wore a tropical helmet after the English style. He was clad in a heavy, brown woolen sweater, which was loosely woven, with a large roll collar and buttons down the front, khaki military trousers, army leggings and heavy riding boots. Zapata in his physiognomy was much more the Indian of the two. His skin was very dark in comparison with Villa's; his face was thin with high cheek bones. He wore an immense sombrero, which at times hid his eyes. These were dark, penetrating, and enigmatic. He was much shorter than Villa and slighter. He weighed about 130 pounds. He wore a black coat, a large light blue silk neckerchief, a lavender shirt, and the tight charro trousers of the Mexican rural dandy, black with silver buttons down the outer seam of each pant leg. Villa pronounced his opinion of the middle class revolutionaries who followed Carranza: 'Those are men who have always slept on soft pillows. How could they ever be friends of the people who have spent their whole lives in nothing but suffering?' The reference to Carranza brought an outburst from Zapata: 'Those cabrones! As soon as they see a little chance, well, they want to take advantage of it and line their own pockets! Well to hell with them! I'd have broken all of those cabrones. They're all a bunch of bastards. I wish I could get my hands on them some other time!' Villa expressed to Zapata his pleasure in knowing the men of the South. 'Well hombre, I have finally met some fellows who

During a brief period in 1914, Mexico virtually had no national government. The dictator Victoriano Huerta had been overthrown and no one had yet assumed the presidency. It was at this time that **Pancho Villa** and **Emiliano Zapata** met in Mexico City and had this historic photograph taken in the presidential palace. Unfortunately, neither cared to assume the presidency. Villa returned to Chihuahua, Zapata to Morelos, and soon the fires of revolution burned again.

While Villa and Zapata occupied Mexico City in 1914, their troops roamed the nation's capital. Here, two of Zapata's well-armed "guerrilleros" enjoy breakfast at Sanborn's, one of Mexico City's most exclusive restaurants for the wealthy. Do you think that the waiter demanded immediate and full cash payment of the check?

are really men of the people.' Zapata returned the compliment: 'And I give thanks that I have at last met a man who really knows how to fight.' They continued to chat, their conversation leaping from hats to the Científicos while outside a military band struck up a tune and finding further conversation impracticable, Zapata and Villa left arm in arm."

Unfortunately, an alliance between these two leaders never came about. Zapata soon withdrew to Morelos and Villa to the north once again.

7. Carranza vs. Villa

More terrible fighting was soon to come. With Villa and Zapata now gone, Obregón entered and occupied Mexico City without a fight. Carranza soon arrived and, with Obregón, began to plot the defeat of Villa.

What followed was perhaps the single bloodiest battle of the revolution. In April of 1915, Obregón waited for the Villistas in the town of Celaya. Villa had, by this time, raised an army of 25,000 men. His famous cavalry seemed unstoppable. For two successive days Villa threw his forces at Obregón with astonishing fury. Obregón, however, used advanced European tactics which included barbed wire, trenches and machine guns. Villa's losses ran as high as 4,000 dead. Obregón had lost little more than 150.

Although Villa did not surrender, he would never again be the dominant force he once was. Obregón chased Villa all the way to Chihuahua, losing an arm in the process. The final stroke, from Villa's point of view, was the U.S. recognition of Carranza as Mexico's president. Villa was greatly angered and he went on a rampage. He stopped a train that had entered Mexico from the U.S. and killed 16 U.S. engineers. Later, in January 1916, Villa invaded the U.S., attacking the town of Columbus, New Mexico. Many Americans were killed or wounded as Villa attempted a bank robbery. Outraged, President Wilson ordered General John J. Pershing into Mexico with 6,000 troops to find and kill Villa. Although he was never found, Villa's career as a national leader was over.

8. The Mexican Constitution of 1917

In November of 1916, Carranza, still acting as first chief, called a constitutional convention to meet in Querétaro. The Villistas and Zapatistas were excluded from the convention. Most expected that Carranza's recommendations for more executive power and few social reforms would be merely rubber-stamped. They were not. In fact, many of the ideas of the Flores-Magón brothers' "Liberal Plan," published in *Regeneración,* were included. The result was the most enlightened and progressive constitution in Latin America to that time. Here are some of the provisions:

In response to the years of Church wealth and privilege and the fact that high Church officials had cooperated with the Díaz dictatorship, Church power was severely cut. Priests would now be like ordinary citizens with no special privileges. They were even forbidden to wear their religious clothing outside of the Church buildings. There were to be no more Church schools and from now on the Church could not own land. Even the Church buildings were to become public property.

There were to be extensive labor reforms. The right of independent labor unions to organize workers and to freely engage in strikes would be protected. A minimum wage was set and child labor was forbidden.

After 34 years of Porfirio Díaz there would now be one six-year term for Mexican presidents. There would be no more re-elections for presidents.

In terms of land reform, the ejido lands of the Indians were to be returned. To facilitate this the Mexican government would be given the power to take lands and property away from individuals if it was "for the public good." Additionally, foreigners were now prohibited from owning land or property in Mexico. This was in response to the Díaz regime's sale of Mexico's best lands to foreigners.

And finally, in a key provision for Mexico's future, all "subsoil wealth" such as oil, natural gas and minerals would be the property of the Mexican nation.

Thus the writers of the constitution had drawn upon some of the great causes of the revolution itself. And they had been able to do so in the midst of the worst fighting! They had limited the president to one term seemingly in answer to the "no re-election" cry of Francisco Madero. They had moved to return the ejido lands of Mexico's indigenous people as if answering Zapata's call for "land and liberty." And they had seen to it that the legal structure would be in place for Mexico to protect itself against the kind of foreign economic domination that men like Hidalgo and Juárez had struggled against for years.

However, merely having the laws in writing is very different from realizing the actual benefits of their provisions. The fighting and bloodshed was still going on, and whether or not these ideas of the constitution would ever be implemented was anybody's guess.

9. The Carranza Presidency

On May 1, 1917, Carranza was elected president of Mexico. But the fighting was still not over. The country was still armed, the economy was still in chaos, transportation was ruined, phony money abounded and there was a shortage of food. Additionally, Carranza ignored the new constitution. He declared that it would be impossible to implement it immediately. Throughout his presidency he did not distribute lands and he used federal troops to put down strikes.

In the states, revolutionary leaders ruled as bandidos. The military under Carranza was undisciplined, engaging in looting and raping. There was no unity in the nation. Each province was ruled by the local chieftain. Carranza as president was unable to maintain order. Once the war with Villa had ended, and with Obregón in retirement, people of integrity and intelligence soon rejected Carranza. A new verb came to be used in Mexico: "carrancer," which meant "to steal." Indeed, while Carranza himself may not have profited from his presidency, those under him surely did.

Because Carranza moved too slowly, or not at all in terms of social reforms, the Zapatistas totally lost faith in him. They preferred to administer Morelos themselves. This, Carranza would not tolerate. He sent thousands of federal troops into Morelos to hunt down and kill Emiliano Zapata once and for all. But Zapata could never be found. Constantly the Zapatistas would embarrass the Carranza regime with victory after victory. The federal troops under General Pablo González burned towns and deported civilians in Morelos. But still the Zapatistas would not give up.

Finally, in 1919, Zapata was killed under Carranza's orders. The warfare in Morelos began to die down and soon an exhausted and disillusioned Mexico lay quiet for the first time in ten years.

For what had so much blood been shed? Why had so many died? Slowly, industry and business were revived but wages were even lower than during the time of Díaz. As we have seen, Carranza was not doing anything to put into practice the much needed economic reforms called for in the Constitution of 1917.

The next presidential election was scheduled to take place soon. At first Carranza did not want to step aside. His personal ambition was seemingly too great. Finally Carranza selected Ignacio Bonillas as his successor. Carranza hoped to use Bonillas as a puppet, run things from behind the scenes, and then return to the presidency six years later. When this became clear to everyone a revolt in Sonora began against Carranza, led by Adolfo de la Huerta. Soon Alvaro Obregón, by now the most respected man in Mexico, allied with de la Huerta. A new army of northerners was formed and began marching on Mexico City. Carranza escaped from the capital but was later shot. In November of 1920, Obregón was sworn in

Venustiano Carranza's career is a mixture of positive and negative events. Governor of Coahuila under Madero, Carranza organized a rebel army of men such as Pancho Villa and Álvaro Obregón to fight against the dictator, Huerta. But Zapata never trusted Carranza and refused to join. As president, Carranza organized the Constitutional Convention of 1917. At the convention, a marvelous document for Mexico was written. Then Carranza proceeded to ignore it until he was overthrown and ultimately shot as he attempted to flee the capital.

as president.

Mexico was finally over the worst of her bloody revolution. The 1920s would in general be calmer than the previous decade. Although it would be another twenty years before the ideas of the 1917 Constitution would be fully realized, at least Mexico could now rest and lick her wounds.

Many people, as they have studied the Mexican Revolution, have become confused with the rush of names, places, battles, killings, presidents and generals. In order that this does not happen in this discussion we are going to look at the events of 1910-1920 once again. But this time we are going to study them through the eyes of perhaps the greatest hero of the Mexican Revolution, the man many feel was the most courageous, idealistic and interesting of all the Mexican revolutionaries — Emiliano Zapata.

10. Emiliano Zapata: Case Study of a Legend

The Mexican state of Morelos lies just south of the Distrito Federal where Mexico City is located. Blessed with pleasant climate, rich lands and abundant vegetation, Morelos is a beautiful state. Its capital city of Cuernavaca is only about 60 miles from Mexico City. In the early 20th century Morelos was suffering from many of the same problems facing other areas of Mexico. Its ancient Indian pueblos and villages had been gradually losing their ejido lands to the wealthy hacendados. Many villages faced outright extinction as they were encircled by the huge sugar plantations. Under the Díaz dictatorship, the state governors had allowed the wealthy sugar barons to do pretty much as they pleased in acquiring peasant land. The experience of one small Morelos town in 1887 is a good example.

Tequesquitengo was a pueblo of several hundred rural Mexicanos. The citizens of the town had come into conflict with the large San José Vista Hermosa sugar plantation. The plantation was attempting to seize public ejido lands from the village. The villagers fought back and appealed to the state governor but they received no help. They appealed to the plantation but were ignored. One day, to punish the peasants for their continued complaints, the plantation owners opened up their irrigation canals, spilling millions of gallons of water into the valley where Tequesquitengo lay. The entire town was flooded. Only the church's tower was visible. The residents lost all their possessions.

Another small town in Morelos had a similar conflict with the sugar plantations. This town, called Anenecuilco, was where the Zapata clan had lived for generations. This family had originally been small land owners who farmed the rich earth of Morelos. But as their lands were gradually seized by the hacendados, the Zapatas had to turn to the raising of cattle and horses to survive. In the Zapata

At Chichen-Itza the Mayans built an observatory, which we see in the foreground. This structure was specifically designed for the study of astronomy, a field of study in which the Mayans were very advanced. From this observatory the Mayans made complex calculations which were used to chart the solar system and even predict eclipses years in advance.

PLATE **17**

At Chichen-Itza we see a Chac-Mool figure reclining in a curious posture. Scientists who study the Mayans are unsure as to this figure's role, but it is speculated that he might be some kind of intermediary or messenger between the gods and the Indians.

PLATE **18**

The Pyramid of the Sun at Teotihuacan; constructed during the Classic Era of Indian Mexico, this pyramid is at least 1200 years old. The size compares favorably to the Great Pyramid of ancient Egypt. The Teotihuacanos and other Indians painted and decorated their important structures in bright colors.

PLATE **19**

The temple of Quetzalcoatl, located at Teotihuacan, features rows of carved statues. The snake head with the feathers as a collar represents Quetzalcoatl. Next to the statues of Quetzalcoatl are representations of Tlaloc, the god of rain. One of the most important structures at Teotihuacan, Quetzalcoatl's temple honored the ruling god of these Mexican Indians.

PLATE 20

Close-up of Quetzalcoatl, the feathered serpent god of Teotihuacan, possibly the most important religious figure in all of Indian Mexico. Quetzalcoatl was the god of learning, fine arts and agriculture. A king of the later Toltecs took the name Quetzalcoatl for himself. Driven into exile, this light-skinned and bearded king predicted he would return to re-claim his throne. Five hundred years later, Hernan Cortés was mistaken for Quetzalcoatl by the Aztec emperor Moctezuma. This was the beginning of the end for the Aztecs and, indeed, for all of Indian Mexico.

PLATE **21**

Detail of a mural by the Mexican, Juan O'Gorman, entitled *La Dictadura* which depicts the cruelty of the hacienda system under Mexico's dictator Porfirio Díaz. Here, the evil mayordomo punishes the pleading peon as he is forced to sign a contract enslaving him to the hacienda under the system of debt-peonage. Note the Tienda de Raya in the background, the company store located on the haciendas, which would cheat the *peones* and keep them forever in debt.

PLATE **22**

Emiliano Zapata and his brother Eufemio are seen here with their wives in front of a hotel in Cuernavaca, Morelos. Eufemio fought bravely alongside Emiliano in the struggle to regain the stolen lands of Morelos's rural poor.

family there were two brothers, Eufemio and Emiliano. Familiar with horses all his life, Emiliano soon gained wide recognition as a rodeo rider. He soon had the reputation of being the finest horseman in the state of Morelos.

In 1909 Emiliano Zapata was elected president of the city's governing council. His common sense, determination and courage made him a natural leader even then. The town had just begun looking for a lawyer to represent them. They wanted to recover their ejido lands from the large Hospital hacienda that bordered their town. In February 1910, Emiliano was drafted into the military of Porfirio Díaz. Zapata clearly did not want to serve in the Díaz military, so he appealed to an acquaintance, Ignacio de la Torre. De la Torre got Zapata out of the service but, in return, Emiliano had to go to work as a groom in de la Torre's horse stables. Mexican folklore has it that it was while tending the de la Torre horses that Zapata came to a very important awareness. He began to see a similarity between the beasts of burden on the ranch and the poor people of his native state. Both, he thought, were forced to toil and labor until exhaustion for the wealthy landowners of Mexico. But in actuality, the horses and farm animals were treated better than the people. A horse was a costly investment and needed to be protected. Human life was cheap and there was no shortage of peones who needed work. This realization is said to have angered and incensed Zapata. He was rapidly moving towards actively opposing the continued enslavement of his people.

Meanwhile, the people of Anenecuilco were still trying to settle their land problem. They wrote letters to State Governor Escandón who was, unfortunately, a typically corrupt Díaz appointee. But the people were growing desperate. It was becoming impossible for them to survive and feed their families without their farming lands. They now faced the possibility of losing their land and going to work as peones for the sugar plantations. This would mean the destruction of a human community that had lived together for nearly seven centuries, since before the Spanish conquest! Their problem was like that of so many other small rural pueblos. Everyone knew the ejido lands were theirs, but they could not prove it by means of legal land titles or deeds. Governor Escandón sent the town's claims to the Hospital Plantation so the patrón there could make a response. His answer is typical of the hacendados' attitude toward the people. In part he wrote: "If that bunch from Anenecuilco wants to farm, let them farm in a flower pot, because they're not getting any land, not even up the side of the hills."

Adding insult to injury, the Hospital *dueño* (owner) then proceeded to lease the disputed lands to the villagers of a nearby town called Villa de Ayala. Soon the Villanos were plowing the lands, preparing to plant. This was too much to take. Something clearly had to be done. Zapata returned from the de la Torre hacienda, still bitter from his experiences there. He decided the time was right to take up arms and fight for his people's land. He gathered a force of about eighty men armed with rifles. They rode to the disputed area where the Villanos were at work. He told them they had no fight with them, but that this land was and always would be Anenecuilco's. If they didn't want any trouble they should leave. Needless to say, they left. News of this soon spread throughout Morelos and even across Mexico. Like the Yaquis of Sonora and a few other village people, Zapata had stood up to the hacendados. The personal reputation of Zapata grew as he began immediately to redistribute the lands to the people of his village.

This would be the pattern Zapata would follow for the next nine years. He fought against Díaz first, then Madero, Huerta, and finally Carranza. Zapata believed that he who worked the land should own it, pure and simple. He had no liking for politics and never sought the president's chair for himself. But off and on for the next nine years he was virtually the law for the state of Morelos. No one, president of Mexico or anyone else, could stop him from attempting to regain the lands he felt had been stolen from his people.

11. Zapata and Madero

When Zapata and his followers heard that Madero had escaped from the San Luis Potosí jail, they knew they were not alone. Later, when Madero issued his call for rebellion on November 20, 1910, Zapata quickly began organizing an effective band of guerrilleros. Other rural chieftains joined with him, most notably Genovevo de la O, a fierce looking *Indio Jefe* who had fought in Morelos and as far south as Guerrero and Oaxaca for as long and as bravely as had Zapata.

These rural *Indio guerrilleros* of the south did not look like other Mexican revolutionaries. Typically, they dressed in white cotton pants and shirts, with broad palm leaf sombreros. These Zapatistas were soon worshiped and protected by the country people and feared by the hacendados and army.

The Zapatistas were never an army in the same sense as the dreaded Villistas from the north. True, the Zapatistas could look fearful with their stern Indian expressions, dark eyes, and ammunition belts slung across their chests; but they were always too busy farming, plowing and planting to be a real army. When they won a town, they immediately began dividing up the land and soon they were at work, farming the land as their ancestors had done for centuries.

In the final days of the Díaz regime, Zapata amassed a strong rebel force of 400 men. On the 12th of May, 1911, only two days after Orozco and Villa's defeat of the Federales in Ciudad Juárez, the Zapatistas took the important Morelos town of Cuautla. Now Zapata was the clear source of order and authority throughout the state. When Díaz resigned a few days later, Zapata put out the word throughout the state that the seized ejido lands should be reclaimed by the pueblos.

Zapata hoped that now Madero, as president, would see to it that the rightful land claims of the people of Mexico would be legally respected. But instead of being supported, Zapata was betrayed.

On May 26, 1911, Madero announced that not all agrarian (land) aims of the revolution could be achieved immediately. It would take time to see to it that legal procedures were followed and that nothing outside of the law was done. Further, under the interim presidency of de la Barra, Zapata was asked to lay down his arms as a gesture of good will. Zapata could not see the logic in this. After all, his men had defeated the Federales. While these troops were to remain armed, he was being asked to lay down his weapons. He wondered what would happen to the lands already reclaimed. Worried and suspicious about Madero, Zapata traveled to Mexico City to meet with him. As John Womack says in his book, *Zapata and the Mexican Revolution,* the meeting between Zapata and Madero was remarkable. Zapata began by stating his overriding concern: "'What interests us,' he said, 'is that right away lands be returned to the pueblos and the promises which the revolution made be carried out.' Madero demurred; the land problem was a delicate and complicated issue, and proper procedures must be respected. What counted more was that Zapata disband his troops .... Zapata then stood up, and carrying his carbine walked over to where Madero sat. He pointed at the gold watch chain Madero sported on his vest ... 'Look, señor Madero, if I take advantage of the fact that I'm armed and take away your watch and keep it, and after a while we meet, both of us armed the same, would you have a right to demand that I give it back?' 'Certainly,' Madero told him. 'Well,' Zapata concluded, 'that's exactly what has happened to us in Morelos where a few planters have taken over by force the villagers' lands. My soldiers, the armed farmers and all the people in the villages, demand that I tell you, with full respect, that they want the redistribution of their lands to be got underway right now.'"

But as we have seen, the legal and official distribution of the lands did not "get underway right now." On the contrary, the planters began spreading wild rumors about the cruelty and savagery of the Zapatistas. Zapata was labeled the "Attila of the South" by his enemies. De la Barra betrayed Zapata by sending General Victoriano Huerta into Cuernavaca with over a thousand men. They were to see to it that the Zapatistas laid down their arms. That is why, on August 8, 1911, de la Barra ordered Huerta to "suffocate any uprising which might start from the opposition Zapata's men might show to their discharge," from Zapata's army. On his wedding day, Zapata learned of the Huerta invasion. Huerta's men began burning villages suspected of protecting Zapatistas. Zapata responded and soon the fires of revolution burned again in Morelos. Zapata declared: "I am resolved to struggle against everything and everybody. Madero has betrayed me ... nobody trusts him any longer." When asked by a reporter what he would like him to tell Madero,

THE MEXICAN REVOLUTION: PART II

Zapata responded: "Tell him this for me, to take off for Havana, or, if not, he can count the days as they go by and in a month I'll be in Mexico City with 20,000 men and have the pleasure of going up to Chapultepec Castle, and dragging him out of there and hanging him from one of the highest trees in the park."

Why then did Madero and Zapata fail to unite? Madero's fatal error was to believe that the revolution was basically a political one. Once liberty and democracy were achieved, Madero thought Mexico's problems could be solved legally and officially. But Zapata believed that there could be no liberty for the people of Morelos without their land also.

Zapata wanted an immediate and unconditional social revolution. He wanted the lands regained to be permanently restored to the people. Zapata was to wage war in Morelos for another eight years fighting for their lands. Madero was soon to lie dead, the victim of an assassin's bullet.

12. Zapata and Huerta

We have seen how the military general, Victoriano Huerta, betrayed Madero and had himself named president after the *Decena Trágica* and the death of Madero. Huerta had personal experience fighting the Zapatistas in Morelos. Now he wanted Zapata killed and Morelos brought into line immediately. Summoning General Juvencio Robles, Huerta ordered him into Morelos. Huerta now told Robles to use "extreme measures, for the government is going to depopulate the state and send the planters new workers." Robles was also ordered to deal with Zapata "... with an iron hand. The best way to handle the rebel chiefs is an eighteen cent rope from which to hang them."

The forces of Robles used every imaginable tactic to capture Zapata and terrorize his supporters in the countryside. But Zapata enjoyed victory after victory, even capturing an entire federal army of 500 men, 330 rifles and 310 horses. The towns of Cuautla (again) and Jonacatepec fell to the Zapatistas and they even blew up a military train on the Mexico/Morelos border, killing over 100 federal soldiers. Robles responded with a furious "burnt earth" policy, attempting to scatter and terrorize the civilian population. From Womack we learn that: "Everywhere in Morelos communities disintegrated. Desolating village after village, federal commanders drove people out of their homes." Throughout Mexico this occurred during the bloody Civil War against Huerta.

Zapata published his famous *"Plan de Ayala"* in which he outlined his revolutionary positions. In part he stated: *"The lands, woods, and water usurped by the hacendados, Científicos, or caciques ... henceforth belong to the towns or citizens in possession of the deeds concerning these properties ... The possession of such properties shall be kept at all costs, arms in hand."*

Zapata's fame grew as did the horror of the bloodshed. Robles continued his devastation of Morelos, but Huerta was fighting a losing battle. Fighting the Zapatistas in the south, Villa and Obregón in the north, and now the U.S. Marines in Vera Cruz, Huerta soon resigned and departed. An exhausted and war-torn Morelos lay quiet for the first time in years. Its lands were burned, few crops grew, towns had been destroyed and over one fifth of the state's population had been killed.

13.   Zapata and Carranza

The national conflict in Mexico now resolved itself into an epic struggle between Carranza and Villa. But Zapata was suspicious. Mistrusting him, as he had Madero, Zapata wrote of Carranza: "I will tell you in all frankness that this Carranza does not inspire much confidence in me. I see in him much ambition and a disposition to fool the people."

As we have seen, it was at this time that Villa and Zapata had their intriguing meeting at Xochimilco. But unfortunately, the two were never able to come together and form an alliance. Zapata, however, appeared to like Villa and approved of his social programs in Chihuahua. But Zapata would not change his mind regarding Carranza. He refused to join forces with Carranza's Constitutionalist Army, stating: "Revolutions will come and revolutions will go, but I will continue with mine."

He personally saw to it that the *Plan de Ayala* was put into practice in Morelos. Villagers reoccupied the ejido lands once again and the Zapatistas tried to breathe new life into the pueblos. Zapata set up rural commissions in the important towns to study the boundaries of the disputed lands. Rulings were made and reinforced with arms if necessary. With peace in Morelos for the first time in four years, the villagers slowly returned. Under the direction of Manuel Palafox, Zapata's administrator, land claims and titles were ironed out. Lands were redistributed, respecting local customs and traditional village land ownership. A social revolution was taking place in Morelos. Apparently, a new age had dawned and the people would be able to work their fields, raise their crops and feed their families as they had always wanted to do.

But storm clouds appeared on the horizon. The social miracle that was occurring in Morelos was not to last for long. In Mexico City, Carranza declared: "This business of dividing up the land is ridiculous." He felt such actions had to be done officially, legally, and from a metropolitan office in Mexico City. He warned Zapata that unless he laid down his arms, he and his men would be shot as bandits.

When Villa was finally defeated by Obregón, Carranza could now turn his full attention to bringing these rebellious Zapatistas under his control.

In the autumn of 1915, Carranza sent Federales into Morelos. As Villa's army of the north collapsed, Carranza called for a total war against Zapata, "a definitive campaign against the Zapatistas, right in their hideouts in Morelos." But Zapata and his chiefs were ready. He and other chieftains like de la O raised armies of two to three thousand men. De la O was active as far south as Guerrero, battling the Carrancistas.

But in Morelos the federal troops under Pablo González were beginning to overtake several important towns. With over 30,000 troops, González took Cuautla and then Cuernavaca. The bloodshed of war had now returned to the people of Morelos. This time it was to be even worse and more vicious than the previous attacks of Huerta or Robles. Ruling as a military dictator of the State of Morelos, González began a genocidal war, designed to exterminate or deport all Zapata followers. He cared not if entire towns were burned. Indeed, he had the towns' populations herded into concentration camps in the big cities so they could be more closely watched. The atrocities of González mounted. Timber was cut, cattle stolen, crops seized, towns burned to the ground, people deported. As one eyewitness wrote: "Robles was little in comparison. The Constitutionalists drove people like a herd of pigs to loading platforms and then shipped them in boxcars and cattle trucks to Mexico City. There they scattered them into the slums around the railroad yards, absolutely destitute."

Zapata decided to disband his regular army of over 20,000 men. He and his men became guerrilleros once again, making small hit-and-run attacks, raiding and ambushing the Carrancistas when they were least prepared. Into the autumn of 1916 there were perhaps 5,000 Zapatista guerrilleros active in Morelos. Zapata's raids grew bolder, even as the brutality of González increased. Zapata was now attempting to embarrass the Carranza government, making it appear that Carranza was unable to keep order. On November 17, 1916, Zapata and his men blew up a train near the Joco Station in the Distrito Federal. Over 400 soldiers and civilians died. González then issued a decree: "Anyone who directly or indirectly lends service to Zapatismo will be shot by a firing squad with no more requirements than identification." Zapata responded a few days later by blowing up another train.

By December of 1916, the Zapatistas had regained the upper hand. Zapata organized coordinated surprise attacks at Cuernavaca, Yautepec, Jojutla, Puebla, and in a dozen other towns. The Constitutionalist forces were on the verge of collapse and began withdrawing to Mexico City.

A short interval of peace settled over Morelos. On the 11th of March, 1917, national presidential elections were held in all states of Mexico except Morelos. Again, the Constitutionalist Army began moving into Morelos. Warfare began in the state for yet another time.

In August of 1918, Zapata sent a letter to Obregón, pleading with him to lead a revolt against Carranza. Obregón refused, although the presidency of Carranza was proving to be corrupt, dictatorial and ineffective in achieving the goals of the new constitution. Now it was only Zapata who continued to fight against Carranza. In March of 1919, Zapata sent an open letter to Carranza. In part it reads:

"From the moment that the idea of making revolution first against Madero and then against Huerta germinated in your brain, the first thing you thought of was to further yourself. And for that purpose you set yourself to use the revolution ... In agrarian matters, the haciendas have been given or rented to favorite generals ... neither have the ejidos been returned to the people ... Do free elections take place? What a lie! ... Nobody believes in you or your ability to pacify any more, nor in your greatness as a politician or governor. It is time for you to retire, it is time to leave your post to more honorable and honest men. It would be a crime to prolong the situation of undeniable moral, economic, and political bankruptcy. Your remaining in power is an obstacle to union and reconstruction."

Zapata was the only revolutionary leader to stand against Carranza after the defeat of Villa. As we have seen, Carranza would never voluntarily step down. Indeed, deeply embarrassed by Zapata's continued warfare, Carranza began plotting a trick that would lead to Zapata's death.

Zapata was led to believe that a leading colonel of Carranza's army wanted to join the Zapatistas. To prove it, this colonel, named Jesús Guajardo, led a revolt and killed many troops loyal to Carranza. Convinced now that Guajardo was sincere, Zapata rode to meet him. But it was a trap. Zapata rode straight into an ambush and, as the corridos say, he "fell, never to rise again."

14. Zapatismo Lives On

To the dismay of González and Carranza, the Zapatistas did not lay down their arms after the murder of their chief. De la O, especially, kept the pressure on the Federales in Morelos. In the decisive days of the Obregón revolt against Carranza, de la O and the Zapatistas would fight with Obregón in defeating Carranza once and for all. De la O became the supreme Zapatista of the south, riding into Mexico City in triumph alongside Obregón. In the new Obregón cabinet many of the Zapatistas were prominent, with de la O becoming a general. It became clear that Obregón intended to at least begin the official redistribution of land as called for in the 1917 Constitution. Obregón established the National Agrarian Commission that was to see to it that all claims over stolen ejido lands would be settled promptly.

On the 26th of September, 1920, Anenecuilco became the first village to test the new land law and the new Agrarian Commission. The village of Zapata had been destroyed more than once during the bloody past decade. But the villagers had returned, determined not to let their town die. On September 28 they received official notification that their pueblo now held legal title to lands on the Hospital Plantation.

By 1927 Morelos had been transformed. Few haciendas now operated there and over 120 pueblos now farmed freely on their traditional ejido lands. Eighty percent of the state's farming families now had land of their own.

Thus Emiliano Zapata's stubborn fighting for nine years had not been in vain. His dream of a restored and prosperous Morelos had finally come true, although he never lived to see it. His call for "land and liberty" had finally been heeded. His desire that the native *Mexicanos,* the Indians and the rural pobres, be respected in their land holdings became a fact of Mexican life. He, more than any of the other revolutionary figures, represented the rights of the native Mexicans.

Mexico's government was now supposed to concentrate on these people. A new sense of pride in Mexico's Indian heritage and culture began to spread throughout the nation. The great mural painters, Orozco, Siqueiros and Diego Rivera, began to decorate public buildings with murals that depicted native Mexican scenes. The struggle and death of Zapata were thus not in vain. Today he is regarded by the Mexican nation as the heart and soul, the conscience, indeed the immortal spirit of the Mexican Revolution. In Morelos the corridos (Mexican songs which tell a story) say that he can still be seen racing through the countryside on his white horse, ready to help the people if they need him.

If the reforms and distribution of lands seemed to slow a bit under Obregón and his successor, Plutarco Calles, the presidency of Lázaro Cárdenas would see a sincere attempt to bring to life Zapata's dream. Let us now conclude our story of the Mexican Revolution with a brief look at Lázaro Cárdenas and find out why he has been called the greatest president of the Mexican Revolution.

15. Cárdenas

Mexican development now depended on the extent to which the Constitution of 1917 would be implemented (put into practice). We have seen that a crucial part of this new constitution dealt with land reform. The large haciendas were to be

Jovita Idar. Her father published *La Cronica*, a Laredo, Texas newspaper, which fought for the rights of Mexican Americans in the early 1900s.

She decided she could help more as a teacher. But Anglo Americans controlled the money and would not provide decent resources for Mexican American schools. She turned to writing for her father's newspaper, where she wrote about the struggle against tyranny and for a decent life.

Then a 14-year-old Mexican American boy was arrested for murder. But the boy did not have a trial. A mob of Anglo Americans kidnapped him from the police, beat him, tied his body to a buggy and dragged it through the streets of Laredo. The outrage drove Jovita to more action.

Jovita and her family, in 1911, decided to form *El Primer Congreso Mexicanista*, dedicated to fight for education, justice, and better labor conditions. Jovita called for women to join in these activities. They did. One month later the women organized *La Liga Femenil Mexicanista*. The Mexican Revolution neared Laredo and Jovita joined other women to become guerrilla nurses who served the revolutionary soldiers in Mexico. She returned to Laredo to continue her journalism fight for the rights of Mexican Americans. In one memorable event, Jovita, alone, faced down the Texas Rangers bent upon trampling upon her constitutional right of free speech. The Rangers backed off.

Jovita Idar
(1885-1946)

Ema Tenayuca

"La Pasionera"

Born in 1916, it has been said that her concern for the poor led her to a place as a pioneer in the women's movement. She lived in San Antonio, Texas. During her last year in high school, in 1934, she went to watch some strikers, most of them women, in their fight against Finck Cigar Company. She landed in jail, the first of many times. With a great sense of injustice, and the need to do something, between 1934 and 1948 she supported almost every strike in the city, and there were many. While still in her twenties, she was the undisputed leader of a labor movement that shook San Antonio. It was the first sign of political liberation of the Mexican American population from the big bosses who had controlled it for decades. Not only did she fight against the Finck Cigar Company; in 1938 she was the guiding inspiration in the pecan-shelling workers strike. Quoted in the San Antonio Light, "It was a horror," she said. "I don't think there was a time when people cried more, especially to see their children hungry."

After the strikes in 1948, no one would hire her, so she moved to California where she graduated magna cum laude from San Francisco State University.

Of her labor organizing experiences she has said, "I was arrested a number of times. I don't think that I felt exactly fearful. I never thought in terms of fear. I thought in terms of justice."

Many young boys fought in the Mexican Revolution as it was truly a widespread social uprising of the people as a whole. Here we see a fifteen-year-old *guerrillero* well-armed to fight with the forces of Pancho Villa. The surprise here is that the youth in this case is none other than the future president of Mexico, **Lázaro Cárdenas** himself!

President Lázaro Cárdenas was in office from 1934 until 1940. Under his administration he not only returned millions of acres of land to Mexico's rural poor, he also seized Mexico's rich oil lands from the United States and created the Mexican oil industry, PEMEX. But what Mexicans especially loved about Cárdenas was his willingness to listen to the concerns of Mexico's people in a non-condescending way. Here, President Cárdenas visits an Indian pueblo to personally hear about the needs and the complaints of the people. It is for this reason that Lázaro Cárdenas is fondly remembered as "Tata Cárdenas" by many Mexicans, even to this day.

broken up and redistributed to the rural peones. This was the revolutionary goal of Villa and Zapata. Another important section of the new constitution called for national ownership of all natural resources. The subsoil wealth — oil, natural gas and precious metals underground — wcrc to be the property of the Mexican nation. No foreigner was ever to be permitted to own land in Mexico. Leases could be worked out but Mexico was clearly reacting here to Díaz's practice of selling Mexico's richest lands to foreigners from the U.S. and Europe. How did the presidents of Mexico go about putting the ideas of this new constitution into practice?

We have seen that under the presidency of Alvaro Obregón (1920-1924) Zapata's state of Morelos began to change. Lands were redistributed to the villagers. But in general, Obregón was cautious and hesitant about land reform. He believed that to break up the large haciendas would ruin Mexico's agricultural production. Indeed, in his four-year term, Obregón distributed only slightly more than 4,000,000 acres of land to Mexico's rural population. This may sound like a large amount but it was quite a limited program in view of the total amount of acreage involved.

Obregón did not alter the subsoil situation greatly. The U.S. and England at this time held Mexico's rich oil fields. Clearly the U.S. was concerned over its oil property in Mexico. Would the Mexican government take the oil lands from the U.S.? Mexico's Constitution of 1917 clearly called for such action. How radical (ready to make big changes) would the Mexican government become? Many in the U.S. called the 1917 Mexican Constitution communistic.

Obregón's successor, Plutarco Calles, proved not to be a threat to U.S. holdings. The Americans and the British were allowed to continue to do business in Mexico. Calles did not go too far in land reform either. He redistributed nearly eight million acres of Mexico's land to the peasants, but although this was twice what Obregón had done, it did not solve the problem. It was not until Calles's successor, Lázaro Cárdenas, took office that the land and subsoil questions were really acted upon.

Lázaro Cárdenas was a Tarascan Indian from the Mexican state of Michoacan. He had been a revolutionary fighter as a boy and had risen to the rank of general. After his election in 1934, Mexico soon saw that Cárdenas would be unlike most Mexican presidents. Cárdenas traveled extensively throughout the nation. He visited the rural poor, listened to their problems, studied solutions, and most importantly, acted in aggressive ways to realize the dreams of the revolution.

He began to spend great sums of money on education for the poor. More and more rural schools were built. Cárdenas spent twice as much money on rural education as any other Mexican president and also acted decisively on land reform. By the end of his administration, almost 50,000,000 acres of Mexico's land had been redistributed. In his one term, he gave back more land than the six previous

Diego Rivera
1886-1957

Perhaps Mexico's greatest painter, Diego Rivera's accomplishments were monumental and his life-long reverence for the Mexican people, their history and their way of life, will always be remembered with special affection.

Born in Guanajuato, he said, "My oldest memory is of myself drawing." He loved to draw on walls, doors and furniture. His father, a chemist and journalist, set up his room with blackboards all around the walls. Diego loved to draw machinery, especially trains.

His family moved to Mexico City where he was enrolled in the prestigious Academy of San Carlos art school. There he was influenced by the great Mexican satirical artist, Guadalupe Posada, one of the leading artistic critics of the Porfirio Díaz dictatorship. Diego said, Posada "...taught me the connection between life and art."

With a scholarship to study in Europe, he spent most of his time in France, visiting Spain, Portugal, Belgium, England and Italy. By 1913 he was embracing the cubist style of modern art,

Continued on Next Page

Diego Rivera: Continued.

a revolutionary idea which questioned all of the existing art forms. But for Diego, "...all of this artistic innovation had little to do with real life."

Receiving news of the Mexican Revolution, Rivera determined that the emerging new society would offer great opportunities. Now he could make art important in peoples' lives. He would become a mural art painter, painting grand frescoes in the Italian style. He envisioned huge murals on the walls of schools, post offices, government and other public buildings.

In 1919, upon his return to Mexico, Rivera was overwhelmed when he saw the people, their festivals, the workers, the children and animals. All seemed so bright and alive! Soon Mexico's government would sponsor a public mural art program, and Rivera would participate along with other great painters such as José Clemente Orozco and David Siqueiros.

In 1923, at the Ministry of Education, blending the natural light with the architecture of the building, he embarked on an ambitious project of numerous murals. He spent four years on these paintings, refining his techniques. He included workers, factories, villages and peasant life. It was this subject matter, the Mexican people in their everyday life, that was so unique and revolutionary about his work.

He had joined Mexico's Communist Party, and he included in this mural series the "Capitalists Banquet" which parodied Henry Ford, J.P. Morgan and John David Rockefeller as they sit at the dinner table while reading the stock market's ticker tape.

His work now became more political, describing the workers' struggle of the Socialist movement. He met Frida Kahlo at the Ministry of Education and they would marry in 1929. She was 22, he was 43. Frida, of course, became a famous painter in her own right.

In 1928 he began a major project at the National Palace in Mexico City, the scene of many of his finest works. It was a massive work with hundreds of faces from Mexico's past and present. A few years later he painted a series of murals at the Palacio de Cortés in Cuernavaca depicting the conquest of Mexico by the Spanish and the resultant enslavement of the Indian people. (See Plates 6 and 7)

As the most famous artist in Mexico, he received a series of commissions in the United States. In San Francisco's Pacific Stock Exchange he painted a huge mural entitled, "Allegory of California," dramatizing the history, agriculture, the future of California and its diverse peoples. At the California School of Fine Art he painted a self-portrait of a mural artist at work.

Other works followed in the 1930s. One of the most outstanding was a monumental tribute to technology painted at the Detroit Institute of Art. After studying factories in Detroit, Rivera chose as his subject the Ford Assembly Plant which was, at that time, the largest in the world. Followed by controversy, some in Detroit demanded that the mural be whitewashed for not being "beautiful enough."

But the greatest controversy came in 1932. Hired by the John D. Rockefeller family to paint a huge mural at the entrance of the not yet completed Rockefeller Center in New York City, the controversy resulted when Rivera insisted on including a portrait of Nikolai Lenin, the architect of Russian Communism.   The mural was destroyed when Rivera refused to change it.

Back in Mexico, Diego Rivera began what many believe are his greatest masterpieces. Following extensive research on ancient Mexico, at the National Palace he painted a series of murals depicting Mexican life during the Aztec period. He showed the cultural and artistic advancements of Mexico's Indians. Rivera spent years on these projects. (See Plates 3, 4, and 5)

Though plagued by poor health, in the 1950s he supervised the construction of a museum which he called Anahuacali. It would house his collection of thousands of pieces of Mexican Indian art. But Frida and Diego were not destined to survive the 1950s. In 1954 she died. Her last painting was that of a bright red watermelon with the words, "Viva la Vida." Three years later, Diego was to die of heart failure. His last painting was also that of a watermelon!

As time passes, thousands of new viewers of Rivera's work are amazed at the sheer size, the complexity, and beauty of his great murals. It will never be forgotten that Diego Rivera chose to use his vast talents in tribute to the common Mexican people, their lives, their culture, their society, and to the greatness of Mexico from ancient times into its unique and challenging future.

presidents combined. Twenty years of promises finally had been kept. Cárdenas had clearly been influenced by Emiliano Zapata of Morelos.

Cárdenas was now ready to tackle the subsoil matter head-on, but to do so he would have to confront the United States. By this time, American oil men were labeling Cárdenas a communist. Who else but a communist would turn so much land over to the poor? Cárdenas himself preferred the label of socialist rather than communist; but clearly, many aspects of socialism or even communism were embodied in Zapata's *Plan de Ayala* and in the 1917 Constitution of Mexico. It was Cárdenas who, in 1938, really pushed Mexico's new revolutionary government to the left.

16. PEMEX

The confrontation between Cárdenas and the foreign oil companies began innocently enough. In 1936 Mexican oil workers went on strike. These Mexican workers raised some of the same complaints often heard during the Díaz years. Mexican oil workers were paid less than U.S. workers for doing the same job. Mexican workers were denied the opportunity to perform the higher paying technical duties. The foreign oil companies would not seriously negotiate with the Mexican labor leaders.

Mexico's oil production began to decline with her oil fields inactive. This began to hurt Mexico's economy. Cárdenas ordered that an Industrial Arbitration Board must listen to both sides and settle the dispute. The profits of the oil companies were examined. The living conditions of the workers were inspected. The Arbitration Board issued an order calling for pay increases of one-third and improved pensions for the Mexican oil workers. The foreign companies thought this was too much and appealed the decision to the Mexican Supreme Court. The court's decision upheld the order of the Arbitration Board. The foreign companies refused to obey the court's ruling. President Cárdenas then stepped in to settle the matter. He stated that the foreign oil companies had disregarded the sovereignty (independent power) of the Mexican nation. Under the subsoil articles of the 1917 Constitution, Cárdenas ordered the nationalization of the oil companies on the 18th of March, 1938. All of the foreign oil lands and equipment on them became the property of the Mexican nation. In this way, Cárdenas created Petroleos Mexicanos (PEMEX), the national oil industry of Mexico.

Needless to say, the U.S. and England's oil men were horrified. They labeled Cárdenas a communist and called the nationalization of the oil lands outright theft. Many conservatives in the U.S. began to call for a U.S. military invasion to recover what they called stolen U.S. property. But Franklin D. Roosevelt was now president of the United States. Roosevelt had already decided on a non-interference policy toward Latin America in general and he was an admirer of Cárdenas. This time there would be no landing of U.S. Marines at Vera Cruz. Celebrations broke out in Mexico as nationalist fever and pride swept the nation. Cárdenas received telegrams of support from other Latin American countries. Mexico had, for the first time in her history, confronted the United States and come out on top.

The early days of PEMEX were difficult ones. The lack of trained Mexican technicians meant reduced production. But slowly and painfully the Mexican oil company has matured. In the late 1970s and early 1980s Mexico made huge new oil discoveries. Mexico may prove to be the second or third largest oil producer in the world. Mexicans are now pleased with Cárdenas's historic seizure of the oil lands. Now Mexico can develop her rich natural resources herself. This was one of the great goals of the Mexican Revolution. Like the land reform successes of the 1930s, Mexico's oil independence shows that, at least in these cases, Mexico's revolutionary hopes have been fulfilled.

17. Mexico Today and Tomorrow

Cárdenas had provided the nation with a sound economic base through his nationalization of the oil lands. Next, he turned his attention to the political arena. Working within a structure begun by Plutarco Calles, Cárdenas continued the integration of important elements of Mexican society in order to ensure political stability for the future. Peasant and campesino organizations were formed. Labor unions were organized together into large labor associations. The military was advised that it, too, must now follow the civilian leadership of the government and not interfere as it had done for so long. Cárdenas brought all these essential elements of Mexican society together into one political party. What emerged was the embryo of the political structure, the Partido Revolucionario Institucional, or PRI, which controls Mexico to this day as it has for the last sixty years.

Enrique Krause, one of Mexico's most noted historians, once made the following comment when discussing the impact the Mexican Revolution has had on present day Mexico: "Francisco Madero initiated the revolution in an attempt to limit the power of President Díaz. Lázaro Cárdenas completed the cycle by enlarging the president's power to a degree that Porfirio Díaz never in his wildest dreams could have imagined. It may have had the advantage of offering the nation a measure of stability. But Cárdenas' actions sowed the seeds of some of the most serious problems Mexico would face in her future."

Let us examine just what señor Krause means and why these ideas are so important to an understanding of Mexico today.

First of all, Mexico's constitution clearly gives the president tremendous powers: the right to take lands and property away from individuals if "for the public good," and it put all of the country's subsoil wealth at the disposal of the president. Cárdenas not only used these powers in positive ways with his land reform program and his creation of PEMEX, he also established a "super" political party which was comprised of the most important elements of Mexican society. All these things made him far more powerful than even Díaz had been. Overall, it provided a much-needed break for Mexico from her long history of political upheaval, military uprisings and civil wars. So what does Krause mean when he says these developments created the conditions for serious future problems?

There is an old saying: "Power corrupts. Absolute power corrupts absolutely." In other words, people tend to enjoy power when they get it. The tendency, then, is to try to hold onto it and even expand it whenever possible. The Mexican Constitution of 1917 did not contain any effective methods for checking or balancing the powers of the president, and since Lázaro Cárdenas created an incredibly effective political system during his term in office, what we now see in Mexico are the unfortunate results of an abuse of governmental authority.

Because of its powerful and pervasive structure, the PRI has won every presidential election in Mexico since the time of Lázaro Cárdenas. The party also controls almost all local and state governments. Many Mexicans believe that the PRI has been so successful on election day because of their willingness to stuff the ballot box. There has also been documented evidence which alleges that government officials embezzle funds in order to enrich themselves.

Since the PRI has won every presidential election for the last sixty years, some call Mexico a one-party dictatorship. Others believe that "every six years they change the head but the body remains the same." Mexicans are often cynical about the honesty of their governmental leaders, and they are doubtful that the system can ever change for the better. Today, many feel that the recent economic problems in the country have been caused largely by governmental waste and theft.

Because of the tremendous power in the hands of the president and the government, events have occurred which have shocked the nation. Using his power to nationalize private property "for the good of the public," President José López-Portillo, in 1976, made all private banks and airlines in Mexico the property of the government. And since all subsoil wealth like oil is also government owned, Jorge Díaz Serrano, Director of PEMEX, was able to embezzle sixteen million dollars of oil profits for himself. Scandals and government actions such as these have shaken the Mexicans' remaining faith in their government. There has been too much power in the hands of the government and the PRI.

Actually, Mexico seems to have sufficient oil and other natural resources to provide her people with a much better life than they currently experience. But the nation is once again faced with a staggering list of problems. The value of the peso has dropped greatly in recent years. The country has managed to accumulate one of the largest foreign debts in the world, and it has taken drastic cutbacks in governmental services just to be able to pay the interest on the loans. In some parts of Mexico unemployment is over a staggering 50% and it seems that almost everyone with work has to hold down two jobs or sell small items in the streets just to make ends meet. Inflation has robbed millions of Mexicans of their savings as the prices of basic foodstuffs such as milk, meat and tortillas have continued to go up and up in the last ten years. In certain large metropolitan areas like Mexico City the pollution and environmental damage has led some to warn of an environmental catastrophe in the near future. Furthermore, a population explosion has continued, stretching available food and resources even thinner. These problems are the reasons why so many Mexicans are choosing to head north to the United States in search of a better life.

What will happen to Mexico in the future? At present it seems that no political party is able to effectively challenge the PRI. Since the party has controlled the government for so long, the line that separates the party and the government has been blurred. The government controls the major television network, "Televisa," and opposition political parties complain that PRI receives much more media coverage than the opposition. Opponents also claim that the PRI uses public tax money to finance the campaigns of its own candidates. There have even been allegations that journalists who seek to expose official corruption have been murdered or threatened.

One of the most interesting contenders for power is the son of Lázaro Cárdenas himself, Cuauhtemoc Cárdenas, who heads a party known as the Partido de la Revolución Democrática, or PRD. Today, many Mexicans feel that Cárdenas actually won the 1988 presidential election when he came in second to President Carlos Salinas de Gotari. Even if there was no vote fraud, Salinas's margin of victory was the smallest in recent history. Whatever the case may be, voter turnout has dropped dramatically in recent local and state elections.

Unfortunately, Enrique Krause appears to be right. Mexico's main problem is a national government and president that are just too strong. The only remedy is a "people power" movement which would demand free and open elections as well as direct accountability to the people on the part of elected leaders. In this sense, the future is up to the Mexicans of today. Regardless of what happens to Mexico in the years to come, the Mexican Revolution has clearly forged the Mexico we see today.

Chapter Five

THE MEXICAN REVOLUTION, PART II:

WRITING EXERCISES

On the following pages you will find the writing exercises for this chapter. For additional explanations, please see "To the Teacher" or "A Note to the Student" on **pages 21 and 26**. Teachers are urged to select the writing exercises most appropriate for their particular classes. Below are the writing exercises for Chapter Five:

1. Sentence or Fragment?

This exercise is designed to help students learn how to recognize incomplete sentences (fragments) and then rewrite them as complete sentences. The most important idea here is that a complete sentence makes sense when read alone. When rewriting the fragments, the students must make sure not to change history!

2. Short Answer Questions

Once a student knows what a sentence is (and is not!), he or she can answer brief questions with one or two sentence answers of their own. This list of questions also makes a good study or review sheet when preparing for a test.

3. Paragraph Questions

These questions require slightly longer answers which are to be written in paragraphs. A sample paragraph along with definitions of such terms as "topic sentence" is included in the writing exercises of **Chapter One**.

4. Clustering and Identification (ID) Items

ID Items refer to and identify important people, places and things. Clustering is a way of brainstorming ideas based on these ID Items. Once the cluster has been made, use it as a guide and write an ID Paragraph. A sample cluster and a sample ID Paragraph can be found in the writing exercises of **Chapter One**.

5. Essay Questions

Very broad or complicated questions require essays or compositions as answers. A sample essay and instructions on how to write essays, both as homework and during in-class essay exams, are provided in the writing exercises section of **this Chapter**.

Sentence or Fragment?

DIRECTIONS:

A complete sentence makes sense when read all alone. An incomplete sentence or fragment does not. Some of the following are fragments. Some are perfectly correct, complete sentences. Rewrite the fragments and make them into good sentences. You may add words, get rid of words, or rearrange the words. **Just make sure that each fragment you rewrite is factually correct according to the chapter and makes good sense when you read it alone.** Leave the complete sentences alone.

EXAMPLE: *The Díaz dictatorship and the Mexican Revolution.*

Clearly this does not make sense when read alone. Although there is **no single correct way** to rewrite it, the following is much better:

The Díaz dictatorship is what caused the Mexican Revolution.

1. Camilo Arriaga's objections to the Díaz dictatorship.
2. The Flores-Magon brothers and *Regeneración.*
3. The Liberal Plan of the Flores-Magon brothers offered solutions to many of Mexico's problems.
4. A strike in 1906 at the Cananea Copper Company.
5. Francisco Madero's book, *The Presidential Succession in 1910.*
6. Díaz spent over 20 million pesos on the Centenario celebration.
7. Madero's *Plan de San Luis Potosí.*
8. A former peon from Durango known as Doroteo Arango.
9. Two important early battles, Ciudad Juárez and Cuautla.
10. The leader of the guerrilleros in Morelos was Emiliano Zapata.
11. Díaz's resignation and his departure to Paris.
12. Madero's desire for a political revolution prior to the returning of the ejido lands.
13. Huerta's traitorous plot against Madero known as the *Decena Tragica.*
14. The Huerta presidency is characterized mostly by military encounters.
15. Venustiano Carranza organized an army to fight against Huerta.
16. The U.S. Marines at Vera Cruz.
17. Huerta's resignation followed by the meeting between Villa and Zapata.
18. The Mexican Constitution of today was written in 1917.
19. The single bloodiest battle between Obregón and Villa.
20. An all out war against the Zapatistas by Carranza.

21. Zapata's *Plan de Ayala*.
22. Obregón and the Zapatistas joined forces to overthrow Carranza.
23. Lázaro Cárdenas and land reform.
24. The establishment of PEMEX by Cárdenas in 1938.
25. The PRI has not lost a Mexican presidential election in over 60 years!

Short Answer Questions

DIRECTIONS:

Answer the following questions by writing one or two complete sentences for each. Be sure that each sentence you write:

a) Is factually correct and helps to answer the question.
b) Is a complete sentence which means it makes sense when read alone.
c) Could be understood by someone who has not seen the question.
d) Begins with a capital letter and ends with a period.
e) Is completely in your own words.
f) Uses correct spelling and is neat.

EXAMPLE: *Why did Camilo Arriaga criticize Church behavior during the Díaz era?*

Arriaga thought the Church was cooperating with the government. The Church was allowed to keep its large land holdings and in return preached obedience to Díaz's dictatorship.

1. Why did the Flores-Magón brothers have difficulty printing in Mexico?
2. What were a few of the most important ideas of the "Liberal Plan"?
3. What important event occurred in 1906 in Cananea?
4. What happened at Rio Blanco in 1907?
5. What did Madero want in terms of political changes for Mexico?
6. What was the outcome of the 1910 Mexican presidential election? What happened to Madero?
7. What had Pancho Villa done before becoming a revolutionary leader?
8. Briefly describe the bands of guerrilla fighters that appeared in 1910.
9. What were the two decisive battles of the revolution against Díaz?
10. What happened to Díaz?
11. What did Madero ask Zapata to do as a show of good faith?
12. What did Zapata ask of Madero?

13. Why did Madero fail as president?
14. How did Huerta make Madero's government look bad?
15. Who were the most important leaders who fought against Huerta?
16. How did the U.S. get involved?
17. What was Mexico's condition after the defeat of Huerta?
18. Why did Villa and Zapata like each other?
19. Why did Zapata continue fighting even after Carranza became president?
20. What are the most important ideas of the 1917 Constitution of Mexico?
21. Who overthrew Carranza?
22. What were the haciendas of Morelos doing with the stolen ejido lands?
23. Once the Zapatistas won a victory, what would Zapata do with the land?
24. Why did Madero and Zapata fail to unite?
25. Who was the only guerrilla chief to fight against Carranza after Villa's defeat?
26. What made Zapata so popular with his people?
27. What was important about Obregón's National Agrarian Commission?
28. Why did Jovita Idar leave Texas and go to Mexico?
29. What are the subsoil articles of Mexico's Constitution?
30. In Texas, Ema Tenayuca was fighting for Mexican Americans. How?
31. How did Cárdenas use the subsoil articles in the creation of PEMEX?
32. What did Cárdenas achieve regarding land reform?
33. How has PEMEX become more important to Mexico recently?
34. What is the PRI? What do they supposedly stand for?
35. What are some of the problems Mexico faces today?

Paragraph Questions

DIRECTIONS:

Answer the following questions by writing a good paragraph for each. Refer back to the sample paragraph on **page 47** for help. Be sure that each paragraph you write:

    a) Is factually correct, helps to answer the question and is in your own words.
    b) Looks like a proper paragraph (see sample).
    c) Has an <u>underlined</u> topic sentence at the beginning of the paragraph.
    d) Contains no fragments.
    e) Uses correct spelling and is neat.

1. Describe the most important ideas of the Liberal Plan as written by the Flores-Magón brothers in *Regeneración*.
2. Why were so many people in Mexico ready to take up arms and revolt against President Díaz in 1910?
3. Explain this statement: "Madero wanted a political and not a social revolution for Mexico."
4. Describe the brief guerrilla revolutionary war that led to Díaz's departure from Mexico.
5. Why did the revolutionary chiefs not trust Madero? Why did they (especially Zapata) fail to support him?
6. Describe the *Decena Trágica* and Huerta's overthrow of Madero.
7. Briefly describe the Civil War of 1914.
8. Why did Villa and Zapata continue to fight even after Huerta was defeated?
9. What are some of the most important ideas of the 1917 Constitution?
10. Why did Carranza hate the Zapatistas in Morelos so much?
11. Why has Zapata become a legendary hero in Mexico?
12. How was Carranza overthrown and by whom?
13. How did Diego Rivera relate to the people of Mexico?
14. Why is Lázaro Cárdenas known as one of Mexico's greatest leaders?
15. How was PEMEX created?
16. What positive progress has Mexico made in recent years?
17. What are some of Mexico's biggest problems today?
18. Why do many Mexicans not trust the PRI?

Clustering and ID Items

DIRECTIONS:

Make clusters and/or ID paragraphs for the following identification items. While making your cluster or paragraph, ask yourself who or what the item is and why it is important in the history being studied. Refer to your book if necessary. A sample cluster and ID paragraph can be found on **page 49.**

Mexican Constitution of 1917	Victoriano Huerta	Jovita Idar
National Agrarian Commission	Venustiano Carranza	Ema Tenayuca
Flores-Magón brothers	Alvaro Obregón	Diego Rivera
Francisco Madero	battle of Celaya	soldaderas
Colonel William Greene	Emiliano Zapata	Lázaro Cárdenas
Pancho Villa	PRI	PEMEX

How to Answer Essay Questions

DIRECTIONS:

Sometimes a question is so broad or detailed that it requires several paragraphs for a complete answer. Such answers are organized into a number of paragraphs and are called essays. Essays are usually divided into three main sections, the introductory paragraph, the body paragraphs and the end paragraph (conclusion).

1. Introductory Paragraph

This paragraph introduces the topic to be covered by making general statements which show where the topic fits in the larger picture. It can act as a summary of the whole essay. It ends with a thesis statement, which is a proposition which you will support with arguments or facts in the rest of the paper.

2. Body Paragraphs

These paragraphs each deal specifically with one aspect of the answer. They should be written in exactly the same manner as individual paragraphs or ID paragraphs; that is, a topic sentence with supporting details. These body paragraphs should provide specific details: facts, dates, names and statistics wherever possible. Remember, write one paragraph for each main idea or main aspect of the essay question.

3. Conclusion

This paragraph ties up or finishes the essay and shows how the body paragraphs prove the thesis statement. Do not repeat anything you have written before. Try to make a strong finish!

Sample Essay

SAMPLE TOPIC:

Choose and describe three of the most important and influential figures of the Mexican Revolution of 1910-1940.

SAMPLE OUTLINE:

Please note that the essay has one paragraph for each of the following topics:

I.   INTRODUCTION and THESIS STATEMENT
II. PANCHO VILLA
III. EMILIANO ZAPATA
IV. LAZARO CARDENAS
V.   CONCLUSION

The Mexican Revolution involved a social upheaval which shook Mexico for nearly thirty years. Over 1,000,000 Mexican people died in the bloody fighting. Once the dictator Porfirio Díaz was overthrown in 1911, a struggle for power resulted which took the form of a civil war. Although most of the fighting was over by 1920, the revolutionary changes lasted into the 1940s. Among the Mexican Revolution's colorful, interesting and influential personalities, three of the most important are Pancho Villa, Emiliano Zapata and Lázaro Cárdenas.

Doroteo Arango was Pancho Villa's real name. He was born into extreme poverty in the state of Durango and worked as a peon on the large *haciendas* of Mexico's corrupt wealthy class. He managed to escape from the *hacienda,* becoming first a *bandido,* and then later a revolutionary guerrilla and general. He consistently fought for retrieval of lands stolen by the *hacendados* from the rural country people. He is most famous for his powerful cavalry and his flamboyant lifestyle. His heart and motives were always with Mexico's poor.

Emiliano Zapata was the son of small landowners in the Mexican state of Morelos. An expert horseman and rodeo rider, he has become the most legendary of all the revolutionary figures. At the height of his power he virtually controlled all of his home state, seeing to it that stolen village lands were returned to the people. His cry for "land and liberty" and his preference to "die on my feet rather than live on my knees" have immortalized him in Mexican history and lore.

Lázaro Cárdenas, as a boy, was a revolutionary fighter with Pancho Villa. He became president of Mexico in 1934. He saw to it that the promises made during the revolution were kept. Under his administration over 50,000,000 acres of rural lands were returned to the people. Tremendous sums of money were spent on a rural school system. Most important, he nationalized Mexico's oil industry, creating a financial base that serves Mexico to this day. He is considered to have been the most aggressive, honest and efficient Mexican president in modern history.

The history of Mexico's revolution is highlighted by many larger-than-life figures. Their deeds have been honored in books, songs, monuments and murals. Pancho Villa seems more like a mythical figure than a real person due to the famous stories and exaggerated accounts of his exploits. Pictures of Emiliano Zapata's serious countenance remind us of his single-minded desire to better the lives of his people. Lázaro Cárdenas, "the FDR of Mexico," serves as the archetypical Mexican president of the modern era against whom all others must inevitably be judged. The careers of these men are a part of the rich heritage of Mexico.

PLEASE NOTE:

The introduction begins with needed background information on the Mexican Revolution as a whole, attempting to put the three men into some context. Notice how the thesis clearly states what the essay will cover.

Further, notice how the body paragraphs each deal with only one man and attempt to be specific and detailed. Finally, notice how the end paragraph (conclusion) provides perspective for what has already been said and does not repeat anything said earlier.

How to Take In-Class Essay Examinations

DIRECTIONS:

High school and college teachers often give essay examinations or tests. In this situation you must write an essay that answers a specific question under the pressure of time and without using notes or other materials. The same basic rules of how to write an essay apply. Below is a suggested step-by-step method for successfully writing in-class essay exams.

1. **Read and Understand the Question being Asked.**   Look for key words. Think! Make sure you answer what the question is really asking.

2. **Plan Your Essay.**   Figure out how many paragraphs you will need and what the title of each will be. Brainstorm. Think of all possible aspects of the answer. Each main idea should become a separate paragraph. Finally, arrange your paragraph topics into the best possible order.

3. **Write a Brief Introduction or Opening Paragraph.**   Give necessary background information or other general information. At the end of the introduction clearly state your thesis or answer the question in such a way that you communicate what you are going to write about.

4. **Write the Body Paragraphs.**   Follow the outline plan you made. Be as specific and factual as possible. Be careful not to get off the subject. Everything you say should relate to your thesis and/or help you answer the question or topic given.

5. **Write an End Paragraph or Conclusion.**   Review what you have said but do not repeat! Draw conclusions on what you have said and tie the entire essay together. Be sure you have proven what you said in your thesis.

6. **Read Over Your Essay.**   Correct errors in fact or writing.

Essay Questions

DIRECTIONS:

The following are essay questions on the content of this chapter. Before attempting to answer any questions, see **page 187** for directions on how to write an essay and **page 188** for a sample essay.

1. What were the actions of Díaz which contributed to the beginning of the Mexican Revolution? Be sure to include: Rurales, foreign privilege, the hacienda system, etc.

2. Compare and contrast the revolutionary beliefs of Emiliano Zapata and Francisco Madero. Who do you think was right? How might the revolution have been different if they had united together?

3. Throughout the presidencies of Díaz, Madero, Huerta, and Carranza, the Mexican Revolution was basically a guerrilla war. Why are guerrilla wars so hard for regular armies to fight? Where do the guerrillas get their weapons and supplies? What are their battle tactics? Why are guerrillas often willing to fight harder than the soldiers in regular armies?

4. Discuss the following ideas from Mexico's 1917 Constitution and how Mexican presidents (especially Cárdenas) implemented these ideas: subsoil articles, land reform, education for the poor.

5. Although the PRI has not lost a Mexican presidential election in over sixty years, its popularity is threatened by many problems in Mexico today. Discuss the PRI and the problems it faces in Mexico.

6. The United States has historically been concerned about communist guerrilla movements in Latin America. Are there any lessons to be learned from the Mexican Revolution?

7. Jovita Idar and Ema Tenayuca fought their own battles. How and why?

8. How did Diego Rivera inform us about the Mexican Revolution and conditions in Mexico?

9. Why and how is it possible that Mexico could have another revolution?

Chapter Six

THE ZOOT SUIT YEARS

1. Mexicans Return to Aztlan

The 1910 Revolution was such an overwhelming catastrophe for Mexico that over ten percent of her population migrated to the United States. Ernesto Galarza's classic autobiography entitled *Barrio Boy* vividly describes his family's trek northward. As evidence of how different things were in the 1920s, U.S. military personnel were there to help as Galarza's family arrived at the United States/Mexico border. Those who came to the U.S. during the revolution would spawn a new, young generation of Mexican Americans. These were the teenagers who became the "pachucos" and wore the "zoot suits."

Unfortunately, it was predictable that these Mexicans would encounter resentment and hostility in the United States. After all, the Southwest had been taken from Mexico in the name of "Manifest Destiny," which took for granted the inferior nature of the Mexican when compared to the European American.

Racism in the history of the United States is not difficult to find. Whether it be the Native American Indians, African Americans, the Irish, the Chinese or the Mexicans, all have suffered the sting of being labeled "unworthy," "inferior," and, as a result, have received second class treatment.

To focus on the experiences of this new Mexican American generation during the decade of the 1940s, it has been necessary to rely upon two very important sources. One is Carey McWilliams. His landmark book entitled *North From Mexico* is absolutely essential for an understanding of this period. Luis Valdéz, the author of the play and film *Zoot Suit,* has dramatically and artistically told the very ugly story of war-time hysteria and prejudice in Los Angeles, California with the Mexican pachucos as the victims.

Luis Valdez

Homes Invaded in Hunt for Pachucos

Ban on Freak Suits Studied by Councilmen

VICTIM OF JAP

U.S. CASUALTIES IN BAT

HERALD Express

GRAND JURY TO ACT IN ZOOT SUIT WAR

LESLIE HOWARD LOST AT SEA

Riot Alarm Sent Out in Zoot War
Servicemen Strip and Beat 50;

When most Mexican Americans today think of racism, they may think only in terms of the treatment of Black Americans in the U.S. They may even know that, during the 1940s, Japanese Americans were taken from their homes and locked up in prisons without having committed any crimes. What many young Mexican Americans may not know is that their ancestors suffered similar racist harassment, discrimination and segregation as did both the Blacks and the Japanese.

Today in the United States the problem of racism in a multi-ethnic and multi-racial nation has yet to be solved. Indeed, in some respects it would seem that racism is currently undergoing a resurgence. No other country in the world has so many different kinds of people living together in the same cities and towns. It is our challenge, therefore, to be able to go beyond the tendency to dislike those who are different. In order to more fully understand the events associated with the "Zoot Suit Years," which often involve racism, prejudice and discrimination, we will take a brief look at the real meanings of these words.

2. Essential Vocabulary

Racism is a difficult subject to discuss since it entails sensitive feelings between different kinds of people. The word racism can be defined as a feeling of racial hatred or superiority toward others. In other words, you may hate or dislike people of another race or you may feel superior to them because they are not the same color as you. Sometimes "racism" is not exactly the most accurate word to use because it may involve dealing with a particular ethnic group or nationality.

Prejudice is defined in much the same way as racism. To practice ethnic or racial prejudice is to prejudge those of different colors or nationalities than ourselves. A Japanese person who dislikes Koreans would be practicing ethnic prejudice since both are members of the same race.

Discrimination is what often results from racism or prejudice. To discriminate **against** someone means to treat them differently or unfairly. If only boys were allowed to see a particular movie at school, the girls could rightly claim that they were being discriminated against. Discrimination can be based not only upon race or ethnic group, but on a person's sex, their age, their appearance, their sexual preference or even upon their religion.

One common type of discrimination has been to segregate people on the basis of color or other such factors. To segregate means to separate. Racial segregation used to be legal when it concerned schools or housing. The laws would not allow people of different races to buy houses next to each other or to go to school together.

People who are racist or prejudiced often stereotype those of other races or nationalities. This means they generalize about certain groups of people in ways that are very unfair. Mexicans have been stereotyped as being violent or lazy. The Japanese ("Yellow Menace") during World War II were portrayed as being sneaky and vicious. Hitler stereotyped the Jews as stingy, greedy people who were creating economic chaos in Germany for their own benefit. Today, stereotypes are not spoken of as openly, yet many people have preconceived notions about how entire groups of people always behave. Actually there are **no true stereotypes**. For every member of a group who fits a stereotype there is another who does not.

Often people stereotype in ways they believe are funny. This is known as telling racial or ethnic jokes. Usually people who like racial humor are actually racist themselves (although they may not realize it). Next time you hear or tell a racial joke, ask yourself how funny it would be if a person of the group the joke is about were there in front of you!

Racism and discrimination are as old as humanity itself. Obviously there are no easy solutions. Generally speaking, the more we know about groups of people different from ourselves the less likely we are to have racist feelings toward them. It is natural for all of us to have some racist tendencies. The trick is to recognize these feelings for what they are, deal with them and try to treat all people you come in contact with openly, fairly and equally.

Racism, in all its ugly forms, has done great damage in human history. Different groups of people such as the Indians of Mexico, or the Africans, were enslaved because others thought they were inferior. As a result, millions of innocent lives have been wasted or lost. In Hitler's Germany, for example, people died in concentration camps because they were believed to be "different" and "inferior." In the *Encyclopaedia Britannica* (1978 edition), it was estimated that in all the camps of Nazi Germany and its occupied territories, 18 million to 26 million persons — war prisoners, political prisoners and nationals of occupied and invaded countries — were put to death through hunger, cold, pestilence, torture, medical experimentation and gas chambers. It is up to us not to teach racism or prejudice of any kind to our children. We must remind ourselves that people of all colors and nationalities are identical under the skin. All of us deserve the same chance in life.

3. World War II

The Second World War provides the backdrop for the experiences of the Mexican Americans in the United States during the 1940s. In many ways, the war made the Mexicans' situation worse as many White Americans saw them as "foreigners" who were not "patriotic Americans." In time of war this led to resentment and bad feelings. But World War II also provided the opportunity for Mexi-

Los Angeles Newspapers

361,692

STIMSON SAYS 15 'SPY' PLANES FLEW OVER L.A.

REVEALS 143C

PLANES, SHIPS HUNT JAP SUB IN SO. CAL. SHELLING

JAPANESE COUNTENANCE

Immediate Evacuation of Japanese Demanded
Southern Californians Call for Summary Action

Storm Grows Over Delay in Alien Ouster
Navy Speeds Evacuation

Spurred to action by yesterday morning's air-raid alarm here and bombardment of the Elwood oil field Monday by an enemy submarine, Southlanders yesterday demanded immediate evacuation of all Japanese aliens and citizens.

Telegrams poured into Governor Olson's office urging him to request Federal authorities to "remove from this state all Japanese, both American born and alien at once.

Children Bound to Nippon Soil

Allegiance to Hirohito Stressed in Japanese Language Schools Here

How American-born children of Japanese aliens are closely bound to their ancestral soil by ties of blood, tradition and culture through operation of Japanese language schools in this country is disclosed in detail for the first time today with publication of the Dies committee on un-American activities report.

Knox Assailed on 'False Alarm'

Whether Los Angeles experienced a bona-fide air raid or reconnaissance in the early morning hours of Wednesday or was the victim either of military practicing, many California and other West Coast legis-

Editor's Note:
Countenance: Noun. **1. The look on a person's face that shows his <u>nature</u> or feelings.**

can Americans to prove their loyalty and bravery, often in extraordinary ways. Let us take a brief look at the war.

In Europe, Hitler's Nazi Germany had been flexing its military muscles. Hitler not only seemed bent on conquering all of Europe in the name of some grand German empire, but he also had made it clear that the Jewish people were to be eliminated. What followed was warfare on a scale never seen before on the face of this earth. Never had so many tens of millions died.

In Asia, Japan was using its military power to challenge the Europeans for colonial control of the rest of Asia. China, Indochina, the Philippines — all fell to the Japanese armies. Then Hitler and the Japanese formed an alliance and, with Italy, came to be known as the Axis Powers. World domination appeared to be their goal.

The Japanese attack on Pearl Harbor, in the Hawaiian Islands, marked the entry of the United States into the war. At the urging of President Franklin D. Roosevelt, the United States Congress declared war on Japan. The following day Germany and Italy declared war on the U.S. Although we had tried to remain out of the fighting, we were now in it whether we wanted to be or not.

A military draft was imposed and able-bodied American men, between the ages of 18 and 40, were called up to fight our enemies. Hundreds of thousands of Mexican Americans served in the Second World War. Women went to work in the defense industries in huge numbers. Gasoline was rationed as were other vital materials like metal and rubber. Air raid drills and other emergency preparations went into effect. Not to sacrifice in the name of the war was considered unpatriotic. After all, many had already made the ultimate sacrifice. Now, particularly on the west coast of the U.S., there was near panic and hysteria. Would California be the next victim of the Japanese Air Force?

4. Setting the Stage

Little more than two months after the sneak attack on Pearl Harbor in Hawaii, a Japanese submarine surfaced off the coast of Santa Barbara, a town about 100 miles north of Los Angeles. The submarine fired several shots at an oil field and then left the area. Reports of this sighting quickly spread up and down the Pacific Coast. Three days later on February 26, 1942, the "Great Los Angeles Air Raid" took place. That night the U.S. Army at San Pedro announced the sighting of incoming enemy aircraft. Approximately 1500 rounds of ammunition were fired at the mysterious planes. Five people died; three from automobile crashes and two from heart attacks. On the following day the Secretary of the Navy announced that there had been no enemy planes.

Los Angeles newspapers

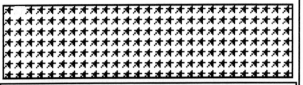

FIX CAL. ZONES FOR BAN ON ENEMY ALIENS

All Japs Will Be Barred From West Coast

The western half of Washington, Oregon and California and the southern half of Arizona today were declared by the Army to be a "military area from which enemy aliens as well as American-born Japanese will be ousted progressively to combat the threat of sabotage and espionage.

Japanese Here Begin Exodus

Nation's Greatest Mass Evacuation Starts as Vanguard of 35,000 Southland Nipponese Move to Owens Valley Concentration Center

America's greatest mass evacuation began yesterday as 86 Japanese aliens and American-born citizens arrived in Manzanar, new evacuees' city in Owens Valley from Los Angeles.

They are the forerunners of some 35,000 of their race who will be moved out of Southern California, first to the Owens Valley camp and later, after classification as to industrial ability, to inland concentration centers.

Eventually, a total of more than 170,000 Japanese, Germans and Italians will be evacuated from coastal communities.

DEWITT VISITS CAMP

The arrival of the first contingent of Los Angeles Japanese at Manzanar was preceded by an inspection visit by Lieut. Gen. John L. DeWitt, chief of the Western Defense Command, who flew down from his San Francisco headquarters with members of his staff to look over the huge establishment now rising in the remote valley.

He expressed himself as pleased with the progress made at the camp, where hundreds of carpenters and other artisans are building houses, assembly halls, a hospital and other facilities for the 10,000 evacuees who will soon people Manzanar.

GROUP OF ARTISANS

The first contingent of Japanese to leave Los Angeles in compliance with Gen. DeWitt's orders was comprised of plumbers, painters, nurses, cooks, waiters, bakers and stenographers, all of whom left voluntarily to aid in preparing the evacuation center for the thousands of others who will be taken there in the near future.

With the small amount of their worldly possessions they were able to take packed into neat bundles, this group climbed into three busses and a truck in the playground of the Maryknoll School, Third and Hewitt Sts., and waved good-by to more than 200 of their friends and relatives who had gathered to see them off.

MOVE SWIFTLY

Here and there, traditional Oriental stoicism cracked and there were a few tears, but for the most part, the voluntary evacuees evinced little emotion. ....

Nevertheless, the citizens of Los Angeles began making preparations for future attacks. A blackout was imposed. Windows were painted black to prevent light from getting out. Strict orders were issued against the burning of lights at night. All anyone could talk about was the war and whether or not California would be bombed by the Japanese.

In March and April of 1942 the roundup of all Japanese and Japanese Americans began. All people of Japanese descent were imprisoned, whether they were American citizens or not. They were allowed to bring only a few belongings with them as they were transported to "relocation centers" (more like prisons) away from the coast. A few concerned Americans complained that we were violating the constitutional rights of these Japanese Americans. Some even dared to suggest that what we were doing to these people was similar to what Hitler was doing to the Jews in Germany. But in the atmosphere of wartime fear and anxiety these arguments were not heeded. America could afford to take no chances, so the reasoning went. Perhaps these "Japs" were spies, secretly working for the Japanese government and only pretending to be loyal, law-abiding Americans. When the round-up and imprisonment of the Japanese in California was completed, most Californians breathed a sigh of relief.

5.   "Pachuquismo"

Once the Japanese and Japanese Americans were out of the picture it appeared that another scapegoat was needed. A scapegoat is someone who receives all the blame for a particular problem or set of problems. Usually a particular society, in such cases, focuses the majority upon a minority and vents its anger and frustrations upon them.

Most Americans were in an understandable state of rage and frustration during World War II. The Germans and Japanese were conquering countries friendly to the U.S. and were responsible for the deaths of mounting thousands of American soldiers. Yet there was no way the average American could personally strike back at the Nazis or the "Japs." The pachuco scapegoat provided such an outlet.

In Los Angeles, by the 1940s, most of the Mexican and Mexican American population lived in "barrios" or "colonias" where sewers, street lighting, trash collection and police protection were often inferior to the same services provided to White communities. Real estate was difficult for Mexicans to purchase outside of the barrios. The property deeds often stated, in so-called "exclusive covenants," that a given home could not be sold to a member of the Black, Asian or Mexican race. The "East Side" of Los Angeles came to be primarily Mexican in rapidly growing colonias such as Chávez Ravine, Belvedere and Maravilla. By 1948, for example, Carey McWilliams estimated the Mexican population of Los Angeles to be as high as 200,000.

Most of the fashionable movie theaters in downtown Los Angeles and Hollywood often would not admit Mexican Americans, or would segregate them into separate sections. Restaurants often openly refused service if the patrons were Mexican Americans. Public parks and swimming pools often had signs posted which read, "WEDNESDAYS RESERVED FOR NEGROES AND MEXICANS ONLY." Even attractions popular with young people, such as ice skating and roller skating rinks, were only open to Mexicans one day a week.

Schools in districts such as Orange County and San Bernardino openly segregated Mexican American children from Whites. In the Los Angeles city schools signs were posted reading "English Only" and students who violated this rule could face suspension. In the elementary schools it was quite common for teachers to change children's Spanish names to Anglo versions.

Similar patterns existed in employment. Mexican American workers were often paid a lower wage for doing the same job as a White person. The established labor unions such as the American Federation of Labor did not even admit Mexican Americans as members. People of Mexican descent were relegated to the lowest paid positions which required the hardest labor.

The younger generation of Mexican Americans, which came of age in the 1940s, therefore had many more problems than the average teenager. In school they were taught that English was the only language that mattered and that U.S. history and literature alone merited serious study. In this manner, the schools turned the young people away from their own families. Their parents, who often did not speak English and who wished to maintain ties with Mexican customs, were often seen by their teenage sons and daughters as being "square," "out of it," or as people of whom they should be ashamed. An outgrowth of these developing attitudes was that American-born or educated Mexican American teens often came to look down upon newly arrived Mexican people.

However, the day came when Mexican American youth sought to test the "freedom" and "equality" they were reading about in school. They tried to be "real Americans." The clothes that the young men wore, which came to be known as the "zoot suit," may have had their origins in the popular 1939 movie, *Gone With the Wind.* The zoot suits, or drapes, were probably the young men's way of trying to look "American." Certainly their Mexican parents did not approve of such an extreme dress style. And it was soon to become abundantly clear that the predominant White society did not approve of this dress style either.

The long broad-shouldered coats, the extra baggy pants that fit tight at the ankles, and a broad-brimmed hat, sometimes with a feather in it, became the stan-

Los Angeles Newspapers

200 Boy Gangster Suspects Held

While an exhaustive Coroner's inquest behind heavily guarded doors failed to reveal new clues yesterday in the death of Jose Diaz, slain Aug. 2 when the 38th St. gang raided a party on the Williams ranch, police last night conducted a showup of 200 youths at Central Station.

Inquest Airs Ranch Killing
Coroner's Jury Fails to Identify Slayer; Authorities Push Drive

INVESTIGATION PUSHED

In another move Dis. Atty. John F. Sockweiler appointed....

COURT CRACKS DOWN

Superior Judge Edward R. Brand cracked down with a sample of the punishment the young hoodlums can expect....

LEAVING INQUEST — Henry Leyvas, front center, alleged member of a youthful gang, is shown as he was led from an inquest yesterday where the death of Jose Diaz was investigated. Other suspected members of the gang shown in background.

AUGUST 3, 1942   ★★★   FIVE CENTS ◄

BLACK WIDOW GIRLS IN BOY GANGS; WAR ON VANDALS PUSHED

Aroused by two new week-end outbursts of youthful gang warfare, in which one young man was beaten to death, another driven into a pool with chains and feared drowned,

Five Mexican youths were arrested after police scattered a big gang fight at Repose and Effie streets. This quintet and the band nabbed at First and Boyle streets were all charged with suspicion of assault with a deadly weapon.

Nab 29 In Boy Gangs
13 Arrested After Alleged Attempt To Kidnap Girls

Twenty-nine suspects, mostly youths, today were being held by police for attacks and robbery and creating disturbances in various sections of the city and county in the wake of a weekend dard pachuco outfit for the boys. The pachucas, or "cholas," favored dark colors, short and tight black skirts, black sweaters, fishnet hose and tall pompadour hairdos. In this manner the Mexican American youth engaged in the time-honored phenomenon of youthful rebellion and assertion of individuality. But soon, to the dismay of many, this superficial fashion came to be seen as a symbol of the worst kind of criminal and unpatriotic behavior.

It was in this context that the first Mexican American "gangs" began to appear. Discriminated against, not permitted into the same lifestyle as White teenagers, the teens turned inward, toward their own, for social support. And since they often had been turned against their own families by the educational system, neighborhood groups often took the place of the family.

Elsewhere in the United States other minority groups have had similar experiences of discrimination, alienation, and the notion that they have not been considered equal; including Italian Americans, Jewish Americans, Black Americans, Russian Americans and others who have banded together in youthful gangs at one time or another.

And so it was in Los Angeles where, during the 1940s, one of the favorite meeting places for the youth was a large irrigation ditch located in a ravine in a rural area of Montebello, near the East Side of L.A. The place served as a swimming hole and "lovers' lane" for the pachucos and their girlfriends. The area was large, but not large enough for everyone who would use it. Minor fights over possession of this place were common. Soon a cycle of violence between Mexican and Mexican American teenagers was underway.

6. Racism Against Mexicans

In the midst of war time anxiety, the Los Angeles newspapers began to run stories describing a "Mexican crime wave." The first stories with their alarming headlines appeared in the newspapers owned by the Hearst family. L.A. residents were told about "a rising tide of Mexican juvenile delinquency." The pachucos, or zoot-suiters, were described as "Mexican baby-faced gangsters" who rode around town getting into all sorts of trouble. The newspapers alleged that they were carrying deadly weapons while accompanied by their equally evil girl friends whom the newspaper accounts called "black widows." Actual arrest statistics of the years just before the outbreak of the war show no great increase in the amount of Mexican American juvenile delinquency, but still the hysteria grew.

A special grand jury of the city of Los Angeles was appointed to investigate the situation. Strong war-time paranoia combined with the newspaper reports may have accounted for the calling of this grand jury. Clearly these young Mexican American zoot-suiters were not angels but, on the other hand, neither were they a threat to the security of the city or the nation. Some newspapers reported that the pachuco gang violence had been organized and manipulated by Fascist organizations in Latin America to distract the U.S. and spoil our war-time unity. No actual connection between Chicano teenagers and any Fascist group has ever been documented. In the midst of this highly charged and emotional environment the newspapers were able to convince most Los Angeles residents that there was indeed cause for alarm.

The Los Angeles County Sheriff's Department appointed an official, E. Duran Ayres, to head their Foreign Relations Bureau. He was to make an investigation of the Mexican crime and juvenile delinquency situation in the city. Ayres prepared a report and testified before the grand jury.

When presented to the grand jury, his written report began by offering an accurate description of the various forms of pervasive discrimination practiced against the "Mexican element" in the city of Los Angeles. Mentioning discrimination in housing, schools, public swimming pools and parks, night clubs, and even employment in the defense plants, Ayres then went on to make some startling statements about certain "biological factors" which "explained" the Mexican's inborn love of violence.

He stated that Mexican Americans are essentially Indians and therefore Orientals or Asians. Throughout history, he declared, the Orientals have shown less regard for human life than have the Europeans. Further, Mexican Americans had inherited their "naturally violent" tendencies from the "bloodthirsty Aztecs" of Mexico who were said to have practiced human sacrifice centuries ago. At one point in his report Ayres even compared the Anglo to a domesticated house cat and the Mexican to a "wild cat," suggesting that the Mexican would forever retain his wild and violent tendencies no matter how much education or training he might receive. That this report was even considered "legal evidence" in a court of law is surprising today.

Soon the essentials of Ayres' theories appeared in the L.A. newspapers which quickly realized that these types of sensational stories were excellent for business. The damage to the Mexican community of Los Angeles was considerable. To be Mexican or Mexican American began to be equated with being a criminal, a hooligan or a gangster.

A stereotype of the "evil" pachuco was beginning to form in the minds of many L.A. residents. Intense (and justified) war-time fear, combined with growing paranoia against this Mexican "enemy from within" created a climate of racism towards Mexicans in the city of Los Angeles just as, at the same time in Germany, the majority population was being fed a steady stream of propaganda which led them to believe that minorities in their midst were a threat to their way of life.

7.   Henry Leyvas — Killer or Victim?

On August 1, 1942, Henry Leyvas, 20, was enjoying the relative calm of the lagoon near the Williams Ranch with his girlfriend. After sitting in their car for a while they decided to take a walk. As they walked, they were suddenly attacked by a group of young pachucos. Leyvas was severely beaten and had to be helped back to his car by his girl. They drove away, returning later with some friends in several other cars, "to get even." Leyvas's attackers are unknown to this day, having been identified only as the "Downey boys."

When Leyvas and his friends returned they found the lagoon deserted. After wandering around for a few minutes they heard the sounds of a party coming from the Delgadillo house, one of the small guest houses that lay at some distance from the Williams Ranch. They decided to "crash" the party. When they got to the door of the house they were attacked by the people inside. It later turned out that the "Downey boys" had earlier tried to "crash" the party themselves and when Leyvas and his friends arrived the people at the party thought they were the Downey boys coming back. The fight was not a serious one and because Henry Leyvas was so weakened by his earlier attack, he did not participate. Leyvas and his friends, who later came to be known in the newspapers as the "38th Street gang," left the party and went home. A man named José Díaz was found the next morning lying unconscious on a road near the Lagoon. He died later at a hospital without regaining consciousness.

An examination was made of the body. Díaz was found to have been drunk at the time of his death. His death resulted from a skull fracture that could have been made by a blunt instrument or even a car. One medical examiner stated that Díaz's injuries looked similar to those seen on the victims of car accidents. But despite the fact that there was no evidence of a murder, despite the fact that the two friends of Díaz, with whom he left the party, were never questioned by police, and despite the fact that no one had seen how Díaz died, 24 members of the "38th Street gang" were arrested and charged with the murder of José Díaz.

When the newspapers learned of the death it immediately became a brutal and senseless "murder" typical of the crimes committed by the "Mexican hoodlum element." Clearly this case called out for "severe punishment" by the courts. In the words of "El Pachuco" in the play *Zoot Suit,* the newspapers were "screaming for blood." It was Henry Leyvas's blood and the blood of his young friends that they were screaming for in articles and headlines.

Ban on Freak
Suits Studied
by Councilmen

"The question goes deeper than just suits.   It is a racial protest. I
have been worried for a long time about the Mexican racial situation. It is a problem with roots going a long way back, and we do
not always face these problems as we should."

ELEANOR ROOSEVELT
June 16, 1943

Above we see the family of Henry Leyvas, his mother
and sisters as they await the verdict on the appeal of
the Sleepy Lagoon murder case.   A picture of his
brother, lower right corner.

8. The Sleepy Lagoon Trial

The newspapers thought they had the proof they had long been seeking that a Mexican crime wave was in full swing. The police were also now ready to begin the crackdown that was "necessary" to teach these "baby gangsters" a lesson "they would never forget."

On the nights of August 10 and 11, 1942, the Los Angeles Police Department sprang into action. Key streets in Mexican neighborhoods in East Los Angeles were blocked by police cars. Any and all cars that had Mexicans in them were stopped and searched. Anyone who had tools — wrenches, hammers, chains, knives, or, as in one case, a bottle opener — in their car was arrested. In these two nights over 600 people were arrested. They were charged on suspicion of armed robbery, assault and other similar crimes. One hundred and seventy-five people were held on such charges. When we look at the list of the 600 people who were arrested we see not one name that is not Spanish. A clearer and more blatant example of discrimination by law enforcement is hard to find.

The newspapers went wild! Six hundred Mexican gangsters arrested in two nights! Here was clear proof that a serious situation existed and someone would certainly have to pay for it.

About the same time as the big round-up, the police began their investigation of the murder of José Díaz. Talking to people who were at the Delgadillo house on the night in question, they heard the name Henry Leyvas mentioned as someone who had been involved in the fighting. For reasons that are still not clear today, the police decided that Henry Leyvas and his "38th Street gang" were responsible for the murder. Warrants were issued for Leyvas and 23 of his friends.

There is clear evidence that police brutality was involved in the questioning of these young men. Several were severely beaten just before facing the grand jury. Some even had blood on their faces when they went in to face the jury.

Because we already know what the grand jury had been seeing, hearing and reading concerning the Mexican crime wave, it isn't hard to understand why these young men were indicted for the murder of José Díaz. Even though there was no eye witness to the crime, no murder weapon was produced, no motive for the crime was established, indeed no proof existed that it had even been a murder, it is still easy to see how the grand jury could indict these boys.

As soon as the indictments came down the newspapers went to work again. They began to run stories of "vicious young killers" who would "get what was coming to them" in the upcoming trial. One reporter gave the lake at the Williams Ranch the name "Sleepy Lagoon" and the press now had the perfect murder story on its hands. Amid this publicity the "Mexican Hoodlum Trial" began.

Throughout the time the boys were in jail, awaiting the start of their trial and for two weeks into the trial, they were not allowed to change their clothes. This was ordered by the district attorney and approved by the judge in the case, Charles Fricke. Their reasoning was that the jury must see the zoot suits the boys wore. Fricke denied repeated attempts by the defense lawyers to allow the boys to change into clean clothes.

Two of the original 24 defendants were tried separately and acquitted. Throughout the trial the remaining 22 defendants **were not allowed to sit with or talk to their lawyers.** This is a right guaranteed every defendant in any trial. Whenever the name of each defendant was mentioned, the boy in question was forced to stand. When they stood up it appeared as if they were admitting guilt, especially when some false and damaging statement was made about one of them.

Seven different lawyers represented the defendants at one time. This made it very hard to organize or coordinate an effective defense. This points out one of the major unfair aspects of the trial: it was a mass trial. With so many defendants it was impossible to keep the evidence and the facts from becoming confused. Later on in the trial, a famous labor lawyer, George Shibley, took over for two of the lawyers. He repeatedly charged Judge Fricke with "legal misconduct." These charges were important later in the appeal of the case. The judge and the jury seemed to have already decided clearly in their minds that the boys were guilty of murder and deserved to be punished.

Because Fricke considered it important that "expert" witnesses were called to testify, E. Duran Ayres was called to the stand to explain his theory of the Mexicans' inborn love for killing and violence. Fricke allowed Ayres's statements to go into the trial record and allowed the jury to listen to everything Ayres had to say.

But the prosecution still had serious problems with evidence. No murder weapon had ever been found. Indeed, as we have seen already, no proof was ever offered that José Díaz was actually murdered. Because of this the district attorney had to rely on evidence based on hearsay (what people have heard from others). Consider this example of hearsay evidence from the official trial record:

District Attorney: Someone got killed, you know that?
Witness: I know now.
DA: Who did you see kill José Díaz?
 W: I didn't see. I saw someone hitting someone else with a stick.
DA: You know now that the boy died as a result of that beating?
 W: I don't know if he is the one that died.
DA: He was beating a boy named José Díaz.
 W: I don't know what the boy's name was.
DA: But you heard since that the boy he was beating had died?
 W: Yes.

Or take this example:

> DA: Did you see a knife in Henry Leyvas's hand?
> W: I didn't see nothing in his hand, but they told mc hc had a knife.
> DA: Who told you?
> W: Everybody said Henry Leyvas had a knife, a big knife.

Or this example:

> DA: Does Henry Leyvas have a reputation among the gang as a leader?
> W: He thinks he has but a lot of guys don't pay any attention to him.
> DA: Does he have a reputation as being a pretty good knife man?
> W: I don't know.

This is the quality of the evidence that was used to send several people to prison for life.

The trial dragged on month after month toward the obvious conclusion. Despite the lack of a murder weapon, motive and evidence, the prosecution was successful. After approximately five months of testimony, on January 15, 1943, nine of the boys, including Leyvas, were found guilty of second degree murder. All nine were given sentences of five years to life. The others were found guilty of assault charges and given shorter prison terms. The nine convicted of murder were sent to San Quentin Prison.

9. The Sleepy Lagoon Defense Committee

Luckily for the nine young men in San Quentin Prison, a group of concerned individuals came together and formed the Sleepy Lagoon Defense Committee. Their goal was to sccurc thc release of the young men who clearly had not received a fair trial and justice. The committee hoped to raise enough money to pay for an appeal to a higher court. The group also wanted to publicize the facts pertaining to the injustice done.

Carey McWilliams, the author of *North from Mexico,* served as the chairman of the committee. His extensive experience as a journalist and writer who had focused on the history of Mexican migration into the U.S. proved invaluable. George Shibley, the primary defense attorney, was responsible for drafting the appeal brief. His job was the most time consuming for he had to sift through five months of court testimony and document instances of miscarriages of justice.

At this time a young Jewish woman, Alice Greenfield, who had been an activist in other progressive causes, became especially involved in the case. It was she who wrote endless letters of encouragement to the boys in prison. She also edited the committee's newsletter, *The Appeal News,* which kept their supporters informed on the progress of the case. In addition, Greenfield was in charge of fundraising. Her work made a deep impression on Luis Valdéz who, years later, made her one of the main characters in his play, *Zoot Suit.*

Many Mexicans and Mexican Americans were involved in the Sleepy Lagoon Defense Committee. This included the families of most of the defendants as well as the well-known Mexican American actor, Anthony Quinn, who had grown up in the Belvedere section of East Los Angeles.

The members of this pressure group did not take the attitude that "you can't fight city hall." Still, it was an uphill battle, for not much later, Carey McWilliams and other members were called before the Un-American Activities Committee of the House of Representatives where they were forced to answer questions about their activities. Soon they were accused of being disloyal to the United States and of harboring communist sympathies. Nevertheless, this harassment by the government failed to stop their efforts.

But the months dragged on and Henry, along with his friends, remained in prison. While they were in jail the ugliest part of our story of the Zoot Suit years was to take place: the so-called "Pachuco Riots" of June, 1943.

10. The Riots

Approximately five months after the Sleepy Lagoon defendants were convicted, an incident took place in the downtown section of Los Angeles. On the night of June 3, 1943, eleven sailors managed to find themselves on the 1700 block of North Main Street, right in the middle of one of the worst sections of town. According to their story, they were walking down the street when they were suddenly attacked by a gang of young Mexicans. They were, supposedly, badly outnumbered in the attack. One sailor was severely injured while the others suffered cuts and bruises. They immediately reported the attack to the police.

But before the citizens of L.A. or even the police could do anything, the sailors took matters into their own hands. A group of about 200 sailors hired twenty yellow taxicabs from the Naval Armory at Chávez Ravine. Their intended victims were anyone wearing a zoot suit. One sailor who was involved proudly stated: "We're out to do what the police have failed to do. We're going to clean up this situation."

As they cruised through the downtown and east side area of L.A., they stopped the cabs whenever they saw someone wearing a zoot suit. Leaping from their cars they would attack the unsuspecting victim, tear his clothes off and leave him unconscious and bleeding on the street. The Los Angeles Police Department did not seem able to intercept a caravan of 20 taxis filled with 200 uniformed sailors. Toward the end of the evening the police "accidentally" came across the group. Nine sailors were taken in, but no charges were filed and the sailors were released.

The next morning L.A. residents opened their newspapers to find the following headlines: "WILD NIGHT IN L.A. — SAILORS AND ZOOTERS CLASH." One article read in part: "Zoot suited roughnecks fled to cover before a task force of 20 cabs." A week of rioting followed.

On the following night, June 5, the sailors were joined by members of the other armed forces. Linking arms and marching down the middle of downtown streets they warned anyone wearing a zoot suit that they had better change their clothes or they would be in serious trouble the next night. Again the police made no attempts to get in the way of the servicemen. Of the several hundred servicemen involved, none were arrested. But 27 Mexican boys, who had gathered on a street corner to watch the goings-on, were arrested on suspicion of assault.

Meanwhile, the mob of sailors continued to parade through the streets. As Carey McWilliams writes: "A squad of sailors invaded a bar on the east side and carefully examined the clothes of the patrons. Two zoot-suited customers, drinking beer at a table, were ordered to remove their clothes. One of them was beaten and his clothes were torn from his back when he refused to comply with the order."

On the 6th of June the rioting began again but this time with a slightly different twist. The police, apparently, had decided on the best way to keep themselves busy. As the magazine *Time* later reported: "The police practice was to accompany the caravans of soldiers and sailors in police cars, watch the beatings and jail the victims." The sailors and servicemen continued on through the evening, covering the Mexican neighborhoods systematically. As McWilliams writes:

"Six carloads of sailors cruised down Brooklyn Avenue that evening. At Ramona Boulevard they stopped and beat up eight teenage Mexicans. Failing to find any Mexican zoot suiters at a bar on Indiana Street, they were so annoyed that they proceeded to wreck the establishment. In due course, the police made a leisurely appearance at the scene of the wreckage but could find no one to arrest. Carefully following the sailors, the police arrested eleven boys who had been beaten up on Carmelita Street, six more victims were arrested a few blocks further on, seven at Ford Boulevard. By morning, some 44 Mexican boys, all severely beaten, were under arrest."

Los Angeles Newspapers

VOL. LXXIII   Two Sections Section A   FIVE CENTS   SATURDAY, JUNE 5, 1943   ★★★ ⬦ NO. 61

Sailor 'Task Force' Hits L.A. Zooters

Send 5 to Hospital In Riots

Two hundred Navy men sailed up the Los Angeles River early today, and in a task force of taxicabs launched a reprisal attack on "zoot suit" gangsters in the East Los Angeles area.

The fleet men, who went methodically about applying fists and rope's ends to the gang terror problem, reported "all's well," following a night of wild rioting which

Riot Alarm Sent Out in Zoot War
Servicemen Strip and Beat 50;

Homes Invaded in Hunt for Pachucos

Ban on Freak Suits Studied by Councilmen

A proposal that it be made a jail offense to wear "zoot suits with reat pleats within the city limits of Los Angeles" was given

PACHUCAS STAND BY BEATEN PACHUCOS

Boys to Face 'Showup' Test

Nearly 300 to Parade Before Crime Victims at Old Central Jail Tonight

Grab a Zooter. Take off his pants and frock coat and tear them up or burn them. Trim the "Argentine ducktail" haircut that goes with the screwy costume....

Web of 'Zoot Suit' Gangs Spreads Over Entire L.A. Area

'Zooters'
Citizens Group Opens Probe of Riots

The Citizens Committee for Latin American Youth today began an investigation into the recent street fights between members of the so-called "zoot suiters" and members of the armed forces.

The committee asked the Council of Social Agencies to prepare a plan for increasing social activities for boys, especially in the areas where the street fights have occurred.

Army, Navy End War on Zooters After Wild Rioting

700 Boys In Latest Riots

More Than 100 Loosely Organized Mobs Now Active

...this routine was varied by an impromptu "tar-and-feather" job, effected with molasses and feathers....

ZOOT SUIT WAR INQUIRY ORDERED BY GOVERNOR

Continued from First Page   Twenty-five boys ranging from

INVESTIGATION LAUNCHED — State Senator Jack Tenney and R.E. Combs, investigator, question Alfred Valencia and Frank H. Tellez in County Jail as Tenney started inquiry yesterday to determine whether local zoot suit rioting was sponsored by Nazi agencies attempting to spread disunion within

The Mexican and Latino community was terrified. No one really understood why all this was taking place. They knew only that anyone with a brown face or an even slightly Latin appearance should not be out on the streets at night.

But if the rioting and bloodshed of June 5th and 6th were shocking, the events on the 7th of June were much worse. Again, the press played a key role.

11. Blood on the Streets

The newspapers reported that the Mexican zoot-suiters were busy planning massive counterattacks on the servicemen. "ZOOTERS PLANNING TO ATTACK MORE SERVICEMEN" was the headline of the *Daily News*. Another read: "ZOOTERS TO MASS 500 STRONG." To virtually guarantee a huge riot, the names of street corners were printed in the papers. These locations were said to be the places where the zooters would launch their counterattacks. Even the times were given.

Judging by the thousands of L.A. residents who turned out to join the servicemen in this rioting, the newspapers were successful. McWilliams wrote:

"On Monday evening, June 7, thousands of Angelenos in response to twelve hours advance notice in the press turned out for a mass lynching. Marching through the streets of downtown Los Angeles, a mob of several thousand soldiers, sailors, and civilians, proceeded to beat up every zoot suiter they could find. Pushing its way into the important motion picture theaters, the mob ordered the management to turn on the house lights and then ranged up and down the aisles dragging Mexicans out of their seats. Street cars were halted while Mexicans, and some Filipinos and Negroes, were jerked out of their seats and beaten with sadistic frenzy. If the victims wore zoot suits, they were stripped of their clothing and left naked or half-naked on the streets, bleeding and bruised. Proceeding down Main Street from First to Twelfth, the mob stopped on the edge of the Negro district. Learning that the Negroes had planned a warm reception for them, the mobsters turned back and marched through the Mexican East Side spreading panic and terror."

At last, however, the Chicanos fought back. Rudy Leyvas, brother of Henry, said to the *Los Angeles Times* as he thought back on the riots of 36 years ago:

"I was involved in the main one at 12th and Central. The sailors had been beating up zoot-suiters for about a week. The radio was even broadcasting when and where they were coming. This time we were going to be ready for them. All day we were just transferring guys from the neighborhoods into the city. The Black people loaned us their cars to use. We called 'em neighborhoods, not gangs. There was 38th Street, Adams, Clanton, Jug Town, Watts, Jardine. We rounded up at least 500 guys. Toward evening, we started hiding in alleys. Then we sent about 20 guys right out into the middle of the street as decoys. Then they came up in U.S. Navy trucks. There were many civilians too. There were at least as many of them as us. They started coming after the decoys, then we came out. They were surprised. It was the first time anybody was organized to fight back. Lots of people were hurt on both sides. I was about 15 then, and I had a baseball bat. I came out OK, but I know I hurt a lot of people."

Finally, at midnight on the 7th of June, the Navy declared L.A. off limits to all sailors. The shore patrol stepped in and the violence stopped almost immediately. Clearly these riots could have been stopped at any time the authorities had wished.

But it is clear today that neither the L.A. city government, the Navy, the police nor the residents of Los Angeles wanted the rioting to end. Indeed, the tone of the newspapers, and the popular sentiment in general, seem to have been to pat the sailors on the back for doing such a fine job "cleaning up the city." McWilliams writes that in the papers: "Huge half-page photographs, showing Mexican boys stripped of their clothes, cowering on the pavements, often bleeding profusely, surrounded by jeering mobs of men and women, appeared in all the Los Angeles papers." Other headlines included the following: "44 ZOOTERS ARRESTED IN ATTACKS ON SAILORS" and "ZOOT SUITERS LEARN LESSON IN FIGHT WITH SERVICEMEN."

The city was finally at peace. But it was an uneasy peace. Many residents of Los Angeles were glad that their "war heroes" had taken on the "evil Mexicans" and taught this "internal enemy" a lesson even though, at the same time, hundreds of thousands of Mexicans and Mexican Americans were not "internal enemies," but were serving with distinction in Europe and the Pacific as members of the Armed Services of the United States.

Inside the barrios the Mexican residents were no doubt wondering just what they had done to deserve the treatment they had received. Even though we know how wartime hysteria can change someone's sense of right and wrong, it seems that the racism was there all along. It took the war and the supportive prompting by the press to bring the feelings to the surface.

Conviction of 12 Reversed in Sleepy Lagoon Murder

Evidence Too Weak for Guilty Verdict, Appeal Court Says

Conviction of 12 youths for the "Sleepy Lagoon" murder of Jose Diaz two years ago was reversed yesterday by the District Court of Appeal in a 121-page decision written by Associate Justice Thomas P. White.

Justice White's opinion, which was concurred in by Presiding Justice John M. York and Justice William C. Doran, held that the evidence presented at the trial was insufficient to establish the guilt of the defendants.

The opinion stated that there was no evidence of racial prejudice in the proceedings during the 13-week trial of the youths.

22 Youths Indicted

Originally 22 defendants were indicted, but five were acquitted of murder charges and five were held on assault charges only. The appeal was instituted by the 12 convicted of murder.

One of the 12, Manuel Delgado, was paroled from the California Institute for Men at Chino last August, while the others were due to be released on parole later on varying dates.

Convicted of first-degree murder were Henry Leyvas, 19; Jose Ruiz, 17, and Robert Telles, 17.

The nine others, Gus Zamora, 20; Henry Ynostroza, 18; Victor R. Thompson, 20; Ysmale Parra, 23; Angel Padilla, 18; John Y. Matuz, 20; Jack Melendez, 21. Manuel Reyes, 18, and Delgado, 18 were found guilty of second degree murder.

Henry Leyvas

12. Justice Served

No story seems right without a happy ending. For the defendants in the Sleepy Lagoon case there was a somewhat happy ending. On October 4, 1944, after the defendants had spent approximately two years in jail, the district court of appeals reversed the guilty verdict in the Sleepy Lagoon trial. Judge Fricke and the jury were found to have been grossly prejudicial. The evidence presented in the case was declared totally insufficient and the general unlawful nature of the trial was criticized by the higher court. Henry Leyvas and his friends were finally able to come home to their families. Nothing, of course, could give them back the two years of their lives spent in jail.

13. End of a War — End of an Era

The war ended in a victory for the United States and its allies. But the cost has been estimated at between 40 and 60 million lives, both military and civilian. Additionally, a new and horrible weapon of war had been unleashed: the atomic bomb. And the seeds of the "Cold War" were planted. Only recently, after more than forty years, has it begun to thaw.

It had been during the pachuco era that we witnessed the beginning of Chicano gangs. Today we can wonder about the role of racism, discrimination and segregation in their development. After all, an entire generation of Mexican American youth has had its history, culture and language considered not worthy of serious attention by our educational system, thus driving a wedge between the youth and their families. Had that generation of Mexican Americans had equal educational attention, as well as equal recreational activities, would the gangs have begun at all? But once started, Chicano pachucos would fight each other for such seemingly insignificant matters as the right to write one's name on a wall. To this day, we have not been able to put a stop to the cycle of violence and revenge.

Although the 1940s saw the beginning of Mexican American gangs in large cities, the end of the war also brought about a positive beginning for Mexican Americans in the United States. It was with exceptional valor that Mexican Americans served in the United States military during World War II. Hundreds of thousands of them saw combat. In fact, the Mexican American soldiers were the most decorated of all American minority groups.

But the real changes began when the Chicano veterans came home. The World War II generation of Mexicans became activists for social change. They were not about to return to their previous status as second class citizens.

It soon became increasingly difficult for sellers of property to deny Mexican American veterans the right to buy homes and other property. As a result, Mexican Americans gradually found themselves able to use their G.I. Bill government loans to purchase homes outside of the traditional Mexican colonias and barrios. New housing developments gave these veterans a chance for a new life. For them the integration of the Southwest had finally begun.

As part of this process the segregation of Mexican school children in California began to end. In Orange County, California, the city of Westminster had traditionally maintained two separate schools; one for Whites and one for Mexicans. On March 2, 1945, Gonzalo Méndez filed suit in the federal courts against the school officials of Orange County. Two years later, in April of 1947, the Ninth Circuit Court upheld a ruling by Judge Paul J. McCormick that segregation of Mexican school children could not be permitted under California law as it violated the equal protection clause of the 14th amendment of the U.S. Constitution.

One year before that important ruling Mexican American residents of Chávez Ravine, near downtown Los Angeles, formed a civic organization to demand that the city provide their area with bus service. The voices of these 4,500 well-organized and angry citizens were heard and soon the buses were running in their area. This victory, however, was short-lived, for their activism could not save their homes ten years later when they were driven out and their barrio bulldozed so that Dodger Stadium could be built!

But other politically active Mexican Americans, mostly war veterans, began to organize. In Texas, for example, when the body of a deceased Mexican American war veteran was denied burial in a community cemetery, the American G.I. Forum was formed. Other organizations, such as the Latino Issues Forum, the Mexican American Political Association and the Community Service Organization (CSO) began to actively work and struggle toward a better life for the citizens of their communities. In 1949, the CSO was instrumental in getting the first Mexican American, Edward R. Roybal, elected to the Los Angeles City Council.

Clearly, a beginning had been made. Similar to the success of the Sleepy Lagoon Defense Committee, the groundwork was being laid for even more aggressive demands for equal justice and treatment. By the 1960s the full flowering of Mexican American activism for civil rights would occur, spearheaded by the resurgence of the farmworkers movement in California. This would lead to the birth of the Chicano Movement.

Chapter Six

THE ZOOT SUIT YEARS:

WRITING EXERCISES

On the following pages you will find the writing exercises for this chapter. For additional explanations, please see "To the Teacher" or "A Note to the Student" on **pages 21 and 26**. Teachers are urged to select the writing exercises most appropriate for their particular classes. Below are the writing exercises for Chapter Six:

1. Sentence or Fragment?

This exercise is designed to help students learn how to recognize incomplete sentences (fragments) and then rewrite them as complete sentences. The most important idea here is that a complete sentence makes sense when read alone. When rewriting the fragments, the students must make sure not to change history!

2. Short Answer Questions

Once a student knows what a sentence is (and is not!), he or she can answer brief questions with one or two sentence answers of their own. This list of questions also makes a good study or review sheet when preparing for a test.

3. Paragraph Questions

These questions require slightly longer answers which are to be written in paragraphs. A sample paragraph along with definitions of such terms as "topic sentence" is included in the writing exercises of **Chapter One**.

4. Clustering and Identification (ID) Items

ID Items refer to and identify important people, places and things. Clustering is a way of brainstorming ideas based on these ID Items. Once the cluster has been made, use it as a guide and write an ID Paragraph. A sample cluster and a sample ID Paragraph can be found in the writing exercises of **Chapter One**.

5. Essay Questions

Very broad or complicated questions require essays or compositions as answers. A sample essay and instructions on how to write essays, both as homework and during in-class essay exams, are provided in the writing exercises section of **Chapter Five**.

Sentence or Fragment?

DIRECTIONS:

A complete sentence makes sense when read all alone. An incomplete sentence or fragment does not. Some of the following are fragments. Some are perfectly correct, complete sentences. Rewrite the fragments and make them into good sentences. You may add words, get rid of words, or rearrange the words. **Just make sure that each fragment you rewrite is factually correct according to the chapter and makes good sense when you read it alone.** Leave the complete sentences alone.

EXAMPLE: *Discrimination not only suffered by Blacks in the U.S.*

Clearly this does not make sense when read alone. Although there is **no single correct way** to rewrite it, the following is much better:

Discrimination was suffered by Mexicans, as well as Blacks, in the U.S.

1. Luis Valdéz and the play *Zoot Suit.*
2. Japanese Americans during World War II.
3. The main events of the zoot suit years rarely appear in U.S. history books.
4. Discrimination which occurs often in many societies.
5. To prejudge or to be prejudiced.
6. Racism involves a sense of racial superiority.
7. Stereotyping or labeling certain ethnic or racial groups.
8. The most common cause for racism and stereotypes.
9. Pearl Harbor located in Hawaii.
10. The draft and women going to work in defense plants.
11. Relocation centers in the U.S.
12. The Great L.A. Air Raid.
13. War-time panic and hysteria in California.
14. The Pachucos and the first Chicano gangs.
15. Discrimination against Mexican Americans in Los Angeles.
16. Speaking Spanish in public schools.
17. The generation gap between the pachucos and their parents.
18. L.A. newspapers during World War II.
19. E. Duran Ayres's racial theories.
20. Henry Leyvas and the "38th St. gang."
21. In two nights 600 Mexicans were arrested in Los Angeles.

22. The Sleepy Lagoon trial.
23. The Sleepy Lagoon Defense Committee.
24. The Pachuco riots.
25. The lessons of the zoot suit years.

Short Answer Questions

DIRECTIONS:

Answer the following questions by writing one or two complete sentences for each. Be sure that each sentence you write:

a) Is factually correct and helps to answer the question.
b) Is a complete sentence, which means it makes sense when read alone.
c) Could be understood by someone who has not seen the question.
d) Begins with a capital letter and ends with a period.
e) Is completely in your own words.
f) Uses correct spelling and is neat.

EXAMPLE: *Why is Luis Valdéz important in the history of the Zoot Suit years?*

Luis Valdéz researched the history of the Mexican experience during wartime L.A. He presented the story in a play called Zoot Suit.

1. Define discrimination. Give an example.
2. What is the connection between racism and discrimination? How are they different?
3. Give an example of prejudice.
4. Why are all stereotypes false and insulting?
5. How can ignorance cause racism?
6. How did the U.S. get involved in World War II?
7. What was done to the Jews in Germany during World War II?
8. How was life in the U.S. affected by the war?
9. What effect did the Japanese submarine in Santa Barbara and the L.A. Air Raid have on the people of California?
10. What happened to Japanese Americans in the U.S. during World War II?
11. Give some brief examples of discrimination against Mexicans in L.A. in the 1940s.
12. Where and what was the "Sleepy Lagoon?"
13. What did the L.A. newspapers have to say about the pachucos?

14. Why was a special Grand Jury called in L.A. in 1942?
15. Why is E. Duran Ayres's theory an example of racism?
16. Why was Henry Leyvas arrested in August of 1942?
17. What was discriminatory about the 600 arrests on August 10 and 11, 1942?
18. Briefly, what was wrong with the Sleepy Lagoon trial?
19. Who was George Shibley?
20. Why was Alice Greenfield important?
21. What did the police do during the pachuco riots?
22. What role did the newspapers play in the riots?
23. What was the ruling of the District Court of Appeals in the Sleepy Lagoon case?
24. What was the role of Mexican American servicemen during World War II?
25. Why is the lawsuit of Gonzalo Méndez in 1945 so important?
26. What did Mexican residents in Chávez Ravine accomplish in 1947?
27. What did the CSO and Ed Roybal achieve in 1949?

Paragraph Questions

DIRECTIONS:

Answer the following questions by writing a good paragraph for each. Refer back to the sample paragraph on **page 47** for help. Be sure that each paragraph you write:

   a) Is factually correct, helps to answer the question and is in your own words.
   b) Looks like a proper paragraph (see sample).
   c) Has an underlined topic sentence at the beginning of the paragraph.
   d) Contains no fragments.
   e) Uses correct spelling and is neat.

1. Why is Luis Valdéz important in the history of the zoot suit years?
2. Why is it important to understand World War II in order to understand what happened to Mexicans at that time?
3. Define discrimination and give several examples.
4. How do we hurt ourselves by being prejudiced and thinking in stereotypes?
5. How were racism and discrimination involved in Hitler's Germany?

6. How did the blackouts, air raid drills, and the locking up of the Japanese Americans change the atmosphere of wartime Los Angeles?
7. Give some examples of discrimination practiced against Mexicans in L.A. in the 1940s.
8. How did the first Chicano gangs grow out of this discrimination as well as the pachucos' misunderstanding by their parents?
9. Describe the L.A. newspapers' coverage of the alleged Mexican crime wave.
10. What were the racial theories of E. Duran Ayres?
11. Why is it questionable that Henry Leyvas killed José Díaz?
12. Describe the Sleepy Lagoon trial.
13. Why was the Sleepy Lagoon Defense Committee so important?
14. Describe the Pachuco riots. Include the role of the police.
15. Could the riots have been stopped sooner? Why weren't they?
16. Why did the District Court of Appeals overturn the conviction of Henry Leyvas?
17. What are some lessons to be learned from these events?
18. How did Mexican Americans fight against racism and segregation after World War II?

Clustering and ID Items

DIRECTIONS:

Make clusters and/or ID paragraphs for the following identification items. While making your cluster or paragraph, ask yourself who or what the item is and why it is important in the history being studied. Refer to your book if necessary. A sample cluster and ID paragraph can be found **on page 49.**

racism	the Sleepy Lagoon
prejudice	E. Duran Ayres
stereotyping	Henry Leyvas
discrimination	the Sleepy Lagoon trial
Holocaust	the Sleepy Lagoon Defense Committee
Adolf Hitler	the Pachuco riots
Pearl Harbor	Carey McWilliams
Franklin D. Roosevelt	the first Chicano gangs
Great Los Angeles Air Raid	the Gonzalo Méndez Lawsuit - 1947
blackout drills	pachuco
relocation of Japanese Americans	drapes

Essay Questions

DIRECTIONS:

The following are essay questions on the content of this chapter. Before attempting to answer any questions, see **page 187** for directions on how to write an essay and **page 188** for a sample essay.

1. Write an essay defining racism, discrimination and stereotyping and give examples for each.
2. How do we hurt ourselves as individuals when we become racist and practice stereotyping and prejudice?
3. Why was World War II such a frightening experience to live through for U.S. citizens?
4. Compare the treatment of German Jews with the treatment of Americans of Japanese and Mexican descent during World War II.
5. Describe the beginning of the Mexican American gangs. Include the discrimination faced by the young Chicanos as well as the alienation from their families. Why is gang violence so hard to stop once it starts? What is the gang situation today?
6. Describe and explain the many examples of discrimination, as well as outright racism, against Mexicans and Mexican Americans in L.A. in the 1940s. Include schools, recreational facilities, entertainment, coverage in the press, police protection (or harassment) and treatment within the criminal justice system.
7. Describe the Sleepy Lagoon trial in terms of the defendants, the evidence, the judge, the verdict and the appeal.
8. Describe the Pachuco riots. Include how they started, the role of the newspapers, the role of the police, the involvement of the military, and why L.A. residents seemed pleased with what the servicemen were doing.
9. How was the reputation of the Mexican American community hurt by the events related in this chapter? What should Mexican Americans learn from these events? How can we make certain that events such as these never happen again?
10. Describe how Mexican Americans organized to fight against racism and segregation after World War II.

César Chávez
1927-1993

Chapter Seven

CESAR CHAVEZ
AND MEXICAN LABOR
IN THE SOUTHWEST

1.   A Traditional Labor Force

Historically, Mexican labor has provided the manpower necessary to build the American Southwest and to make it what it is today. Ever since the Mexican War ended in 1848 and the Southwest became a part of the United States, Americans have had to depend upon Mexican labor. In the 19th century the Mexicans helped build the railroads that connected the Southwest with the rest of the U.S. Mexican "charros" herded the livestock for the large ranches during the era of the "cattle barons." Mexican miners worked in the large gold, silver and copper mines for their American bosses. Characteristically, these Mexican workers often received less than a White person for performing the same work.

In the 20th century this southwestern pattern of Mexican labor continues. Most prevalent are the large numbers of Mexican people working in the productive agricultural fields in states such as California and Texas. Construction workers are often Mexican, as are factory workers, hotel employees, housekeepers, and maintenance personnel, such as janitors. Increasingly, it has been the jobs that White and African Americans will not do that are performed by Mexicans and Mexican Americans. Over time, this pattern of Mexican labor has seemed immune from any particular immigration law or regulation.

Mexican Americans need to know their historic contribution in the development of the Southwest and how indispensable their labor has been in its development. Throughout the years the Mexicans and Mexican Americans have struggled to avoid exploitation and to receive equal treatment in the workplace. Today, workers of Mexican descent appear to be more determined than ever to demand recognition and fair compensation for the work they perform.

2. Labor and Unions: The Basics

When speaking of the associations of workers for a particular purpose, it is necessary to define some of the basic terms. A labor union is a group of workers who have organized together for the purpose of protecting their labor rights. In the 19th century, in the U.S., such organizations of workers were illegal. The earliest attempts by workers to organize together to protect themselves against exploitation were seen by the courts as "criminal conspiracies to restrain trade." As such, most attempts by labor unions to do something about their low pay or poor working conditions were often met by force, violence and arrest by law enforcement agencies or by private security guards hired by employers.

A group of workers may get together in an organization because they are unhappy with some aspect of their work. Usually the workers will begin by drawing up a list of demands to present to their employer. If these are not granted they may decide to stop working in order to put more pressure on the employer to meet their demands. To stop work is to go "on strike." Usually, while on strike, workers make up "picket signs" which may announce their demands and complaints. Workers will then set up a "picket line" around their place of work. The workers want to prevent the use of replacements in their jobs, such as strike breakers, or "scabs." When management tries to break a strike by sending in scabs, strikes often become violent.

3. Mexican Labor: Early Organizing

Many people are unaware of the fact that Mexican labor organizing is not recent, but dates back into the 1800s. In his book, *North From Mexico,* Carey McWilliams has written that: "Mexican immigrants have been the pioneers of the trade union movement in the Southwest." In fact, the beginnings go far back into the history of the region. In 1893, for example, several hundred Mexican cowboys in Texas attempted to form a union to seek better pay. In 1903, 1,000 Mexican and Japanese sugar beet workers began a strike in California's Ventura County. Then in 1910, Mexican streetcar workers organized and began a famous strike in downtown Los Angeles which ultimately led to the dynamiting of the offices of the *Los Angeles Times.* In 1922, Mexican grape pickers in Fresno County, Califor-

An early Chicano wall painting from 1968, known as the *Del Rey Mural*, painted by Antonio Bernal. Here we see the legacy of Mexican and Mexican American dissent, tracing its roots from Villa and Zapata during the Mexican Revolution through Cesar Chávez and the United Farm Workers Movement.

PLATE **25**

Chicano mural entitled *Nuestra Experiencia en El Siglo XX (Our Experiences During the 20th Century)*, painted by Emigdio Vásquez in 1980. Pictured on this wall in a residential neighborhood of Anaheim, California, are some of the most important Chicano leaders of recent times. From left to right: Rubén Salazar, Corky González, Bert Corona, Cesar Chávez, and Reies López Tijerina.

PLATE **26**

One of the most important Chicana muralists is Judith Baca. In this impressive mural painted in 1990, Ms. Baca shows the vastness of the California Agribusiness Industry and the important role of Mexican farm workers. This mural, entitled *Pickers*, is one of the best examples of the artistic style and talent of the Chicano artists of Aztlan.

PLATE **27**

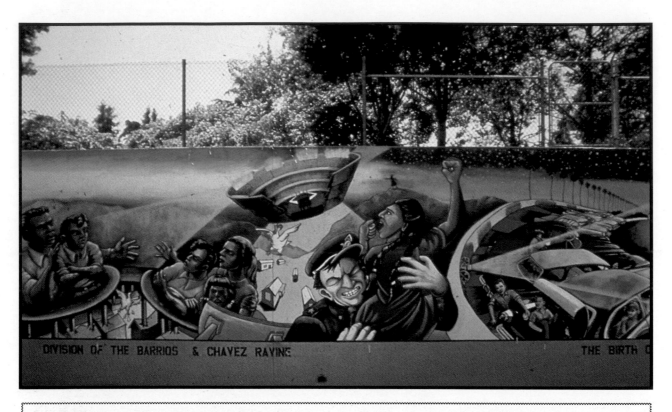

DIVISION OF THE BARRIOS & CHAVEZ RAVINE   THE BIRTH

Judith Baca has organized a major mural project in Los Angeles known as *The Great Wall*. Now over one-half mile long, the numerous murals in this series tell the story of California. Here we see the "Division of the Barrios & Chavez Ravine" which graphically shows the displacement of the Chicano community, Chavez Ravine, in order that Dodger Stadium could be built. Also playing a role in the division of Mexican neighborhoods is the construction of freeways. Have you ever noticed how few freeways are built through affluent neighborhoods?

PLATE **28**

This Chicano mural entitled *Geronimo* was painted in 1981 by Victor Ochoa. It commemorates the important Centro Cultural de La Raza located in Balboa Park in San Diego, California. Chicano cultural centers play an important role in the Chicano community. They create, disseminate, and preserve the art, history, dance, theater and music that has always been a part of the daily life of Mexican and Mexican American people.

PLATE **29**

This is one of the classic Chicano murals, important for its style, location and message. The title is *We Are Not a Minority*. It was painted in 1978 by the Congreso De Artistas Chicanos en Aztlan. The location of the mural is the Estrada Courts housing project in East Los Angeles. The residents of that housing project took it upon themselves to decorate their own homes with colorful, artistic and politically significant murals which became a very important feature of the Chicano movement. Current population statistics (as of 1992) indicate that the Latinos are indeed no longer a minority but, rather, the largest single ethnic group in areas such as metropolitan Los Angeles. Will the political power and control that should come with such numbers also be realized?

PLATE **30**

Painted in 1975, David Botello's *Read Between the Lines* is a masterpiece of Chicano art. Here we see a stylized protest against the mind control of American culture by television and other media. Seated in the foreground is a young Chicano reading a book entitled *The History of Mexico*. The message here is that a knowledge of his people's history will help him to learn who he really is.

PLATE **31**

Detail of Botello's *Read between the Lines* in which the artist pays tribute to the written form of communication and to the need to know one's own historical roots.

PLATE **32**

nia, began efforts to form a labor union. In 1927 the "Confederacion de Uniones Obreras Mexicanas" was formed in Southern California with over 3,000 workers in twenty local union chapters. A few years later, in June of 1933, over 7000 Mexicans went on strike in the berry, celery and onion fields in Los Angeles County. Up to that time, this was the largest strike by agricultural workers in California.

In almost all of the above cases the Mexican workers' attempts to organize were met with violence on the part of public and private law enforcement agencies. Equally often, the use of tear gas was followed by the deportation of the Mexican union leaders. Through it all there was no help forthcoming from the more established national labor unions such as the American Federation of Labor (AFL) or the Congress of Industrial Organizations (CIO). Both of these labor groups had clear policies which excluded Mexican workers from their membership.

Often, the Mexican workers were protesting discrimination on the job. They encountered separate and higher wage scales for Whites while they received less pay. It was also common to assign dead-end work to the Mexicans in which there was no opportunity for advancement. Equally often, Mexicans were assigned work with other Mexicans who worked only in one section of a given business.

During the 1930s organizing among Mexican and Mexican American workers had become stronger and stronger. World War II, however, scattered the people both into the armed services and other lines of work. The agricultural organizing was interrupted by the war and, therefore, it did not succeed in establishing a permanent and organized labor force. However, the effort was to surge again in the form of the first Mexican American labor union to actually succeed in altering not only working conditions, but also state and national labor legislation. This was accomplished by the United Farm Workers Union, led by César Chávez.

4. The California Agribusiness Empire

The story of César Chávez's UFW vs. the California Agribusiness Industry is similar to the story of David vs. Goliath. In terms of agricultural production California is the number one state in the nation. And agribusiness is the number one industry in California. Fruits, vegetables, nuts, rice, table and wine grapes all prosper in the fertile California soil and its ideal climate. California wines have become especially famous worldwide for their high quality. In addition, a wide array of splendid and healthy looking fresh fruits and vegetables are displayed in the supermarkets, both in California and in other states to which the produce is shipped. Increasingly, it has been by means of Mexican workers that this rich harvest has been produced.

The growers and owners of the huge farms and agricultural companies of California often preside over investments valued in the millions of dollars. In fact, each year the total profits from agribusiness in California exceed fifteen billion dollars! The huge profits have been aided by means of a steady stream of cheap labor. At one time or another most nationalities have been forced to provide farm labor in California in order to survive. The Chinese, Japanese, Blacks, "Okies," Filipinos, Mexicans, Mexican Americans, and most recently, Central Americans have all taken their turn in this most back-breaking labor. The Mexicans became the favorite of the California growers during World War II due to the "Bracero Program" in which thousands of Mexicans were imported to fill in for the man-power shortage created by the draft.

The *braceros* were Mexican workers legally brought to the United States. In reality, however, the Bracero Program only legalized what had been going on illegally for decades. Agribusiness was very happy with the program. Mexicans would work for much less than American citizens. And Mexicans had the reputation of being hard workers who got the job done well.

One would think that the end of World War II would have seen the end of the braceros. But the agribusiness industry was so influential that they were able to exert influence on the U.S. Congress to extend the Bracero Law until 1964, almost 20 years after the end of the war. Finally, a combination of severe exploitation, shocking living conditions and pressure from church and labor groups forced an end to the Bracero Program. It was at this point that César Chávez entered the historical picture.

5. Chávez: the Early Years

In 1927 César Chávez was born of Mexican parents in Yuma, Arizona. One of five children, his parents managed to get by on the profits from their small family farm. When the Chávez farm went broke, like so many others during the Great Depression, the Chávez family was forced to become migrant farm workers. Attending so many schools through the years that today he cannot even remember how many he went to, César was forced to drop out of school completely in the eighth grade to work full time to help support his family. Once, when he and his family had just arrived in Brawley, California, the family had to sleep in their car for three nights until they could earn enough money to rent a place to live. In 1939 the family lived in a tent for the entire winter because the parents did not make enough money from picking peas to be able to rent a house. Some days they did not even have enough money to pay for their transportation to and from the fields.

As a teenager and young adult, Chávez set out on his own to follow the crops as a migrant worker. Settling in Delano, California for a short time, Chávez met and married Helen Favela. Helen became one of César's closest fellow workers in his future work, in addition to raising their family of eight children.

As a young farm worker, Chávez joined many short-lived unions, walked many picket lines, and engaged in many strikes, mostly unsuccessful. All throughout the bracero years he struggled to survive as his parents had done.

6. Delano

Into the mid-sixties, after the end of the Bracero Program, there were many more Mexican American workers in the fields, but farm workers were not protected by any of the basic labor laws which covered all other U.S. workers. There was no effective union or organization of farm workers to protect their rights. One of the worst aspects of the situation was the system of farm labor contractors who would supply squads of workers for the growers. Like a middleman, the contractor would supply the workers for the growers and would also take a share of the workers' pay for himself. Although wages were higher than during the time of the braceros, they were still very low despite the fact that agribusiness was a multi-billion-dollar-a-year industry in California.

Because farm workers were not included under basic labor laws, they could legally receive less than the minimum wage. Nor were they entitled to overtime, unemployment or disability compensation. The National Labor Relations Act (NLRA) is the basic labor legislation of the U.S. Through the pressure of lobbyists, growers had convinced Congress that agribusiness should be exempted from any national labor legislation. They argued before Congress that crop failures due to droughts, floods or insects made their business too risky to be able to guarantee their workers a set wage. Therefore, when the National Labor Relations Board (NLRB) was established, agricultural workers were left out completely. Wages were so low (often only $1.00 an hour) that most farm workers had to follow the crops as migrant farm workers. They could not afford to put down any roots. The constant traveling severely affected the children of these migrant families. In the early sixties, 84% of all farm worker families in Delano earned less than $3,000 per year. The average income was $1,300 per year. In Fresno County, 80% of all welfare cases were from farm worker families. Their living conditions were also poor. Some migrants lived in their cars when they could not afford to rent a house or apartment. Some farm workers slept in "houses" they made for themselves from cardboard and plastic sheeting.

Delano, California, the scene of the famous Delano grape strike, is a small

Dolores Huerta

Dolores Huerta

As co-founder and first vice-president of the United Farm Workers, Dolores Huerta is one of the best-known women in the American labor movement, as well as the U.S. in general. The slightly-built 60-year-old mother of 11 and grandmother of 10 has been arrested 22 times, usually for disobeying growers' anti-picketing injunctions.

Huerta was born in New Mexico where her father was a miner, fieldworker, union acti- vist and state assemblyman. Her parents divorced when she was five and Dolores, with her brothers and sisters, was raised in Stockton, California. Her mother worked as a waitress and cannery worker, and later ran a 70-room hotel which often put up farm worker families for free.

After college Huerta taught grammar school. But she quit because, in her words, "I couldn't stand seeing kids come to class hungry and needing shoes. I thought I could do more by organizing farm workers than by trying to teach their hungry children."

In 1955 she joined the Community Service Organization, an Hispanic civil rights/civic action movement with a reputation as the largest and most militant group of its kind in the nation. Huerta battled segregation and police brutality, led voter registration drives, pushed for improved public services, and fought to enact new laws that provided state disability insu- rance to farm workers and old age benefits for non-citizens.

In 1962 Huerta and another CSO organizer, César Chávez, founded the National Farm Workers Association. By 1965 their infant union boasted 1,200 member-families, mostly His- panics. That year they joined a walkout against Central Valley grape producers that was start- ed by a mostly Filipino union sponsored by the AFL-CIO. It became known as the Delano Grape Strike.

Huerta negotiated contracts with growers, lobbied in Sacramento and Washington, D.C., organized field strikes, directed UFW boycotts and led farm worker campaigns for polit- ical candidates. She negotiated the Union's first contract with a grape grower, faced down burly company goons on tense picketlines and was arrested nearly two dozen times, often for violating anti-strike court orders. She spoke out early and often against toxic pesticides that threaten farm workers and consumers.

"Dolores is totally fearless, both mentally and physically," César Chávez once re- marked.

La Causa—the farm workers' cause—came first, even during pregnancies. She changed diapers between organizing meetings and nursed babies during breaks in negotiations. Huer- ta's 11 children sometimes lived with friends or supporters, ate donated food, and coped with frequent moves.

For more than 20 years Dolores Huerta has been one of the UFW's most visible sym- bols. Senator Robert Kennedy acknowledged her help in winning the 1968 California Demo- cratic Primary movements before he was shot in Los Angeles. She was co-chair—with now Assembly Speaker Willie Brown and Assemblyman John Burton—of the California delegation to the 1972 Democratic Convention.

In 1988, Huerta was passing out news releases on the UFW's current grape boycott out- side San Francisco's St. Francis Hotel—where then Vice-President Bush was speaking—when she was battered to the pavement by baton-wielding police officers. She underwent emergen- cy surgery to remove a ruptured spleen and repair three broken ribs.

Dolores Huerta still works long hours for the farm workers' union she founded and nurtured. Many days find her in cities across North America, promoting the grape boycott and campaigning against the pesticide poisoning of farm workers and consumers.

central California town in the San Joaquin Valley which owes its existence to the vineyards of the neighboring growers. Mexican American workers and their families were not treated fairly in Delano, for in the years before the grape strike, César Chávez himself was once arrested for sitting in the "Anglo Only" section of a Delano movie theater. Despite all these obvious injustices, Delano growers maintained that their workers were happy with the way things were and that it was "outside agitators and troublemakers" like Chávez who were the problem.

7. The Birth of the UFW

The United Farm Workers Union was first known as the National Farm Workers' Association, started by Chávez in Delano, California in 1962. No one can tell the story of how it all began better than Chávez himself:

"By hand, I drew a map of all the towns between Arvin and Stockton, 86 of them, including farm labor camps — and decided to hit them all. For six months I traveled around planting an idea. We had a simple questionnaire, a little card with space for name, address, and how much the worker thought he ought to be paid. My wife mimeographed them and we took our kids for two or three-day jaunts to these towns, distributing the cards door-to-door and to camps and groceries. Some 80,000 cards were sent back from eight Valley counties. I got a lot of contacts that way, but I was shocked at the wages the people were asking. The growers were paying a dollar and a dollar fifteen and maybe ninety-five percent of the people thought they should be getting only one twenty-five an hour. Some people scribbled messages on the cards like: 'I hope to God we win' or 'Do you think we can win?' or 'I'd like to know more.' So I separated out the cards with penciled notes, got in my car, and went to those people."

His wife, Helen, worked in the fields while César traveled the San Joaquin Valley. But money was tight, as always, and Chávez had to take a job digging irrigation ditches on Sundays. The first year was very tough and discouraging but some progress was being made. By means of the contacts Chávez had made, he would soon hear if a worker or group had been mistreated. As Chávez said: "If I thought someone had been cheated, I'd raise hell; you always knew a friendly priest who would pay a call, a friendly lawyer who would write a letter threatening a lawsuit." By this time (1965) Chávez figured that by 1968 he would perhaps be organized enough to take on the power of the Delano grape growers. Unfortunately, the first big strike came three years ahead of schedule.

In the spring of 1965, Filipino grape pickers, members of the small Agricultural Workers Organizing Committee (AWOC), walked off their jobs demanding higher wages. Larry Itliong, Filipino leader of the AWOC, asked Chávez for help because the grower was calling in lots of Mexican "scab" labor to break the strike.

Although Chávez knew at this time that his own workers' organization was not fully ready, he also felt it would be wrong not to help the Filipinos. He and his union took a vote and decided to go on strike in support of the AWOC. Because overall there were many more Mexican and Spanish speaking farm workers in Delano, leadership of the strike soon fell to Chávez. This is how the historic Delano grape strike of 1965 began.

One reason why this strike brought César Chávez, and the problems of the Mexican Americans, to the attention of the U.S. was the way in which Chávez went about organizing this strike. From the very beginning Chávez was certain that without the help of powerful outside groups, as well as the support of the U.S. as a whole, this strike would fail as had all other similar strikes in the past. Chávez thought that what was at stake was a moral issue (a question of basic right and wrong). If he could generate enough publicity throughout the entire nation he could get enough powerful and influential outside help to stand a good chance of winning.

8. The Strike Itself

At first, Chávez appealed to the Catholic Church for help. However, none of the priests in Delano cared to get involved with the striking farm workers. They thought it was not the duty of a church to deal with economic and political issues. But other priests actively supported the UFW. The priests volunteered their time, helped organize the workers and lent moral support to the cause. Soon church groups from all over the U.S. began to hear of the poverty of the striking farm workers. In the tradition of church charity, food and clothing drives were organized and donations came pouring into Delano from all over the nation. The more publicity Chávez generated, the more donations the UFW received. The support of churches and synagogues throughout the U.S. was vital because when workers are on strike they are not being paid. Unlike other more established unions the UFW had no fund of accumulated union dues to help its members during the strike period.

The more established labor unions also came to the aid of the farm workers. Lending support, mostly in the form of money, food and clothing donations, their help and aid helped to keep the strike going. Especially helpful was Walter Reuther, the president of the United Auto Workers (UAW), who came to Delano, personally, to give Chávez a check for $5,000 and the promise of an equal amount each month for the remainder of the strike. Of all the outside help the UFW received, this financial support was most important because it allowed Chávez to establish support services for his union members. Meanwhile, the growers were vowing to hold out as long as possible, clearly hoping that when the workers went completely broke they would forget about their demands and return to work.

The growers began to threaten the striking workers with being "blackballed." They told the workers that unless they came back to work they would never be able to get a job in Delano again. But despite the obvious financial pressures, the unity of the strike held. Due to the inspirational leadership of Chávez and his associates, the farm workers stuck together. The old union saying "United we stand, divided we fall" was never more true. Poor by union standards, and even more poverty stricken as individuals, the only thing these farm workers had going for them was their common desire to remain united so as to ensure a better life for themselves and a better future for their children.

Throughout its history the strike continued to be a David vs. Goliath confrontation. The grape growers of Delano were representatives of the wealthiest industry in the richest state in the U.S. Chávez, however, represented the poorest group of workers in the nation. They were officially second-class workers, whether they were American citizens or not. They had been specifically denied the rights of other workers by U.S. laws and, as a result, they had no financial resources whatsoever. What was to prove instrumental, however, was their feeling that what they were doing was right, was long overdue and would prevent their children from having to suffer as they had. Their other key advantage was their method of organization which called out for support from a country that was coming to the aid of other progressive causes, such as the Black Civil Rights Movement and the Peace Movement against the war in Vietnam.

Relations between the police and the strikers were tense. Any striker who set foot in the fields would be arrested immediately by the Delano police for trespassing. Chávez contended that his strikers must be given access to the fields as other unions are given access to their work place. The growers did not agree and continued to insist that Chávez's people were scaring and intimidating workers and even threatening them with violence if they did not join the strike.

In March 1966, Senator Robert F. Kennedy came to Delano with a U.S. Senate Subcommittee investigating the situation of the farm workers and the charges of violence by the union, the police and the growers. Senator Kennedy, in open hearings, at one point was asking Kern County Sheriff Roy Galen about the arrest of some striking farm workers:

Kennedy: *What did you charge them with?*

Gaylen: Violation of, uh, unlawful assembly.

Kennedy: *I think that's most interesting. Who told you they were going to riot?*

Gaylen: The men right out in the fields that they were talking to said if you don't get them out of here we're going to cut their hearts out. So rather than let them get cut, we removed the cause.

Kennedy: *That's the most interesting concept, I think. How can you arrest someone if they haven't violated the law?*

Gaylen: They were ready to violate the law.

Kennedy: *Can I suggest that during the noon recess the Sheriff and the District Attorney read the Constitution of the United States?*

But despite public relations successes, such as this, the strike wore on and the growers held out. They refused to grant the union's demand for higher wages and better working conditions. They also flatly refused to agree that their workers wanted or even needed a union. They refused to sit down and negotiate with César Chávez. Seeing that something dramatic was needed, Chávez and his associates decided that they would march the 280 miles from Delano to the California State Capital of Sacramento. They would march, they said, to present their case in person to the governor of California, Edmund G. Brown. As they walked they picked up more and more supporters along the way. When they reached Sacramento they were told the governor was not there. Nevertheless, Chávez was pleased with the televised publicity they received.

When the march to Sacramento had ended and the strike still dragged on, Chávez got the idea that was to prove to be the most powerful weapon of the UFW: the grape boycott (to boycott something means to avoid it). Chávez publicized the names of the wine companies that were holding out. He began to ask everyone in the United States not to buy any wines from these companies. He asked people not to buy table grapes. Picket lines began to appear at supermarkets across the nation as shoppers were asked to boycott grapes in support of Chávez and the UFW. As people throughout the United States began to learn of the conditions the farm workers worked and lived in, the boycott began to have an effect.

Sales of the boycotted wines and of all table grapes went down dramatically. The growers lost money, lots of money. The dock workers union helped by refusing to load or unload any crates of grapes which did not have the UFW label, in the name of union solidarity. This served to help publicize the UFW strike further.

But the strike went on even with the boycott. Both sides held firm. Anger and hatred grew on both sides. Reports of violence, both by the strikers and the

During the famous Delano Grape Strike, **César Chávez** wanted to inform as many people as possible about his efforts to improve the lot of the farmworkers. This would help to ensure greater success for the boycott of non-UFW picked grapes. In 1966, Chávez and his followers decided to march 280 miles, from Delano to Sacramento, the state capital. Here we see them on their way.

Eventually, the efforts of **César Chávez** and the farmworkers became well-known not only in the United States and Mexico, but internationally as well. Here we see him in New York City, during 1982, with some of his followers promoting another boycott of non-union produce. For Chávez the struggle had never stopped!

growers' private security guards, spread.

Chávez was an admirer of the nonviolent philosophies of Gandhi in India and Martin Luther King, Jr. in the Civil Rights Movement. Chávez feared that if the strike became violent, all that the farmworkers had worked for might be lost. Again he decided that something new was called for. He decided that he would begin a fast and would not eat until all the violence on both sides stopped. As the days passed and Chávez grew weaker and weaker, people on both sides began to see that he was sincere in his demand for nonviolence and an end to the strike. Then on March 10, 1968, after 25 days with only water, Chávez ended his fast. Barely able to walk, he was helped to a platform to address a waiting crowd that included Senator Kennedy. He managed to give a stirring speech that day, calling for an end to the violence in the fields and for a victory for the farm workers.

At last, because of the effectiveness of the boycott, one of the largest growers agreed to hold a union election at his farm. The workers voted for whether or not they wanted to be represented by the UFW. Watched by the police, the news media and indeed the entire nation, the election was held. When the votes were counted the UFW had won. It was a small first victory. Some of the other growers began to come around and other elections were held.

The UFW won all of these early elections and some contracts calling for higher wages and better working conditions were signed. Other elections were held and soon it was just a matter of time until all the grape growers in Delano would give in. On the 29th of July, 1970, Chávez signed a contract with John Guimarra, a representative of the remaining growers. The long awaited victory of the UFW had been won, nearly five long years after that first small strike by the Filipino grape pickers. An extremely poor group of workers had taken on representatives of the largest industry in California and had won.

9. The Impact of the Delano Huelga

The most immediate impact of the UFW's victory came by way of the contracts the farmworkers were able to negotiate with particular growers. For once the farmworkers could negotiate for themselves, thereby eliminating the farm labor contractors' hated practice of acting as middlemen and skimming off money which should have gone to the workers themselves.

As a result of the new contracts, wages went up almost immediately. Working conditions improved. As part of the negotiations the farmworkers now had fresh drinking water in the fields, sanitary restrooms, rest periods and medical plans.

Another important result of the strike was seen at the national level. Final-

A new union comprised mostly of Mexican, Mexican American and Latino workers is known as Justice for Janitors. In 1991 this group conducted some highly organized strikes in the Beverly Hills area of Los Angeles. They were protesting very low wages and no medical insurance. Despite a violent attack by the Los Angeles Police Department, this organization was able to win a new and much better contract with the owners of the high rise office buildings they maintain. This and other similar groups signify a greater activism on the part of Mexican workers in the United States and a willingness to stand up for their labor rights. This action also highlights the vital services they provide to the community.

ly, the National Labor Relations Act was amended to include farmworkers. No longer would they be the second-class citizens of American labor. All basic labor rights now applied to the farmworker. This was clearly a major victory and the 1970s and 1980s were better times for California farmworkers. The State of California passed a farm labor review law which called for an agricultural review board which was to make regular inspections of the working conditions in the fields.

But the struggle has not ended there. For many years Chávez and the UFW have been alerting Californians about the dangers of chemical pesticides. The chemicals are said to be harmful to the health of agricultural workers who come in contact with them in the fields. It has been reported that increasing numbers of farmworkers and their children are suffering from serious illnesses and diseases which seem to be caused by agricultural insecticides used to produce those beautiful and healthy-looking fruits and vegetables grown in California.

The well-known environmental concerns of Californians, as well as the desire of many to consume natural foods, would seem to make Chávez's message especially timely in the 1990s. With this in mind, Chávez had been urging another boycott of grapes and certain supermarket chains which continue to sell farm products which the UFW believes to be unsafe for public consumption.

Clearly the achievements of the UFW have been pioneering and historic, even though the increased immigration, legal and illegal, of Mexican and Central American workers has undercut the union's ability to effectively organize a larger membership. The California farmworkers movement sparked a broader crusade by Mexicans and Mexican Americans which came to be known as the Chicano Movement. The Chávez union also provided a successful model for other Latino labor associations in the Southwest.

10. Justice for Mexican Workers

The face of the American Southwest is rapidly changing. Increased Mexican and Central American immigration, a large Latino birthrate, improved nutrition and health care, all are contributing to a population increase among Latinos in this area of the United States.

In Los Angeles, one of the most active and recently successful labor unions is known as "Justice for Janitors." These workers, who provide the maintenance for the large high-rise buildings of the largest city of the U.S., assert that they are tired of working for the minimum wage with no health benefits. In emotional and well-organized strikes they recently captured the attention of the rich and powerful who employ them. Despite violent reaction by the L.A. Police Department to their peaceful rally in front of some office towers in Beverly Hills, the janitors have won salary increases and improved medical benefits. The janitors now vow to continue their struggle at other similar work locations.

Another job dispute is currently underway between the County of Los Angeles and its public service employees. Recently, walkouts by these workers caused chaos at county offices where residents go to receive public assistance. Many of the county public employees are Latinos, as are their young bilingual leaders. Clearly the economy of the Southwest is vulnerable to strikes and other job actions by organized Latino workers.

Of the clothes that are made in the U.S., most are sewn by Latino garment workers. Most of the service industry employees in large hotels and restaurants are Latinos. Whether they are in this nation legally or not, the vast majority of these workers are underpaid and many work in unsafe or unhealthy conditions. We may be on the verge of an explosion of labor agitation by the very people who keep the economy running. The new, younger generation of Latino workers and their leaders clearly understand the importance of their role in the American economy. They see no reason why the vital services they provide should not be compensated with more equality as compared to others in the U.S. labor force.

Their leaders have organized them well and have demonstrated an increasing willingness to engage in strikes in order to achieve what they see as reasonable demands in the work place: decent wages, medical care and other benefits which will provide a better life for them and for their children. Many today believe that such equity is long overdue because of the second-class role the Mexican and Mexican American workers have traditionally had in the history of the United States.

Finally, many prominent Mexican intellectuals, such as Jorge Castañeda, have made a connection between the history of Mexican labor in the U.S. and the current debate over a "free trade" agreement between the two countries. The Mexicans have argued that if U.S. products are to enter Mexico freely, then Mexican labor ought to freely enter the U.S. where their services are needed. This would mean an historic re-evaluation of the border as we know it. Whatever the outcome, the truth is that, since 1848 to the present day, the border has been invisible for the northern employers of Mexican workers. A more open border policy would recognize publicly what exists today in reality.

Los Angeles Times Photo

Ana Navarette

Ana Navarette is one of the most important organizers of the Service Employees International Union's "Justice for Janitors" movement. Ana frequently gets the toughest jobs, like sneaking into buildings to organize unrepresented workers, even when the security guards are trying to keep her out. As a result of this union's aggressive and unorthodox tactics, tremendous gains have been made in this primarily Latino union movement.

Ana Navarette is part of a labor movement in the Southwest United States which was begun by Mexican and Mexican American laborers as early as 1870, which flowered during the powerful labor movement among Mexican Americans during the 1920s and 1930s and, after considerable success, moved from the agricultural fields to the urban centers of the West. This movement was interrupted by deportations of Mexicans and Mexican Americans and World War II, after which it returned back to the agricultural fields. From there it peaked again during the UFW's organizing activities in the 1960s. Now, in the present, as it did in the 1930s, the quest for decent labor conditions (in the form of "Justice for Janitors") among Latinos moves again to the urban centers of the West. Currently in 1993 this movement is meeting with considerable success. Some people believe that this success in labor is triggering an anti-immigrant backlash.

Chapter Seven

CESAR CHAVEZ AND MEXICAN LABOR:

WRITING EXERCISES

On the following pages you will find the writing exercises for this chapter. For additional explanations, please see "To the Teacher" or "A Note to the Student" on **pages 21 and 26**. Teachers are urged to select the writing exercises most appropriate for their particular classes. Below are the writing exercises for Chapter Seven:

1. Sentence or Fragment?

This exercise is designed to help students learn how to recognize incomplete sentences (fragments) and then rewrite them as complete sentences. The most important idea here is that a complete sentence makes sense when read alone. When rewriting the fragments, the students must make sure not to change history!

2. Short Answer Questions

Once a student knows what a sentence is (and is not!), he or she can answer brief questions with one or two sentence answers of their own. This list of questions also makes a good study or review sheet when preparing for a test.

3. Paragraph Questions

These questions require slightly longer answers which are to be written in paragraphs. A sample paragraph along with definitions of such terms as "topic sentence" is included in the writing exercises of **Chapter One**.

4. Clustering and Identification (ID) Items

ID Items refer to and identify important pcoplc, places and things. Clustering is a way of brainstorming ideas based on these ID Items. Once the cluster has been made, use it as a guide and write an ID Paragraph. A sample cluster and a sample ID Paragraph can be found in the writing exercises of **Chapter One**.

5. Essay Questions

Very broad or complicated questions require essays or compositions as answers. A sample essay and instructions on how to write essays, both as homework and during in-class essay exams, are provided in the writing exercises section of **Chapter Five**.

Sentence or Fragment?

DIRECTIONS:

A complete sentence makes sense when read all alone. An incomplete sentence or fragment does not. Some of the following are fragments. Some are perfectly correct, complete sentences. Rewrite the fragments and make them into good sentences. You may add words, get rid of words, or rearrange the words. **Just make sure that each fragment you rewrite is factually correct according to the chapter and makes good sense when you read it alone.** Leave the complete sentences alone.

EXAMPLE: *Traditionally, Mexican labor in the United States.*

Clearly this does not make sense when read alone. Although there is **no single correct way** to rewrite it, the following is much better:

Traditionally, Mexican labor has been very important in building the United States.

1. In the 19th century the Mexicans and the railroads.
2. Mexican "charros" who worked for American ranchers.
3. Mexican miners worked in large gold, silver and copper mines in the United States.
4. Mexican workers, who usually received less pay for the same work.
5. Service employees such as janitors, restaurant workers.
6. Mexican and Central American agricultural workers.
7. A labor union is when workers organize to protect their employment rights.
8. A strike or work stoppage.
9. Picket lines and "scabs" or strike breakers.
10. The California agribusiness industry.
11. The "Mexican Bracero Program" began during World War II.
12. César Chávez was born in Yuma, Arizona in 1927.
13. The National Labor Relations Act and farmworkers.
14. The Delano Grape Strike of 1965.
15. Walter Reuther of the United Auto Workers Union.
16. Senator Robert F. Kennedy and Sheriff Roy Gaylen.
17. The farmworkers' march from Delano to Sacramento.
18. The UFW decided to call for a national boycott of grapes.
19. César Chávez's fast, or hunger strike.

20. The NLRA was amended to protect farmworkers.
21. Farmworkers today face the peril of agricultural pesticides.
22. The Justice for Janitors movement.
23. Mexican and Central American labor is vital to the economy of the American Southwest.
24. More and more Latino workers in the Southwest are organizing.
25. The vast majority of Latino workers in the U.S. are underpaid.

Short Answer Questions

DIRECTIONS:

Answer the following questions by writing one or two complete sentences for each. Be sure that each sentence you write:

a) Is factually correct and helps to answer the question.
b) Is a complete sentence, which means it makes sense when read alone.
c) Could be understood by someone who has not seen the question.
d) Begins with a capital letter and ends with a period.
e) Is completely in your own words.
f) Uses correct spelling and is neat.

EXAMPLE: *What jobs did Mexicans do in the U.S. in the 19th century?*

Mexicans worked as miners, as railroad workers, and as "charros" or cowboys.

1. What kinds of jobs do Mexican workers do in the U.S. now?
2. What is the definition of a labor union?
3. What is a strike?
4. Why do most workers go on strike?
5. What do "scabs" do during a strike?
6. What was the policy of the AFL or CIO toward Mexican workers?
7. How were Mexican workers segregated while on the job?
8. Give some examples of crops grown in California.
9. What is the reputation of California wines?
10. What was the purpose of the "Bracero Program?"
11. Why did the "Bracero Program" last so long after the end of World War II?

12. What was César Chávez's educational experience?
13. Why did farmworkers not have the same rights as other workers?
14. When did César Chávez first begin to organize farmworkers?
15. Why did Chávez become the leader of the Delano grape strike?
16. What type of donations did the UFW receive?
17. Why was the help of the UAW especially important?
18. Why did Senator Kennedy tell the sheriff to read the Constitution?
19. Why did the UFW decide to march to Sacramento?
20. What was the purpose of the grape boycott?
21. Why did Chávez go on a twenty-five day fast?
22. What ended the Delano grape strike?
23. How was the NLRA changed after the Delano strike?
24. What is Chávez's message concerning pesticides?
25. What are some other Latino labor unions that are active today?

Paragraph Questions

DIRECTIONS:

Answer the following questions by writing a good paragraph for each. Refer back to the sample paragraph on **page 47** for help. Be sure that each paragraph you write:

a) Is factually correct, helps to answer the question and is in your own words.
b) Looks like a proper paragraph (see sample).
c) Has an underlined topic sentence at the beginning of the paragraph.
d) Contains no fragments.
e) Uses correct spelling and is neat.

1. Describe the various jobs Mexican labor performed in the U.S. during the 19th century.
2. Why are Mexican workers, documented or not, vital to the economy of the U.S. Southwest?
3. What happens during a typical labor strike?
4. List some of the earliest attempts of Mexicans to organize labor unions or go on strike.
5. How were Mexicans discriminated against while on the job?
6. Why has the California agribusiness industry been so profitable?
7. Describe the causes and results of the "Bracero Program."

8. Write a paragraph describing César Chávez's youth.
9. What were the working conditions for farmworkers (even American citizens) in California **before** 1965?
10. Describe how Chávez first began to organize farmworkers in the Sixties.
11. What role did Dolores Huerta play in organizing the farmworkers?
12. What were the UFW's demands in the Delano strike?
13. Why was outside help and publicity especially important to the UFW during the Delano strike?
14. Describe the outside help given to the UFW during the Delano strike.
15. What was the purpose of the grape boycott?
16. Why did Chávez go on a fast?
17. How did the lives of farmworkers change after the Delano strike ended?
18. Why was César Chávez concerned about pesticides?
19. What is the Justice for Janitors organization?
20. What types of jobs do Mexican workers do in the U.S. now?
21. What do Dolores Huerta and Ana Navarette have in common?

Clustering and ID Items

DIRECTIONS:

Make clusters and/or ID paragraphs for the following identification items. While making your cluster or paragraph, ask yourself who or what the item is and why it is important in the history being studied. Refer to your book if necessary. A sample cluster and ID paragraph can be found on **page 49**.

Mexican labor unions	NLRA
Mexican workers in the U.S. today	UFW
job discrimination vs. Mexican workers	Delano Grape Strike
California Agribusiness industry	Grape Boycott
the "Bracero Program"	pesticides
César Chávez	Justice for Janitors
Dolores Huerta	Ana Navarette

Essay Questions

DIRECTIONS:

The following are essay questions on the content of this chapter. Before attempting to answer any questions, see **page 187** for directions on how to write an essay and **page 188** for a sample essay.

1. Write an essay describing the role of Mexican labor in the U.S. in terms of the following industries: farm labor, factory work, and service occupations.
2. Why and how do workers organize themselves into unions? Why were unions illegal at first? What usually occurs during strikes? Include examples of current or recent strikes.
3. Describe the California agribusiness industry. Include: crops, profits, labor force, the situation with water, and current debates over pesticides.
4. Write a biographical essay about César Chávez.
5. Describe the Delano grape strike. What were the workers fighting for? What were their tactics? Why was publicity and the boycott so important? What were the short term and long term results?
6. Why are Mexican workers, documented or not, so vital to the economy of the Southwest? What types of jobs do they perform today? How are they discriminated against? Give examples of recent organizing attempts.

Chicano Studies Library
University of California, Berkeley

Tonatiuh-Quinto Sol International, Inc.
Since 1967
Publishers of Chicano Literature
Berkeley, California

Chicano/Latino Literary Contest
University of California,
Irvine

Centro Cultural
de la Raza
San Diego,
California

M.A.L.D.E.F.
Mexican American Legal
Defense and Education Fund
California, Texas,
Illinois, Washington, D.C.

El Teatro Campesino
San Juan Bautista,
California

United Farm Workers
Keene, California

Mexican American Commission
State of Nebraska

Detroit, Michican

Chicano Studies
University of Texas,
El Paso

1981

**NATIONAL
HISPANIC
UNIVERSITY**
San José, California

Pueblo, Colorado

Chapter Eight

LOS CHICANOS

1. A Decade of More Changes

In the United States, and much of the world, the 1960s were a turbulent decade. It seemed that institutions were being challenged everywhere and long-established norms of behavior were rapidly changing. In the U.S. specifically, the Sixties saw major societal movements toward the new. The Black crusade for civil rights was in full swing under the inspirational leadership of such legendary figures as Martin Luther King, Jr. and Malcolm X. The anti-Vietnam War peace campaign saw marches and street demonstrations of tens of thousands of people. There were protests against the draft and in favor of womens' liberation. A new "counter-culture" among America's young people was born.

It was also in the 1960s that the voices of Mexican Americans for change began to enter the national consciousness. The young farmworkers who supported César Chávez's union saw to it that America learned who they were. The call by César Chávez for a national grape boycott brought the plight of the campesinos and also of the Mexicans as a whole to the attention of the U.S. But these young protesters had adopted a different name for themselves. Just as the African Americans marching and protesting in places like Birmingham and Selma, Alabama, preferred to call themselves "Black," the followers of Chávez proudly proclaimed themselves "Chicanos." What was born in the midst of this decade of upheaval was a mass movement by Americans of Mexican descent: "The Chicano Movement of Aztlan."

2. Phase One: Viva la Raza and Chicano Power

Initially, the Chicano Movement emulated the Black Civil Rights struggle and the anti-Vietnam War protests in tactics and style. The idea was to organize, mobilize, confront the authorities, march, demonstrate, occupy, and be as militant as necessary. Even violence was not totally disavowed by some groups as long as it was being used for "la causa."

In New Mexico one of the legendary leaders of the early Chicano struggle was Reies López Tijerina. He had grown up the son of a share cropper whose grandfather had been hung by Texas Rangers so that a White farmer could seize his farmland. In New Mexico, Tijerina began an exhaustive search through the old Spanish land grants in the area. This was an attempt to establish a claim for the return of these lands to their original Mexican owners. Tijerina's organization, the Alianza Federal de Mercedes, contested Mexican Americans' historic loss of vital lands after the Treaty of Guadalupe Hidalgo. Tijerina claimed that, as with the treaties made with the American Indians, the promises made to the Mexicans had also been broken.

Tijerina's followers consistently claimed it was necessary to arm themselves for protection against New Mexican law enforcement authorities. The police viewed Tijerina as a dangerous militant who was inciting the Mexican and Indian people of New Mexico for an unjust cause. The climactic moment came when Tijerina and his followers occupied the county courthouse at Tierra Amarilla, New Mexico, in 1966 and performed a citizen's arrest of the local district attorney, charging him with not enforcing the laws according to the original land grants. A gun battle ensued between Tijerina's followers and the police. Though acquitted of charges in this particular case, Tijerina subsequently was sent to prison on another charge.

Two years after Tijerina's raid at Tierra Amarilla, the scene would shift from the rural to the urban for the next major manifestation of the Chicano Movement. In 1968 Chicano students in East Los Angeles had become convinced that they were receiving an inferior education in the L.A. Unified School District. A group of students at Lincoln High School had taken a trip, as part of a student exchange program, to a predominantly White school in the San Fernando Valley. They came away from this experience convinced they were being denied the educational benefits the White students received. In truth, the educational conditions for Mexican American students in the 1960s were not good. In most schools in the Southwest male Mexican American students were encouraged to take industrial arts or shop classes. The female students were guided into home education classes. The very small numbers of Chicano college students at this time bear out the results of low expectations on the part of educators.

These students at Lincoln told their teacher, Sal Castro, that they were very upset about what they had seen and wanted to "blow out." Castro told them not to walk out. He told them to organize, establish clear demands, make contacts with other schools, and to plan speeches and other peaceful demonstrations.

Soon there was a network of concerned Chicano students at the predominantly Chicano high schools in East Los Angeles: Garfield, Roosevelt, Wilson and Lincoln. The students prepared a list of demands: they wanted to learn Mexican history in their classes; they wanted to read Mexican and Mexican American literature; they wanted more Mexican American teachers and administrators; they wanted better school facilities and equipment like the White schools; and, most important, they wanted an education that stressed college preparation rather than the industrial trades.

Just before the students were to present their demands to the board of education, the principal at Wilson High School canceled a performance of a play that the student body was eagerly anticipating. At this point all of the pent up activism that had been circulating throughout the East Los Angeles schools exploded. To protest the cancellation of the play, the students at Wilson spontaneously decided to walk out of school.

When word of Wilson's walkout reached the other schools in the area, one-by-one the student bodies chose also to walk out in unity with the kids from Wilson. Soon the focus of the walkouts developed into a list of demands drawn up by the students. Sal Castro became the recognized teacher spokesman on behalf of the students. Thus began nearly two weeks of walkouts, speeches, picketing, sit-ins and arrests that followed sporadic outbreaks of violence. What was most encouraging to the students was the fact that they had the strong support of their parents who, for their part, often jammed community and school board meetings to lend their support for the demands the students were making.

Throughout these days of protest the students stressed that they were Chicanos and were intensely proud of their Mexican identity. Slogans such as "Brown is Beautiful," "Viva la Raza," and "Chicano Power" were often heard. And there was a militancy, too. A number of young Chicanos had organized a group which called itself the "Young Chicanos for Community Action." This group was also known as the "Brown Berets." They wore semi-military style clothing with boots and khaki shirts. They pledged themselves to do all in their power to "defend themselves from the oppressors." They were very visible at the school walkouts and often managed to get themselves between the students and the police. In turn, the law enforcement officials called them dangerous "outside agitators" and "communist sympathizers." The police authorities blamed the Brown Berets for instigating the "blowouts" themselves, even though there was no evidence to support this accusation.

Los Angeles, California

Delano, California

a bilingual newspaper

Milwaukee, Wisconsin

Lansing, Michigan

San Antonio, Texas

Oakland, California

The writing of history, science, and ideas in Mexico dates from before the arrival of the Europeans. Then, in 1539, the first book printed in the "New World" was published in Mexico. Written expression, therefore, dates back to antiquity through both branches of the Mexican American Mestizo tradition. It is not surprising, therefore, that during the 1960s Chicanos made maximum use of this tradition through expressions in both Spanish and English in their own newspapers, books and graphics.

Finally, although twelve activists and Sal Castro were arrested and charged with "conspiracy" to commit a crime, these charges were later dropped. Eventually the "blowouts" calmed down and the students went back to their classes. But more importantly, many of their demands were met. Mexican American Studies and Mexican American Literature classes were added to the school curriculum as elective classes. Significantly, there also began a re-evaluation of the way in which Mexican American school children were taught in the United States. The major educational achievements in the areas of bilingual and multi-cultural education all came about after the students of East Los Angeles had told the world they wanted to learn about themselves and would settle for nothing less.

In 1970 the Chicano Movement and the anti-Vietnam War movement merged, momentarily, in what was to become a landmark in Chicano history. On August 29, a group calling itself the National Chicano Moratorium Committee organized a march through the streets of East Los Angeles. The protest had a dual purpose. First, the intent was to protest the war itself. Second, it was to protest the disproportionately high death and casualty rate of Mexican American soldiers in Vietnam. Chicanos, they argued, were being drafted in large numbers by, frequently, all-White draft boards. In addition, Chicano draftees were often sent on the most hazardous duty in combat. Many people saw this as the result of a lack of representation by Mexican Americans at the decision-making level for the conduct of the war.

A crowd of fifteen to twenty thousand showed up to march to Laguna Park where speeches and entertainment were scheduled. During the planning stages the police had been informed of all plans by the organizers. In addition, the Los Angeles County Sheriffs had been involved during the planning stages. However, after the crowd reached Laguna Park things began to turn ugly. Reports of the looting of a nearby liquor store apparently aroused the sheriffs into thinking that the peaceful crowd was about to riot. For reasons that to this day are still not clear, the sheriffs chose to attack the crowd with billy clubs and tear gas. This panicked the crowd. People began to run, rocks were thrown at the police, and in the resulting chaos there was the inevitable loss of property and lives. Two young bystanders were killed in the fighting that ensued. Then, most tragic of all, Rubén Salazar, the noted Mexican American journalist for the *Los Angeles Times*, was killed when struck in the head by a tear gas shell while sitting inside a nearby restaurant. He had been having lunch with an associate. Under circumstances which are still questioned by many people, one of the most eloquent voices of the young Chicano Movement had been silenced.

3. Phase Two: Chicano Intellectuals and Artists

The militant, confrontational phase of the Chicano Movement seemed to fade after the tragedy of the Chicano Moratorium. There was much anger over police brutality, poverty, the gang problem and other societal ills. But as one Chicano college student at UCLA remarked: "I think we learned from the Sixties that we can't march and protest our way into full economic prosperity." Indeed, the strong emotions that had erupted during the Sixties had raised people's consciousness but had not brought about the goals of the movement. This ultimately led the Chicano playwright, Luis Valdéz, to comment in 1969: "What La Raza needs is the arts to tell itself where it is ... we have lacked the poets, novelists, and essayists ...." Valdéz may have been right. Little did Valdéz and the Chicano community expect, however, that one of the great voices of the Chicanos would be silenced during the Chicano Moratorium.

Rubén Salazar was a native of Mexico who had worked as a journalist in both Texas and California for many years and who later became an important reporter and columnist for the *Los Angeles Times.* At the time of his death, he had taken a position as news director of a Spanish language television station in Los Angeles while still writing a weekly column for the *L.A. Times'* opinion section. His commentaries are "must" reading, for they defined the great issues which confronted the people of Mexican descent, not only in Los Angeles but in the Southwest as a whole. He wrote of young zoot-suiters or gang members, of police brutality, of inadequate schools, of racist judges and/or government officials. But he also wrote of the colorful and positive elements of Mexican and Chicano culture.

One of the most memorable columns appeared on February 6, 1970. It is titled, "Who is a Chicano? And What is it the Chicanos Want?" In this column Salazar provided the now classic definition for the word "Chicano." "A Chicano," he wrote, "is a Mexican American with a non-Anglo image of himself." Salazar went on to point out that Chicanos resent being told that Columbus "discovered" America because their own ancestors, the Mayans and Aztecs, developed highly sophisticated civilizations long before the Italian explorer became lost in the eastern shores of the "New World." Chicanos also, Salazar went on to point out, resent being called "culturally deprived" or told that because they often speak Spanish, they have a "problem."

Salazar then succinctly described what Chicanos want: "Mexican Americans, though indigenous to the Southwest, are on the lowest rung scholastically, economically, socially and politically. Chicanos feel cheated. They want to effect change. NOW." Meanwhile, other Chicano voices were asserting themselves in the same vein as the philosophy of Rubén Salazar.

In Berkeley, California, Octavio I. Romano, a Chicano professor at the

Rubén Salazar, a native of Mexico, came to the United States and worked as a journalist for the *Los Angeles Times.* His hard hitting reporting and editorial columns for the *Times* have become classics of non-fiction Chicano literature. Tragically, this eloquent voice of the Chicanos was killed under very questionable circumstances by a tear gas canister fired by the Los Angeles County Sheriffs during the Chicano Moratorium in East Los Angeles in 1970.

University of California, announced that, as an anthropologist, he was extremely dissatisfied with the treatment of Mexican Americans by the academic social sciences because they totally ignored the intellectual, artistic and creative aspects of Chicano culture in an historical context. "Mexican Americans are not mindless blobs without a significant history, as the social scientists would have us believe," Romano insisted. "The truth is that Chicanos have never lacked intellectuals, creators and inventors, and their true history has never been told." The only thing lacking, Romano believed, was an adequate forum for expression of these aspects of Chicano culture. It was with this in mind that Professor Romano and a small group of students, almost all of them Chicano undergraduates, came together and founded a non-university publishing enterprise called Quinto Sol ("The Fifth Sun") Publications. Their first publication was "A Journal of Contemporary Mexican American Thought" called *El Grito,* which they translated as "The Battle Cry." Soon Romano's belief was proven to be true, for *El Grito* began to publish an almost endless stream of Chicano fiction, poetry, scholarly articles, art, essays and photography. Romano and his associates demonstrated that the academic social sciences had attempted to "box in" the Mexican American population into the untrue image of having no goals, no intellectuals, no art, no philosophy, no technical ability, no opinions about the world outside of the Chicano community, and whose only efforts to think were restricted to the continuous repetition of "unimaginative folklore."

Romano, who had obtained a Ph.D. in anthropology and taught behavioral sciences at Berkeley, contributed some of the most important scholarly articles. His work was very influential for it led to a complete re-evaluation of the Mexican Americans' differences from Anglo Americans. To be different, Romano argued, is not to be inferior or somehow deficient. The articles which appeared in *El Grito* also stressed the strengths of Mexican culture in the society of the United States.

Not long after its founding, Quinto Sol Publications published the first contemporary anthology of Chicano literature, followed by the publication of the first anthology of scholarly articles which dealt exclusively with Mexican Americans in the modern world. Within a few years the Chicano publications of Quinto Sol were distributed from Alaska to Argentina and from Tokyo to Eastern Europe. In a publishing world where any book that sells over 5,000 copies is considered a "success," the Chicano anthologies were surpassing 40,000 copies sold!

But Quinto Sol Publications, with all of its success, was not the only publishing venture among Mexican Americans during the Sixties. In Albuquerque, New Mexico, José Armas began an energetic and prolific publishing enterprise called Pajarito Publications. A true pioneer with boundless energy, dedication and intellect, José Armas truly inspired many, many Mexican Americans to write, to study, and to bring out the best of the Chicano intellectual world. In El Paso, Tex-

Chicano Poetry
A CRITICAL INTRODUCTION

La Voz Poética Del Chicano

CHICANO PERSPECTIVES IN LITERATURE
A CRITICAL AND ANNOTATED BIBLIOGRAPHY

EL ESPEJO-THE MIRROR
Selected Mexican-American Literature

BETWEEN BORDERS:
Essays on Mexicana/Chicana History

In 1967 Chicano intellectual and creative history was made again, this time in Berkeley, California, by the Chicano publishing group Quinto Sol, which published *El Grito* (First contemporary journal of Chicano intellectual thought), *El Espejo* (first anthology of Chicano creative writing), and *Voices* (first anthology of academic writings dealing exclusively with Chicanos and by Chicanos). All were edited by Octavio Romano. This tradition continues with a profusion of writings which are emanating from the Chicano community and Chicano publishers today.

Estela Portillo Trambley

Estela Portillo Trambley (left), poet, playwright, author of short stories and novels, was born in El Paso, Texas. Consequently, she has always lived within the harsh and intense meeting of three major world cultures: England-Europe; Spain/Moors-Mexico; and Maya-Aztec-Yaqui. This experience is reflected in her writing which ever seeks the eternal of the human condition; the confluence of humans as they dance the dance of life while they wear the seemingly different garbs of cultures, histories and individualistic idiosyncrasies. Her multicultural and multi-disciplinary foundations have propelled her to the position as one of the foremost Chicana writers of our day.

No transitory ideologue, her major publications include *The Day of the Swallows, Sun Images, Rain of Scorpions, Trini, Puente Negro, Autumn Gold, Blacklight, Sor Juana*, and a collection of Haiku.

Her works have won her the Third Annual Quinto Sol Literary Award, the second-place award in New York's Shakespeare Festival's Hispanic American Playwrights competition, and the Second Annual Women's Plays competition at St. Edward's University. Presently she is completing *Masihani*, her new novel that deals with Toltec mysticism and which continues her focus on the transcendental elements of major world cultures.

Sandra Cisneros (right), poet, essayist and author of fiction, was born in Chicago and educated in the schools of the midwestern United States. She has been rapidly propelled into relative prominence in the field of Chicana letters by her two books of poetry *(Bad Boys, My Wicked Wicked Ways)* and her two works of fiction *(The House on Mango Street, Woman Hollering Creek)*.

Woman Hollering Creek won the PEN Center West Award in 1991, the Anisfield-Wolf Book Award and the Lannan Foundation Literary Award. Selections from her works have been chosen, among others, for *The Oxford Book of American Short Stories, The Best Short Stories by North American Women since 1945* and *American Voices.*

Sandra Cisneros has an extensive teaching background: grades two through twelve in Illinois; at a Latino youth alternative high school in Chicago; grades two through five in San Antonio, Texas; and literature director at the Guadalupe Cultural Arts Center which is also in San Antonio. She has been a guest professor in the California State University system, at the University of California at Berkeley and Irvine, the University of Michigan at Ann Arbor, and the University of New Mexico at Albuquerque.

At present she is at work on a novel, *Caramelo.*

Sandra Cisneros

as, Truchas Publications also began to publish heretofore unpublished Chicanos. And at the University of Illinois, the Arte Publico Press followed in the same trend. With their own publishing outlets, now Chicano writers and artists did not have to "water down" or change their thinking in order to satisfy the "establishment" editors of the New York publishers. And the Chicano reading public now had something to read that did not endlessly focus on gangs and violence. The early phase of Chicano literature began a current which is present to this day.

Dr. Raymund Paredes of the University of California at Los Angeles, one of the leading authorities on Chicano literature, has made an important distinction concerning this literary genre. Not every writer who happens to be of Mexican ancestry, or who has a Spanish surname, can be said to write Chicano literature. As Paredes says: "If a Mexican American writer chooses not to engage his or her ethnic heritage, then it seems to me what that writer is producing is not Chicano literature." In other words, Chicano literature, by definition, must provide the means by which Mexican Americans can gain insight into their identity and psyche.

One of the earliest authors of quality Chicano literature is none other than Luis Valdéz of *Zoot Suit* fame. Valdéz, the son of farmworkers, attended California State University, with major studies in drama. After graduation he returned to his home town of Delano where he came upon César Chávez's United Farm Workers. The now famous Delano grape strike was in full swing. Valdéz soon formed "El Teatro Campesino," The Farmworkers Theater, which began to perform short skits, or "actos," which were intended to educate and entertain the workers about the realities of their lives and their strike. Valdéz and his troupe of actors have performed dozens of his plays across the United States as well as in Europe. Valdéz's humor has always been laced with biting satire while *Zoot Suit*, his play and movie about the pachucos as racism's victims in the 1940s, is a dizzying blend of surrealism, music and dance. His work with "El Teatro Campesino" and beyond has helped Chicanos understand where they have come from and where they are going.

The first famous Chicano novelist of the present era is Rudolfo Anaya of New Mexico. A professor at the University of New Mexico, Anaya's landmark work is titled *Bless Me, Ultima* (1972). In this novel Anaya tells the story of a seven-year-old boy named Tony Mares as he is growing up on the llano (prairie) of rural New Mexico in the 1940s. Deeply symbolic and poetically written, in *Bless Me, Ultima* Anaya evokes visions of the glories of the natural landscape, as well as the mystifying powers of the Mexican curandera (healer), Ultima. By choosing to embrace not only his Catholic roots but Ultima's Indian spiritualism as well, Tony becomes almost a mythic figure symbolizing the Chicano himself. A prolific writer, Anaya has written other novels, short stories and works which embrace the depth of Chicano culture today as well as its Mexican origins.

Other writers from the early phase of Chicano literature include Tomás Rivera (*And the Earth did not Part*), a native of south Texas who went on to become the chancellor of the University of California at Riverside. The poet Alurista also made major contributions through his many works that found their way into many publications. Meanwhile, Corky González, a Chicano activist in Colorado, wrote an epic poem called *I am Joaquín* which has become a classic in Chicano literature.

Just as important as the literary works which have defined the identity of Chicanos are the early Chicano muralists. All over the Southwest, Chicano painters chose to portray their pride in their culture by means of public mural art in the Mexican mural tradition of men like Diego Rivera.See Plates 24 to 26 and 29. One of the early Chicano muralists in Los Angeles was Judy Baca whose "Great Wall" mural now stretches in excess of 800 yards!See Plates 27 and 28. The "Great Wall" has incorporated the work of many Chicano muralists and tells the history of California and its people through the decades. Other Chicano muralists of importance have included Eduardo Carrillo and David Botello who has organized a group known as the "Streetscapers." See Plates 31 and 32.

Schools and universities have become interested in the increasing amounts of Chicano literature, arts and scholarly articles, and they are now including it in their curriculum. Some universities have even established Chicano Studies Departments whereby students can select from a wide range of classes dealing with Chicano history, literature, art or social science. Notable among these is the California State University at Northridge where the Chicano Studies Program is headed by Dr. Rudolfo Acuña, the author of the book, *Occupied America.*

Artists and intellectuals have provided a focus and a direction for the Chicano Movement. They have articulated a sense of Chicano identity in terms of their Indian and Spanish origins. And they have forced the general American society to re-examine its traditional view of the Mexican living in the United States. The next logical step was to redefine the educational experiences of the younger Chicano generation to ensure as bright a future as possible.

4. Focus on Education

At the University of Southern California, in 1961, Fred W. Marcoux wrote a masters thesis entitled *Handicaps of Bilingual Mexican Children.* Following a "study" of Mexican and Mexican American school age children, Marcoux attempted to explain the students' poor performance on standardized tests. In one of his concluding remarks he wrote that: "Mexican children had a lower average intelligence rating than the non-Mexican children and a higher frequency of mental re-

Brad Shirakawa

Rosa María Escalante, as La Virgen de Guadalupe/ Tonantzin-Nuestra Madre Tierra, in El Teatro Campesino's 1974 version of *La Virgen del Tepeyac,* performed in the historic Mission of San Juan Bautista. This work is now a classic in the repertoire of El Teatro.

Rosa María Escalante (center) as the mother in *Simply María,* by Josefina López, a play about Mexican tradition and American reality, performed at the Playhouse of El Teatro Campesino.

Brad Shirakawa

Wilma Bonet (L) and Rosa María Escalante (R) portray two women caught up in a mid-life crisis in the play by Evelina Fernandez, *How Else am I Supposed to Know I'm Still Alive?*

Rosa María Escalante is a 20-year veteran performer of El Teatro Campesino. Currently she is Education Director of El Teatro, as well as a performing member.

"Theater is more than entertainment. It is educational. It serves to teach ourselves, and those who do not know us, about who we are as a gente, our cultura, tradiciones, historia, y nuestros anhelos por el futuro."

"For you, as an individual, theater teaches you to express yourself, to explore and to develop physically, mentally, emotionally and spiritually. It is a wonderful way to learn how to work with people. You cannot do theatre all by yourself. The lessons learned in theater can be applied to any work or life experience. Your ability to express yourself, with self-confidence, will always serve you well."

"As a gente, we must stay true to who we are, and how we want to see ourselves represented. It is my goal, as a theater person, to inspire and encourage our people of all ages to start speaking up for themselves."

Rosa María Escalante

Judith F. Baca
Standing in front of "Triumph of the Heart," one panel from the *WORLD WALL*.
10' x 30' acrylic on canvas.

In 1975, when the Great Wall of Los Angeles was still a dream, I never imagined it would lead me, the more than 200 young "Mural Makers" and the 35 other artists on my team through such a moving set of experiences. Nor could I have imagined that eight years later it would still be a work in progress. When I first saw the wall, I envisioned a long narrative of another history of California; one which included ethnic peoples, women and minorities who were so invisible in conventional text book accounts. The discovery of the history of California's multi-cultured peoples was a revelation to me as well as to the members of my teams. We learned each new decade of history in summer installments; the 20s in 1978, the 30s in 1980, the 40s in 1981, and the 50s in 1983. Each year our visions expanded as the images traveled down the wall. While our sense of our individual families' places in history took form, we became family to one another. Working toward the achievement of a difficult common goal shifted our understandings of each other and, most importantly, of ourselves.

I designed this project as an urban environmental artist concerned not only with the physical aesthetic considerations of a space, but the social and cultural as well. I am not a social worker, though people mistakenly call me one, and I am not a teacher although I have teaching skills. I draw on skills not normally used by artists. I've learned as much as I've taught from the youth I've had the good fortune to know, working alongside of them. They've taught me among other things how to laugh at myself, how to put play into hard work, and how not to be afraid to believe in something. I am extremely grateful.

Perhaps most overwhelming to me about the Great Wall experience has been learning of the courage of individuals in history who endured, spoke out, and overcame obstacles that were dealt them. It was true both of the people we painted and of ourselves, the Mural Makers.

JUDITH F. BACA 1983

Judith F. Baca

Full Professor, 1992-present
   University of California, Irvine.

Artistic Director: Social and Public Arts
   Resource Center (**SPARC**) Venice,
   California 1981-present.

Masters Degree in Art
   California State University,
   Northridge, 1979

Intensive Course in Mural Techniques
   Taller Siqueiros, Cuernavaca,
   México, 1977

Bachelors Degree in Art
   California State University,
   Northridge, 1969

AWARDS AND ACHIEVEMENTS

Hispanic Excellence Award
   Awarded by Northern Trust Bank

Certificate of Distinguished Recognition
   Awarded by National Association of
   Chicano Studies.

Rockefeller Fellowship Awardee
   Awarded by the UCLA Chicano Studies
   Research Center.

**One of America's 100 Most Influential
Hispanics.**
   Awarded by Hispanic Business
   Magazine.

Recognition for Achievements in the Arts
   Awarded by the Mexican American Bar
   Association.

Certificate of Appreciation
   Awarded by the Korean Daily News for
   work in the Korean Community.

Educator of the Year
   Awarded by the National Association of
   Art Educators.

Outstanding Latina Visual Artist
   Awarded by the Comisión Femenil de
   Los Angeles.

Certificate of Appreciation
   Awarded by Los Angeles County
   Supervisor Edmund Edelman.

Award of Appreciation
   Awarded by the Los Angeles Cultural
   Affairs Commission.

The longest mural in the World
THE GREAT WALL OF LOS ANGELES

Outstanding Woman of Color Award
   Awarded by National Association of
   Women of Color.

Arts Award-Hispanic Women
   Awarded by the City of San Francisco.

**Labor Award of Honor for Community
   Service in the Arts**
   Awarded by the Los Angeles County
   Federation of Labor, AFL-CIO.

Hispanic of the Year in Art
   Awarded by the California Department
   of Justice Hispanic Employees Advisory
   Committee.

Achievement Award
   Awarded by California Assemblymen
   Richard Alatorre and Art Torres.

Judith Baca has exhibited in Chicago, Illinois, Mexico, Texas, California, Arizona, Colorado, Washington, D.C., Moscow, USSR , Finland, Vancouver, B.C., Seattle, Washington, New York, Ohio, Mexico City, Rheims, France; Paris, France; and Brussels, Belgium.

tardation. They also are deficient on intelligence tests. This is due to environmental and cultural factors ... such as a lack of rewarding human relationships which incites feelings of inadequacy."

Unfortunately, these and more were the images that students in colleges and universities were taught about Mexican Americans. After graduation, these college students went on to become school teachers, administrators, social workers and counselors. Equally unfortunate was the fact that attitudes such as those found in the work of Marcoux formed the basis of the educational experiences that most Chicanos received during the 1960s. A vicious cycle existed in American schools when it came to the teaching of Mexicans and Mexican Americans. Molded by much of their professional training, most teachers had very low expectations of their Mexican American students. It followed, therefore, that such students were shunted into the industrial arts or the shop classes. At Belmont High School, near downtown Los Angeles, a school from which students participated in the East L.A. Blowouts of 1968, one of the student leaders noted that the shop classes were "full of Mexican kids," while the college prep classes were attended by mostly White and Asian American students. As a result of these practices, few Mexican Americans went on to college and even fewer went on from there to become teachers. In this way, the cycle of low expectations produced a self-fulfilling prophecy.

Change is in the air, however. Once the right to study Mexican and Mexican American history and literature was established as legitimate electives, the principal educational focus of the Chicano Movement became bilingual education. This focus took into account students who arrived from Mexico speaking no English but who had been studying advanced subjects such as algebra and physics. Should such students completely stop their technical education until they learned English? With this in mind, Chicanos began to demand bilingual educators who could teach advanced subjects in Spanish to Mexican students until they became fluent in English. From this point of view the idea of bilingual education developed into a realization that children's knowledge of Spanish is an advantage and not a "social problem."

Proponents of bilingual education believe that it is educationally wrong to throw Spanish-speaking students into "English only" classes where they quickly fall so far behind that they almost never catch up to their normal grade level. All too often such students are labeled as "retarded" or of "low intelligence."

The damage is not only intellectual, however. Students of Mexican descent are totally separated from their own backgrounds when they are thrust into classes where they are taught that the only legitimate language is English and that the language of their parents and ancestors is of no value whatsoever. The result is a separation of the young people from their own families who have been devalued as a consequence.

For these reasons, bilingual and bicultural education for Mexican American school children of all ages is one of the continuing and most important demands of the Chicano Movement. In short, the call for bilingual and bicultural education is really a call for educational innovation in a society which often prides itself on its ability to change and progress.

But some people do not understand the innovative aspects of the Chicanos' demands in education. Some, for example, have come to believe that Chicanos do not want their children to learn English. Nothing could be further from the truth! Chicanos fully recognize and appreciate the importance of English in the United States in order to be successful and fully participating citizens. What the Chicanos propose, however, is that when some of the rules and ideas of English are explained in the native tongue of the students, they learn faster. Fortunately, instruction for all students in their native language is now legally recognized in the United States. In addition, more and more parents of non-Spanish speaking students are enrolling their children in bilingual classrooms at the elementary grades, for they are beginning to realize the importance of being able to speak both English and Spanish in the future of the Southwest.

Another result of pressures from the Chicano Movement deals with the educational goals of the Mexican American population with regard to higher education. High schools across the Southwest have begun to realize the importance of high expectations for all students. The fact that more and more Chicano students are going to college has meant that more Chicano teachers are filtering back into the classrooms. And with higher expectations, more and more Mexican American students are being challenged to take an increasing number of college preparatory courses. In fact, many of these students are choosing to take high school advanced placement classes and to attempt the rigorous Advanced Placement (A.P.) Exams, given nationally, which grant college credit to those who pass. More Chicano students are passing these exams each year, thus earning their way into better universities.

The Chicano Movement has also been successful in obtaining increased governmental programs for college scholarships and tuition fees. In California, for example, the Cal Grant Program provides families of low income the opportunity to send their students to college. The Educational Opportunity Program (EOP) also allows promising students of low socio-economic levels the chance to be admitted to college. The EOP provides tutoring and counseling for students after they are enrolled. Today, more than in the past, there are numerous opportunities for Chicanos to obtain a college education.

Gloria Molina

Gloria Molina

Gloria Molina was first elected to office in 1982 as State Assemblywoman for the 56th District of California. In 1987 she was elected to the Los Angeles City Council where she served as the councilwoman from the First District until 1991. In February of 1991 she was elected to the Los Angeles County Board of Supervisors. Ms. Molina is the first Latina in history elected to the California State Legislature, the Los Angeles City Council and the Los Angeles County Board of Supervisors.

Prior to being elected to public office, she served in the Carter White House as Deputy for Presidential Personnel. Following this service she became Deputy Director for the Department of Health and Human Services in San Francisco.

Molina has a reputation for candor and independence which has made her known for her strong, issue-oriented style and her commitment to community empowerment. Consistent with her reputation, she has a legislative history of standing up for the average citizen, often against almost insurmountable odds. She has introduced bills, as assemblywoman, to protect consumers from unfair bank charges, insurance redlining and utility company rip-offs.

She continued her public spirited efforts in the City Council, where she worked for better protection from toxics, for city-funded child care after school hours and to "get tough" on drug dealers and criminals.

As a Los Angeles County Supervisor, she has enhanced her reputation as a watchdog for taxpayers' dollars.

Supervisor Molina is active in national issues. She serves as board member for the Los Angeles County Transportation Commission, the National Association of Latino Elected Officials (NALEO), the Mexican American Legal Defense and Education Fund (MALDEF), and the National Hispanic Leadership Agenda. She is also a member of the California Hispanic Supervisors Caucus.

Molina is the eldest of 10 children; her father is a retired laborer and her mother is a homemaker. She is married to Ron Martinez and has one daughter, Valentina.

A Los Angeles native, Molina represents the cities of Azusa, Baldwin Park, Bell, Bell Gardens, Commerce, Cudahy, El Monte, Huntington Park, Industry, Irwindale, La Puente, Rosemead, South El Monte, Santa Fe Springs, South Gate, Vernon, and also parts of Los Angeles including Atwater, Boyle Heights, Downtown, El Sereno, Eagle Rock, Elysian Park, Glassell Park, Highland Park, Lincoln Heights, Mount Washington, Silverlake and Westlake.

As County Supervisor, she also represents several unincorporated communities.

Her work has been nationally recognized by *Working Women* magazine, *Time* and *Hispanic Business* magazine.

5. A People and a Movement Come Together

With a better sense of who they are, and with some improvement in the field of education, the Chicanos are now poised to make greater strides.

In the Sixties, Chicanos had tried various political approaches as a means to realize their goals. In Texas, a separate third party was formed, the La Raza Unida Party. Distrustful of the established Democrat and Republican leaders, Chicanos chose a separate party which had some early successes in local elections for positions such as mayors and members of school boards. However, in time, this phenomenon began to die out.

Still, the United States is a democratic country and the most fundamental rule of democratic politics is "majority rules." Unfortunately, for the Chicanos who are rapidly becoming the majority in many parts of the Southwest, this has not been the case. See Plate 30.

One of the obstacles has been that not all Mexican Americans living in the U.S. are American citizens. In addition, there are those who have lived in this country for many years who have chosen not to change their citizenship to become Americans and, therefore, eligible to vote. What many Mexicans who live in the United States do not realize is that they can become American citizens and still retain their Mexican citizenship. Certain Mexican American advocacy groups, such as the Mexican American Legal Defense and Education Fund (MALDEF), are currently encouraging as many Mexicans in the U.S. as possible to become American citizens and exercise the fundamental right to vote.

MALDEF has become one of the most important and effective organizations dedicated to ensuring the civil and political rights for people of Mexican descent in the United States. This non-profit group, which retains some of the best and brightest Chicano attorneys on its staff, is a watchdog or pressure group in the tradition of the Sleepy Lagoon Defense Committee. It is not a "one issue" group, however, for it is committed to becoming a permanent guardian of Chicano political and educational rights.

"Maldef," as it is often called by people who know about this legal group, recently won a landmark case which may open tremendous political opportunities for Mexican Americans. The community of East Los Angeles, which has the largest concentration of people of Mexican descent in the United States, is not a city. It is a part of the County of Los Angeles. As such, it is dependent for its municipal government on the Los Angeles County Board of Supervisors. Services such as police protection, street maintenance, trash removal, street lighting, parks, and recreational facilities all are allocated to East L.A. by the five-member Board of Supervisors. In the entire history of the county there had never been a person of Mexican descent on the supervisorial board. The reason for this lack of representation was that East L.A. had been divided up among three separate supervisorial districts to intentionally weaken the voting power of the Mexican American voters.

Maldef, along with the United States Department of Justice and the American Civil Liberties Union (ACLU), brought a lawsuit against the Board of Supervisors, charging them with political "gerrymandering" (slicing up an area for political advantage). The case moved through the courts and finally all the way up to the Supreme Court of the United States. In 1991 the court ruled that East Los Angeles residents had indeed been taken advantage of, politically, by the Los Angeles County Supervisors. A major legal and political victory had been won. For many Mexican Americans, this proved that you <u>can fight</u> city hall and win!

Maldef submitted a map for the re-drawing of the political boundaries of Los Angeles County which would keep all of East Los Angeles in one solid district. This re-mapping was approved by the court and a special election was called. The election was won by Gloria Molina, a Mexican American member of the Los Angeles City Council, who thus became the first person of Mexican descent in the history of the county to win a seat on the Board of Supervisors. She was also the first woman to realize such an accomplishment. The court ruling and subsequent events may open the door for other re-districting efforts, to prevent the gerrymandering that had reduced the Chicano people's rightful role in a nation which is a democracy.

Another significant event occurred in the city of Bell Gardens which is located in the southeast area of Los Angeles County. That city had been traditionally governed by White city council members, although the population had been increasingly changing with more Mexican Americans within the city limits. In the past there had been a relatively low voter turnout during elections. But, in 1991, the Bell Gardens City Council passed a re-zoning law limiting the construction of new dwellings. The Latino community perceived this as a measure to attack their interests. Angry, the Latinos organized a recall effort to remove the members of the city council. Voter registration efforts were initiated. In the resulting recall election, all four members of the council were removed. They had been "fired" by the people. An election was recently held and three of the newly elected members of the city council are Latinos who have promised to listen to the needs of the majority.

Many political observers, in Los Angeles as well as elsewhere, are now predicting that this may be the beginning of increasing political activity and power for the Latinos. Throughout the Southwest more Mexican American mayors, city councilmen, congressmen and other political representatives are appearing on the political scene.

A key to increased political power, accompanied by the enhanced self-image of the Mexican American people in the Southwest, is the existence of Spanish language mass media such as television stations, radio stations, newspapers and magazines. Not only do these provide positive role models for the community, but the major advertisers have become aware of the buying power of the Latino communities, not only in the Southwest but in the nation as well. No longer are Mexicans and Mexican Americans invisible on TV. Even English language programming now finds roles for Mexican Americans and other Latino actors in performances which are not consistently those of maids, gang members or drug smugglers.

In the world of Chicano literature new voices are coming forth to expand and clarify Mexican American identity. *House on Mango Street* by Sandra Cisneros, *Moths and Other Stories* by Helen María Viramontes and *The Last of the Menu Girls* by Denise Chávez are all excellent examples of the importance of Chicana authors' influence and female perspectives in this growing body of contemporary literature. Gary Soto's poetry, Max Martínez's short stories and novels, the fictional works of Arturo Islas, all give Chicano literature an ever growing richness and expanding dimensions which are attracting attention both in the U.S. and abroad, where they are received as examples of world literature.

In the realm of the cinema Luis Valdéz followed the success of *Zoot Suit* with *La Bamba,* the story of the Mexican American rock-and-roll legend, Richie Valens (Ricardo Valenzuela). Similarly, Gregory Nava wrote and produced the powerfully dramatic *El Norte*, a film which describes the plight of Guatemalan refugees who come to live in the United States. Another filmmaker of note is Moctezuma Esparza, one of Sal Castro's students and a leader of the 1968 East L.A. Blowouts. He has co-produced *The Milagro Beanfield War,* which details the struggle of indigenous Mexican culture to survive in rural New Mexico. Chicano cinema is a growing field. Currently it is challenging many of the more creative artists to produce innovative works which will find a ready audience among Chicanos as well as within the general American public.

Muralists continue to contribute to the enhancement of American culture. Willie Herón and Gronk continue their contributions with their public art. It is because of muralists such as these that Chicano murals now adorn public buildings and businesses throughout the Southwest. Art galleries which have specialized in Latin American art are finding that their patrons are willing to invest in Chicano art, in all of the endlessly creative forms that it takes.

There have been recent developments in the realm of Chicano and Latino theater arts. In the tradition of Luis Valdéz's El Teatro Campesino, an innovative trio of Latino performers calling themselves "Culture Clash" have begun to make a name for themselves. Their satirical skits or "actos," contained in the play known as *A Bowl of Beings,* recently performed at sold-out performances in San Francisco and Los Angeles. In 1991 the Los Angeles Theater Center's "Latino Theater Lab"

Evelyn Cisneros

PRINCIPAL DANCER
The San Francisco Ballet

Born: Long Beach, California

Training: School of American Ballet,
  San Francisco Ballet School

San Francisco Ballet:
  Joined the Company in 1977

Awards:

Honored as Outstanding Artist of the Year by City of Huntington Beach, California - 1993

Honored as one of the Most Gifted Women in San Francisco Bay Area - 1991

Evelyn Cisneros in Kudelka's *The End*

Marty Sohl

Isadora Duncan Performer's Award by Bay Area Dance Coalition, for outstanding performance as Odette/Odile in Helgi Tomasson's *Swan Lake* - 1989

La Raza Lawyers' Association Award for Outstanding Achievement in the Performing Arts - 1989

Guest Speaker and honoree, Familias Unidas Annual Dinner - 1989

Equal Rights Advocate honoree at the organization's 15th Anniversary Luncheon - 1989

Voted a Bay Area Classic by San Francisco Focus - 1989

Honoree for outstanding achievement in the field of performing arts - California State League of United Latin American Citizens (LULAC) - 1988

Outstanding Member of the Hispanic Community - National Concilio of America - 1987

"Outstanding Young Americans" - Esquire Magazine - 1986

Annual Cultural Award - MALDEF (Mexican American Legal Defense and Education Fund) - 1985

Achievement Award - Hispanic Women Making History - 1984

Guest Appearances: British Columbia, Canada; Bellas Artes, Mexico City; Detroit, Michigan; Los Angeles, California; Madrid, Spain; Monterrey, Mexico; New Zealand; Tucson, Arizona; Havana, Cuba .

Carlos Moreno, Jr. and Alma Delia Moreno
Instituto del Ballet Folklorico Mexicano de Carlos Moreno
Oakland, California
Now in its 27th year, the dance troupe has performed
throughout the U.S. and Mexico.

produced a play called *August 29th* which re-examines the death of Rubén Salazar and looks into the continuing relevance of his writings to the Chicanos and Latinos of today.

The field of music has been no exception to this contemporary burst of artistic creativity and production. Veteran Chicano rock-and-rollers such as Carlos Santana are being joined by groups such as "Los Lobos" whose music richly combines the many influences of Mexican American music: Mexican Norteño styles, the corridos and rancheras, and blues as well as rock-and-roll. "Huayucaltia," a group made up of Mexican, Mexican American, South American and Anglo members, is combining indigenous Latin American Indian musical traditions with jazz forms.

In the Southwest, and outside of it as well, Chicano culture has had an influence on our modern institutions; not only in the universities which teach Chicano literature and history but also in cultural centers such as the "Plaza de la Raza," located in Lincoln Park in East Los Angeles, "El Centro Cultural de la Raza" in San Diego, California, and the "Guadalupe Cultural Center" in San Antonio, Texas. All of these centers are oriented to the community for which they perform a number of important functions which include classes in Mexican dance, arts, crafts, and a focus for the celebration of holidays such as Cinco de Mayo and September 16. Although these centers' principal focus is their respective communities, their functions also have a national, as well as an international, vision which allows them to incorporate the contributions of people from throughout the United States and from other nations.

Today, more and more Mexican Americans find themselves with more formal education and an improved financial situation. The Mexican American middle class is growing again, and Chicanos are increasingly invading the previously exclusive suburbs of affluent America. Mexican American businesses and professional associations now provide a focus for like-minded and community oriented professionals who provide services in business and legal assistance. These groups, by and large, continue the desire and respect for formal education which has always been present in the Mexican American community. Their efforts to provide assistance and scholarships for Chicano students have motivated many needy Chicano students to pursue their goals through educational attainment.

A continuing commitment to demand the best in educational opportunities for the young, an increase in parental involvement for the childrens' education, and more political activity to ensure equal services are measures which can help to solve some of the problems we face today. In this sense, Mexican Americans have been and will continue to be an integral part of American culture, introducing variations and helping to sustain its evolving democratic institutions.

The United States is on the verge of entering a new phase of close relations with Mexico, and perhaps opening a "common market" with the entire Western Hemisphere. As a result, Mexican Americans may find themselves in a unique position to achieve better international relations between the United States and its neighbors by utilizing their bilingual skills and their bicultural sensibilities.

As we approach the 500th anniversary of the birth of the Mestizo people it is clear that this new race, "La Raza," will continue to endure and thrive on both sides of the United States/Mexico border. Hopefully, the commemorations which are held to note this historic beginning will enlighten more and more Mexican Americans as to their unique history. In the words of a noted Chicano writer: "We the Chicanos are Mexican, yet American. We must see to it that our youth will truly understand who they are so they may face their future with the confidence which only self-knowledge can bring." To reach this goal, Mexican Americans must know their past history so that it may light the way to the future.

Chapter Eight

LOS CHICANOS:

WRITING EXERCISES

On the following pages you will find the writing exercises for this chapter. For additional explanations, please see "To the Teacher" or "A Note to the Student" on **pages 21 and 26**. Teachers are urged to select the writing exercises most appropriate for their particular classes. Below are the writing exercises for Chapter Eight:

1. Sentence or Fragment?

This exercise is designed to help students learn how to recognize incomplete sentences (fragments) and then rewrite them as complete sentences. The most important idea here is that a complete sentence makes sense when read alone. When rewriting the fragments, the students must make sure not to change history!

2. Short Answer Questions

Once a student knows what a sentence is (and is not!), he or she can answer brief questions with one or two sentence answers of their own. This list of questions also makes a good study or review sheet when preparing for a test.

3. Paragraph Questions

These questions require slightly longer answers which are to be written in paragraphs. A sample paragraph along with definitions of such terms as "topic sentence" is included in the writing exercises of **Chapter One**.

4. Clustering and Identification (ID) Items

ID Items refer to and identify important people, places and things. Clustering is a way of brainstorming ideas based on these ID Items. Once the cluster has been made, use it as a guide and write an ID Paragraph. A sample cluster and a sample ID Paragraph can be found in the writing exercises of **Chapter One**.

5. Essay Questions

Very broad or complicated questions require essays or compositions as answers. A sample essay and instructions on how to write essays, both as homework and during in-class essay exams, are provided in the writing exercises section of **Chapter Five**.

Sentence Or Fragment?

DIRECTIONS:

A complete sentence makes sense when read all alone. An incomplete sentence or fragment does not. Some of the following are fragments. Some are perfectly correct, complete sentences. Rewrite the fragments and make them into good sentences. You may add words, get rid of words, or rearrange the words. **Just make sure that each fragment you rewrite is factually correct according to the chapter and makes good sense when you read it alone.** Leave the complete sentences alone.

EXAMPLE: *Chicanos who are Mexican Americans.*

Clearly this does not make sense when read alone. While there is **no single correct way** to rewrite it, the following is much better:

Chicanos are Mexican Americans who are proud of their Mexican heritage.

1. The Black Civil Rights Movement of the Sixties.
2. The war in Vietnam and the peace movement.
3. Reies López Tijerina studied land grants in New Mexico.
4. Tijerina's methods which were quite militant.
5. Tijerina's 1966 raid at Tierra Amarilla.
6. In 1968 students in East Los Angeles felt they were receiving an inferior education.
7. Inferior school facilities and too many shop classes.
8. The Chicano students' list of demands.
9. The Brown Berets and the walkouts.
10. The achievements of the Chicano student walkouts.
11. Mexican American Studies classes were added to the official school curriculum.
12. The 1971 Chicano Moratorium in East Los Angeles.
13. The Chicano Movement and the anti-Vietnam War cause.
14. Chicanos protested that too many Mexican Americans were being drafted and were dying in Vietnam.
15. A crowd of fifteen to twenty thousand in East L.A.
16. Rubén Salazar, a writer for the *Los Angeles Times.*
17. Salazar's definition for the word "Chicano".
18. Octavio Romano and Quinto Sol Publications.

19. Luis Valdéz and El Teatro Campesino.
20. Luis Valdéz wrote the play and the film, *Zoot Suit.*
21. Rudolfo Anaya's classic novel, *Bless Me, Ultima.*
22. Judy Baca, who along with many other muralists in Los Angeles.
23. Chicano studies programs at many colleges and universities.
24. Bilingual and bicultural education for Mexican and Mexican American students.
25. The Cal Grant and EOP Programs.
26. More Chicano students are taking Advanced Placement classes in high school.
27. "Maldef" and the L.A. County Board of Supervisors.
28. Gloria Molina was the first person of Mexican ancestry elected to the Los Angeles Board of Supervisors.
29. Spanish language newspapers, TV and radio stations.
30. Many new writers of Chicano literature.
31. Plaza de La Raza and El Centro Cultural de La Raza.
32. The many problems which still face the Mexican American community.
33. Keeping Mexican traditions alive helps young Mexican Americans understand their identities better.

Short Answer Questions

DIRECTIONS:

Answer the following questions by writing one or two complete sentences for each. Be sure that each sentence you write:

a) Is factually correct and helps answer the question.
b) Is a complete sentence, which means it makes sense when read alone.
c) Could be understood by someone who has not seen the question.
d) Begins with a capital letter and ends with a period.
e) Is completely in your own words.
f) Uses correct spelling and is neat.

EXAMPLE: *Give an example of the Chicano Movement in the Sixties.*

The Chicano students' school walkouts for better education took place in 1968.

1. What other important social movements were occurring in the Sixties?

2. Why did Reies López Tijerina study the old Spanish land grants?
3. Why did Tijerina and his followers arrest the district attorney in Tierra Amarilla in 1966?
4. What convinced the Chicano students at Lincoln High in 1968 that they were receiving an inferior education?
5. What did Sal Castro tell his students to do instead of walking out?
6. What were some of the Chicano students' most important demands in 1968?
7. Who were the Brown Berets?
8. Which of the Chicano students' demands were granted?
9. What were Mexican Americans protesting at the 1971 Chicano Moratorium?
10. What happened at the end of the Chicano Moratorium march?
11. Why are the circumstances of Rubén Salazar's death so suspicious?
12. What is Rubén Salazar's definition for the word "Chicano"?
13. What was the purpose of Octavio Romano's Chicano journal, *El Grito?*
14. Name some Chicano publishers.
15. Name one of Luis Valdéz's greatest accomplishments.
16. What is Rudolfo Anaya's best known novel?
17. What are Chicano murals?
18. What is the purpose of the Chicano Studies Programs at universities?
19. What was the attitude of most educators about Mexican American school children in the Sixties?
20. Why did Chicano students demand more college preparatory classes?
21. What is bilingual education?
22. Why did Chicano activists demand bilingual education?
23. Why is it an advantage to be bilingual today?
24. What do Cal Grant and EOP programs do?
25. What is an Advanced Placement high school class?
26. Why should it be possible for Mexican Americans to gain political power now?
27. Why did "Maldef" file a law suit against the Los Angeles County Board of Supervisors?
28. Of what was Gloria Molina the first?
29. Name some new writers of Chicano literature and their works.
30. Name some Chicano artists and their works or types of art.
31. What are some important problems still facing the Mexican American community?
32. Name one way in which Mexican Americans can help to solve the problems they face.
33. Why is it important for Mexican Americans to keep their Mexican traditions alive?

Paragraph Questions

DIRECTIONS:

Answer the following questions by writing a good paragraph for each. Refer back to the sample paragraph on **page 47** for help. Be sure that each paragraph you write:

a) Is factually correct, helps to answer the question and is in your own words.
b) Looks like a proper paragraph (see sample).
c) Has an <u>underlined</u> topic sentence at the beginning of the paragraph.
d) Contains no fragments.
e) Uses correct spelling and is neat.

1. Describe other important social movements of the Sixties besides the Chicano Movement.
2. What was Reies López Tijerina trying to accomplish in New Mexico in the Sixties?
3. What did Chicano students in Los Angeles mean when they said they were receiving an inferior education?
4. Describe the Chicano students' walkouts of 1968 in Los Angeles.
5. What effect on the education of Mexican Americans did the Chicano students' walkout have?
6. Why were 20,000 people marching through East Los Angeles in the Chicano Moratorium?
7. Who was Rubén Salazar?
8. Describe Salazar's famous article which defined the word "Chicano."
9. What did Luis Valdéz mean in 1969 when he said the Chicano Movement needed more artists, poets and essayists?
10. Why was Octavio Romano's *El Grito* and the ideas it contained so important?
11. Why were Quinto Sol and other Chicano publishers so important to the beginning of Chicano literature?
12. What is Dr. Raymund Paredes's explanation of what Chicano literature is?
13. Who is Rudolfo Anaya? Why are his works so important?
14. What is the role of Chicano murals?
15. What was the common attitude toward Mexican school children in the Sixties? How were they educated?
16. Why and how do English-only classrooms turn many Mexican American students away from their own families?

17. Why have bilingual and bicultural educational programs become such important demands for Mexican Americans?
18. Why are high expectations of students so important on the part of teachers?
19. What are the political implications of the increase in the Mexican American population?
20. On what basis did "Maldef" sue the Los Angeles County Board of Supervisors in 1990?
21. Describe "Maldef's" victory and the election of Gloria Molina in 1991.
22. What important role do Spanish language media play in the U.S.?
23. Describe some of the new Chicano literary writers and their works.
24. Describe some recent successful films with Chicano or Latino themes.
25. What is the importance of Plaza de La Raza and El Centro Cultural de La Raza?
26. What are some of the most important problems facing Mexican Americans today?
27. What solutions should Mexican Americans adopt to try to improve their situation today?
28. Is it important for young Mexican Americans to learn about and maintain the traditions of Mexico? Why or why not?

Clustering and ID Items

DIRECTIONS:

Make clusters and/or ID paragraphs for the following identification items. While making your cluster or paragraph, ask yourself who or what the item is and why it is important in the history being studied. Refer to your book if necessary. A sample cluster and ID paragraph can be found on **page 49**.

Reies López Tijerina	A.P. Classes
East L.A. "Student Walkouts"	"Maldef"
1971 Chicano Moratorium	Gloria Molina
Rubén Salazar	Spanish language mass media
Chicano	new Chicano literary writers
Octavio Romano / *El Grito*	Los Lobos
Chicano publishers	Rosa María Escalante
Estela Portillo Trambley	Judith F. Baca
Sandra Cisneros	Evelyn Cisneros

Essay Questions

DIRECTIONS:

The following are essay questions on the content of this chapter. Before attempting to answer any questions, see **page 187** for directions on how to write an essay and **page 188** for a sample essay.

1. Discuss the militant phase of the Chicano Movement. What were some of the successes and failures?
2. In what ways did the early Chicano Movement of the Sixties "emulate the civil rights struggle and the anti-Vietnam War protests in terms of tactics and style"?
3. Discuss Reies López Tijerina, his movement in New Mexico, what he may have accomplished and why he may have failed.
4. Discuss the Chicano students' walkouts of 1968. Include what sparked their interest, what their complaints and demands were, the events of the walkouts and the results.
5. Do some research on other Chicano protests that may have happened in your community and write an essay on the causes, demands, events and results.
6. Write an essay on Rubén Salazar. Include his background, his writings, the circumstances of his untimely death and his impact on the future of the Chicano Movement.
7. As a whole, what role have Chicano / Chicana intellectuals and artists played in the Chicano Movement itself?
8. Write an essay on some of the most important works of Chicano literature and their authors.
9. What reforms in education have Chicanos demanded? Why these reforms? What reforms do you think still need to be made?
10. Why could Mexican Americans one day play a major political role in the U.S.? How did "Maldef's" case in Los Angeles help this cause? What has prevented Mexican Americans from gaining more political control than they currently have?
11. Discuss current achievements among Chicanos / Chicanas and Latinos in the mass media, the arts, motion pictures, literature and music. Why is this artistic activity important?
12. What is the stereotype many people have of Mexican Americans? Why and how is this stereotype changing? Is there a growing Mexican American middle class in your community? Why or why not?

13. What are some of the most serious problems facing the Mexican American community today? What do you see in your community and schools that need changes? How should Mexican Americans go about finding solutions for their problems?

14. Many Mexican Americans know little or nothing about Mexican history or about their own historical and cultural background. How are they likely to view themselves and other Mexican and Mexican American people? How does learning about their heritage help them to see themselves and others differently?

Credits: Color plates and photos:

Cover: José Lott, Artist.
Plates 3, 4, 5, 6, 7, 11, 12, 14, 15, 16, 17, 19, 20, 21, 22, 23: Carlos M. Jiménez.
Plates 9, 10, 13, 18: Virginia Peñaloza Jiménez.
Plate   1: Photo: Shige Kajiwara.
Plate   2: Los Mexicas de México.
Plate   8: Photo: Rob Cowan.
Plate   24: Andy Zermeño, Artist, and The Archives of Labor and Urban Affairs,
         Wayne State University.
Plate   25: Antonio Bernal, Artist. Photo: Robert Sommer.
Plate   26: Emigdio Vásquez, Artist. Photo by the artist.
Plate   27: Judith Baca, Artist. Photo courtesy of the Social and Public Art
         Resource Center (SPARC).
Plate   28: Judith Baca, Artist. Photo courtesy of the Social and Public Art
         Resource Center (SPARC).
Plate   29: Victor Ochoa, Artist. Photo courtesy of the Social and Public Art
         Resource Center (SPARC).
Plate   30: Congreso de Artistas Chicanos en Aztlan and Mario Torero. Photo: Tim Drescher
Plate   31: David Rivas Botello, Artist. Photo by the artist.
Plate   32: David Rivas Botello, Artist. Photo by the artist.

Black and white illustrations and photos:

Page: Title page illustration: Logo of Chicano Studies Library, University of California, Berkeley
  2: La Danza Azteca de Berkeley
 39: Códice Mendocino
 43: Desde México
 52: MEXIC-ARTE Museum, Austin, Texas, Centro Cultural de la Raza, San Diego, California
 64: Desde México (Miguel Covarrubias)
 73: Carlos M. Jiménez
 76: Desde México
 84: Carlos M. Jiménez, TQS Graphics
 87: Anonymous, Museo Nacional de Historia, Mexico
 88: Library of Congress
 91: Bancroft Library
102: Carlos M. Jiménez, TQS Graphics
116: Bancroft Library
121: Arizona Historical Society
124: Brown Bros.
127: Brown Bros.
129: Arizona Historical Society
130: Brown Bros.
141: Keystone
144: Brown Bros.
145: Casasola
149: Culver
150: Culver
154: Culver
155: Casasola
159: Brown Bros
161: Casasola
162: Casasola
163: Casasola
172: (Top) U.T. The Institute of Texan Cultures, The San Antonio Light Collection
172: (Bottom) U.T. The Institute of Texan Cultures

173: Unknown
174: Steinheimer
176: Desde México
192: Teatro Campesino
195: Carlos M. Jiménez, TQS Graphics
197: Carlos M. Jiménez, TQS Graphics
200: Carlos M. Jiménez, TQS Graphics
204: Roberto Rodríguez
210: Carlos M. Jiménez, TQS Graphics
213: Roberto Rodríguez
222: TQS Archives
228: Courtesy of Lori Huerta
234: The Archives of Labor and Urban Affairs, Wayne State University
235: The Archives of Labor and Urban Affairs, Wayne State University
237: Jono Shaffer
240: The Los Angeles Times
247: Carlos M. Jiménez, TQS Graphics
248: Romano / TQS logo collection
252: TQS Archives and Graphics
255: TQS Archives
257: TQS Archives and Graphics
258: (Top) Courtesy of the author
258: (Bottom) Ruben Guzman, S. Cisneros
261: El Teatro Campesino - Brad Shirakawa
262- 263: Social and Public Arts Resource Center (SPARC) Venice, California
267: Courtesy of Supervisor Molina
271: The San Francisco Ballet
272: The Ballet Folklorico Mexicano de Carlos Moreno

Book layout, design, TQS Graphics and Index by: Octavio I. Romano-V., Ph.D. Senior Editor, TQS Publications

The Author

Carlos M. Jiménez was born in Los Angeles, California, where he grew up attending local public schools. After completing two years at Santa Monica College, he transferred to the University of California's Santa Barbara campus where he completed his undergraduate studies. Following his graduation with a major in History and a minor in English, he received a California State Teaching Credential. Thereafter, he began his teaching career in the Los Angeles public schools in 1973.

Mr. Jiménez has always had an interest in Mexico and Mexican culture, probably inherited from his Mexican-born father and Cuban-born mother. In 1978, while teaching at Belmont High School, he eagerly accepted an offer to teach a class of Mexican American Studies. This was the first impetus toward writing *The Mexican American Heritage.*

Subsequently, Jiménez was transferred in 1981 to James A. Garfield High School in East Los Angeles where he currently teaches. In addition to teaching Mexican American Studies and Literature, he also teaches Advanced Placement in U.S. History. In addition, he is Head Coach of Boys Track and Field.

Over and above his teaching and coaching duties, Jiménez has been involved with the UCLA Writing Project since 1981. The writing exercises in *The Mexican American Heritage* are, in part, the result of this association. In addition to being a strong advocate for the incorporation of writing instruction within the social sciences, he has also championed a greater inclusion of Mexican American History and Literature within the traditional U.S. History and American Literature frameworks.

Over the years, he has given numerous presentations and workshops on these and many other topics in conjunction with UCLA's Center for Academic Interinstitutional Programs, as well as with the Achievement Council, the English Council of Los Angeles, *The Los Angeles Times* and many other organizations. He has served on committees and task forces organized by the California State Department of Education as well as the National Board for Professional Teaching Standards. Carlos M. Jiménez continues to make himself available for presentations at schools and other institutions.

He is married to Virginia Peñaloza Jiménez, who is a television news reporter for a Spanish language station in Los Angeles. They have a daughter, Daniela, who was born in May of 1992. Their favorite activity away from work is traveling, especially to places like Mexico, Guatemala and the U.S. Southwest.

Carlos M. Jiménez, standing: Teacher of Advanced Placement in U.S. History and Mexican American Studies.

Teacher as track and field coach of the Garfield Bulldogs

Teacher on working vacation in Yucatan— research for the classroom

A.

Tonatiuh-Quinto Sol International, Inc.
Publishers of Chicano Literature
Berkeley, California

M.E.Ch.A.
Movimiento Estudiantil Chicana/o en Aztlan
University of California at Berkeley

M.E.Ch.A.
University of Utah
Salt Lake City, Utah

M.A.L.C.S.
Mujeres Activas en Letras
y Cambio Social
University of Illinois at Chicago

Chicano Studies Library
University of California at Berkeley

United Farm Workers
Keene, California

M.A.L.D.E.F.
Mexican American Legal
Defense and Education Fund
Los Angeles, California

M.E.Ch.A.
University of California at Riverside

CASA ZAPATA
Stanford University
Stanford, California

El Teatro Campesino
San Juan Bautista,
California

Mexican American Commission
State of Nebraska

Houston, Texas

Centro Cultural de la Raza
San Diego, California

Chicano Studies Program
University of Texas
at El Paso

Texas Association of Chicanos
in Higher Education
San Antonio, Texas

NATIONAL HISPANIC UNIVERSITY

San José, California

Mexican American
Engineering Society
Placentia, California

Chicanos por la Causa
Phoenix, Arizona

José Antonio Burciaga
Author - Artist, Casa Zapata
Stanford University, California

Chicano newspaper, Colorado

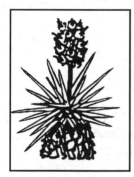

South Broadway
Cultural Center
Albuquerque, New Mexico

Chicano Press Association

Esther Hernandez, Artista
San Francisco, California

Mexican American Studies Program
University of Houston, Texas

Movimiento Artistico Chicano
Chicago, Illinois

Chicano / Latino Literary Contest
University of California
Irvine

M.E.Ch.A.
University of Texas
Austin

EL POPO

M.E.Ch.A. Newspaper
Chicano Studies Department
California State University, Northridge

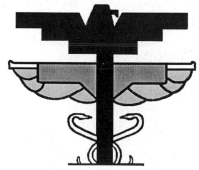

CLINICA DE LA RAZA
Oakland, California

CHIBAS
Chicano Barrio Associates
El Paso, Texas

Comisión Femenil
Los Angeles, California

Chicano Secret Service
Comedy Group at University of Utah
and Weber State Performances

Publishers of Chicano Literature
San José, California

César Augusto Martínez
San Antonio, Texas

San Francisco, California

Committee on Chicano Rights
San Diego, California

Latina Leadership Network

The Mexican Museum
San Francisco, California

Quinto Sol Publications
Berkeley, California
1994 27th Year

TELACU
Community Development
East Los Angeles, California

Los Angeles, California

San Diego, California

Midwest Consortium for
Latino Research
East Lansing, Michigan

Revista Chicana
con un poquito de todo
San Antonio, Texas 1977

Rogelio Cárdenas
Muralist, Instructor, Graphics
Petaluma, California

Cristal, Tejaztlan
Raza Unida de Cristal 1975

Carmen Lomas Garza
Prints, Paintings, Graphics
San Francisco, California

Chicano Comedy Group
Hollywood, California

Aztlan Communications
Lowrider Magazine
San José, California

Kansas City, Kansas

IMAGINE
International Chicano
Poetry Journal
Boston, Massachusetts

American G.I. Forum

League of United
Latin American
Citizens

Midwest
Canto al Pueblo
Milwaukee, Wisconsin
1977

Tucson, Arizona

Third World Writers Symposium
California State University
Sacramento, California

Anonymous
Los Angeles

National Chicano Forum
Salt Lake City, Utah

National Council of La Raza
Washington, D.C.

Raza Recruitment and Retention
University of California
Berkeley

Washington, D.C.

El Paso, Texas

Chicago, Illinois

G.

EAST LONG BEACH NEIGHBORHOOD CENTER
LONG BEACH, CALIFORNIA

D-2 University

Native Americans and Chicanos
Davis, California

Centro Cultural

Cornelius, Oregon

Reno, Nevada

L.A. Moratorium
Los Angeles Moratorium Committee
Los Angeles, California

Washington, D.C.

Bowling Green, Ohio

Centro
Cultural
de la
Misión

San Francisco, California

Mexican American
Chamber of Commerce
Fort Worth, Texas

N.A.C.S.
National Association
of Chicano Studies

Sacramento Concilio, Inc.
Sacramento, California

EL CENTRO
COMMUNITY MENTAL HEALTH CENTER
SERVICIOS DE SALUD MENTAL
Los Angeles, California

Centro Chicano de Nueva York
New York City

S.A.C.N.A.S.
Society for Advancement of Chicanos
and Native Americans in Science
University of California, Santa Cruz

National Image, Inc.

O.L.A. Raza
Organization for the Legal
Advancement of Raza, Inc.
Bakersfield, California

Tony Martinez
Detroit, Michigan

Instituto Laboral De La Raza
San Francisco, California

Raza in Higher Education
California Chicano / Latino
Intersegmental Convocation

Cenzontle
Chicano Short Stories and Poetry
University of California, Irvine
1979

Association for the Advancement of
Mexican Americans
Houston, Texas
1977

SOMOS UNO

BRACERO
Organo Informativo de la Liga
Ricardo Flores Magon
San Antonio, Texas

Raza Newspaper
Appleton, Wisconsin
1973

Cosmopolitan Club
Rock and Mexican Music
Boulder, Colorado
Sam Chavez

Boulder, Colorado

El Espuelazo
Springfield, Massachusetts
1975

Chicano Cultural Center
University of California, Berkeley
1975

César E. Chávez Memorial March
1994

A PUBLICATION OF THE NATIONAL
NETWORK OF HISPANIC WOMEN
Los Angeles, California

South San Francisco,
California

CENTRO BELLAS ARTES
Fresno, California

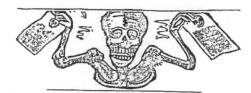

La Calavera Newsletter
MECha
University of Oregon, Eugene
1977

Newspaper
San Juan, Texas

Newspaper
Phoenix, Arizona

University of California, Davis

Mi tierra
Cafe y Panaderia
San Antonio, Texas

Mission Economic and Cultural Association
San Francisco, California

Mexican Grocery
Fresh Tortillas
Tamales – Chorizo
Seattle, Washington

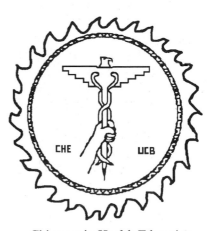

Chicanos in Health Education
University of California, Berkeley

Chicano Studies Newsletter
University of Wisconsin, Whitewater

Chicano
Humanities
and Arts
Council

Denver,
Colorado

RAUL GARCIA
Inmigración Counseling Center
Denver, Colorado

Chicano Student Programs
University of California, Riverside

S T A T E W I D E

M E C h A

C O N F E R E N C E

E A S T L O S A N G E L E S
C O L L E G E
M A Y 22-23, 1987

DE NUESTRA RAZA

San Francisco, California

Chicana
Service Action Center
Los Angeles, California
1973

Chicano / Latino Net
Chicano Studies Research Center
at University of California, Los Angeles
and
The Linguistic Minority Research Group
University of California, Santa Barbara

Farm
Labor
Organizing
Committee

"Hasta la victoria"
Toledo, Ohio

La Raza Bookstore/Galeria Posada
Sacramento, California

Royal Chicano Air Force

Art and Service to the Community
Sacramento, California

"Día de los Muertos #3"
por
Ricardo Favela
Esteban Villa
Sacramento, California
1977

TEZCATLIPOCA
Aztec God of Education
University of Texas - El Paso
Library: Chicano Services Section

Centro Cultural de la Raza
San Diego, California

National City, California

Newspaper
La Mesa Redonda Publication
1977
Wichita, Kansas

EL NUEVO SOL

Movimiento Estudiantil Chicana / Chicano en Aztlan
University of Southern California
1977

Noticiero

Chicano

University of Arizona
1976

" Serving the Barrios of Houston"
Texas
1972

South Florida Migrant Workers
Immokalee, Florida
1970

LATINO RUN
Fiesta de Champaign
Tacos, tamales, tostones, arroz con gandules.
La Casa Student Organization
c/o La Casa Cultural Latina
Champaign, Illinois

Newspaper
Eagle Pass, Tejas
1977

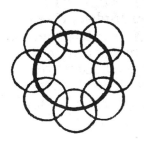

CASA DE UNIDAD

Cultural Arts and Media Center
Southwest Detroit,
Michigan

Chicano Humanities and Arts Council
Denver, Colorado

HISPANIC
CULTURE
FOUNDATION

Albuquerque, New Mexico

Caracol
Chicano Journal
Subscription form
San Antonio, Texas
1977

California
1972

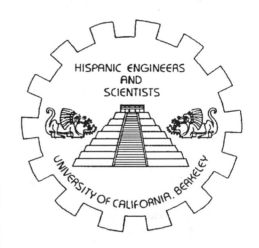

**La Academia de la Nueva Raza
Dixon, New Mexico
1972**

Third National Chicano Literature Festival

LITERARY RECITALS - MUSICA - TEATRO
WORKSHOPS - BAILE - ART EXHIBIT
1976

Somos Aztlan
United Mexican American Students (UMAS)
University of Colorado, Boulder
1972

Newspaper
Los Angeles, California
1969

Zopilote News

The Newsletter for
Displaced Chicanos & Chicanas
Tempe, Arizona
1994

SAMORA
JULIAN RESEARCH
INSTITUTE

Michigan State University
East Lansing

**The Chicano
Quarterly Review**

Journal of the
Chicano Renaissance

Department of Spanish
Yale University
New Haven, Connecticut
J. Bruce-Novoa — P.D. Ortego, Eds.
1975

Distrito de la Misión
San Francisco, California

Hayward, California

Mira como nos tienes

A Musical Tragicomedy
about the life of Emiliano
Zapata by Arte Andariego

Santa Cruz, California

Newspaper
Kansas City - Topeka,
Kansas

Newspaper
Denver, Colorado
1971

EL PAPEL
ALBUQUERQUE. NEW MEX.

LA RAZA SILK SCREEN CENTER INC.

San Francisco, California

LA VOZ ★ DEL LLANO

Topeka, Kansas

¿DÓNDE ESTÁ MI RAZA?

Volume 1, No. 6　　　　March 1977

Kansas City, Kansas

San Francisco, California

Boalt Hall
University of California
Berkeley

V.

Organización Nacional de la Salud de la Mujer Latina
National Latina Health Organization
Oakland, California

Mexican American Women's National Association
Northern Virginia Chapter
Springfield, Virginia

California Chicano / Latino Medical Student Association
CMSA
University of California
School of Medicine
Los Angeles

Santa Rosa, California

The National Chicano
Human Rights Council
San Francisco, California

Congreso Nacional
De Asuntos Colegiales
Washington, D.C.
1976

THE
GUADALUPE
CULTURAL ARTS CENTER

San Antonio, Texas

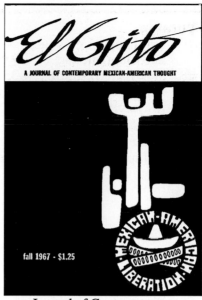

Journal of Contemporary
Mexican American Thought 1967

GRITO DEL SOL: A Chicano Quarterly 1980

1970

Cinco de Mayo Celebration — 1994
Berkeley, California
MUSIC: Dr. Loco and his Rockin' Jalapeño Band
Mariachi Los Monarcas
Eddie Reyna y su Orquesta
Banda Toritos Musical
Los Compas

Danza Xitlalli

Raza Recruitment and Retention Program, University of California
Berkeley

INDEX

by Octavio I. Romano-V., Ph.D.

For the collection of logos

Special Thanks to

Lillian Castillo-Speed, Librarian, along with members of her staff, Marisol Zapater and Luis A. de la Garza, of the Chicano Studies Library, University of California, Berkeley, for their generous and dedicated assistance in compiling this collection.

Also, many thanks to José Antonio Burciaga, artist - author, Casa Zapata, Stanford University, for use of his personal collection of Chicano logos; and to Bob Postawko, Mexican American Studies, University of Texas at Austin, as well as to Martín Flores of the Raza Recruitment and Retention Office, University of California, Berkeley for their interest and assistance.

Logo Graphics by: TQS Graphics
HP Scanjet, HP Laser Jet 4M, Macintosh Quadra 840av